☞ Romantic Rebels

Books by

Emily Hahn

Hongkong Holiday

China A to Z

Picture Story of China

Raffles of Singapore

Miss Jill

England to Me

Purple Passage

Love Conquers Nothing

Chiang Kai-shek

Diamond

The Tiger House Party

China Only Yesterday

China to Me

Africa to Me

With Naked Foot

Romantic Rebels

Romantic Rebels

☞ An Informal History of
Bohemianism in America

Emily Hahn

Illustrated with Photographs ☜

Houghton Mifflin Company Boston
The Riverside Press Cambridge
1967

First Printing   c

810.9
H

ACKNOWLEDGMENTS

I would like to thank the following people for the help they so graciously extended me during the preparation of this book: Mr. Robert Clairmont, Mr. Gregory Dawson, Mrs. Rose Dawson, Mr. Floyd Dell, Mrs. Bernadine Fritz, Miss Mildred Gilman, Mr. Albert Goldstein, Mr. John Goodwin, Mr. Harnett Kane, Mr. and Mrs. Melvin Livingstone, Mrs. John McClure, Mrs. Frances Bryson Moore, Mr. Felix Pollak, and Mrs. Alice Rossin.

Contents

Contents

Illustrations

Illustrations

Mabel Dodge Luhan
Determined experimentalist in her Indian period

Isadora Duncan and Serge Essenine
" 'My husband and I are revolutionists. All geniuses worthy of the name are.' "

Edna St. Vincent Millay
"Miss Millay was the Village."

Floyd Dell
Textbook case

Mary Austin
Excellent witness

Joe Gould
The outer fringe

Allen Ginsberg
"But then, everything in Bohemia changes, or ought to."

Introduction

On a summer evening in 1964, three of us — my nephew Greg, his friend Mark and I — were battling our way through the streets of Greenwich Village. I had not visited the district for years, and we were bound on what I had envisaged as a sentimental pilgrimage to the haunts of my youth, but it wasn't working out that way. The sidewalks were no wider than I remembered, but they were bedizened with lights and thronged with more people than I'd ever seen in New York except for some special event like the circus at Madison Square Garden. Yet these characters had no apparent errands. Most of them were young, carelessly and lightly dressed: they ambled, courted, talked or merely stood silent in clotted groups. Anyone who, like us, was bent on getting somewhere, had to thread a twisted path: we ourselves went single file. Cars nosed slowly, honking, through the crowd that spilled into the streets.

"What is it?" I asked. "Are they waiting for the latest baseball score or something?"

Greg was astonished. "They're not waiting for anything. This is the Village: they come down to look around. Wasn't it always like this?" Greg is an authority on the Village, because he and Mark live on Tenth Street.

"It wasn't a bit like this in my day," I said indignantly. "We never had all these shops and bars, and of course there were no neon signs. This is terrible. If it's just an ordinary night, what's it like on the Fourth of July?" With an exasperated burst of vigor I pushed past an immovable fat girl, the boys following. Over my shoulder Mark said, "Just the same it's a fun place, isn't it?"

Before I had time to wince at the anachronism (for my mood it was an anachronism), we had arrived at Lee Chumley's. I had to look for the number because I wouldn't have recognized the front door. It was probably unaltered, but my nostalgia hadn't gone far enough for me to cherish such details. The few steps of descent, however, I did remember. As the door swung shut behind us there was complete silence, a change so sudden that I felt stunned and unable, for a few moments, to make any more observations. The silence of the tomb, perhaps? We tiptoed to a table, where it was a relief to see that we had a neighbor after all, a boy reading. Moreover, as ears readjusted themselves I heard evidence of other people in the inner room — the muted chink of fork on plate, and a murmur at the bar. There was the famous fireplace. Everything was fitting together, but there was much more light than I remembered: in earlier days that boy couldn't have read his book in the candlelight. Though on each table candles still stood stuck in upright bottles, skirted by masses of varicolored drippings, the drippings were dusty, the candles unlit: they were only for atmosphere. Reverently, Greg pointed out the frieze of faded book-covers running around the room head high, bearing the names of writers who used to frequent Chumley's.

"I suppose you knew them all," Mark said to me, with flattering trust.

"Well, as a matter of fact a lot of them were gone by the time I came here."

"Life in the Village must have been a real ball then." He sighed.

For a moment I thought of setting him right, but it would have taken too much time to explain that though the Village was certainly a good place in its time, the great days were over before I arrived. It is a way the great days have, I discovered long ago — they're forever escaping you. According to the old-timers in Shanghai, London, Paris and Bombay, they were over there too, before I arrived. "You should have seen it in the old days," people are always saying.

Another thought struck me. Even if the Village was as much fun as they say, back in some bygone era such as 1915, would it amuse Mark and Greg with their neon tastes? Things change, people change, and I doubted it. Plunged into 1915 the boys would probably be bored.

We gave our order to a sallow youth in shirtsleeves. "I don't know how the food used to be," said Greg, "but the dinner you get here now is as good a value for the money as you'll find anywhere in town." After all, there are things that remain constant, like the appetite of youth.

"The Village must have seemed more Bohemian at that time," said Mark. I nodded firmly. It's gayer and more crowded now, and noisier, I found myself thinking, but something was missing. I was wondering what it was when Greg said, "Oh, I wouldn't say that. It's still pretty Bohemian. You get lots of espresso bars where beatniks congregate to read poems and play guitars, stuff like that. Let's look for one after dinner."

But Mark objected, saying that beats don't like strangers butting in, and if we crashed such a party we'd only spoil it. Bowing to his decision, we finished dinner and went home.

In my hotel room I couldn't get to sleep. My head was full of scenes from the modern Village —the drifting youngsters choking the streets, jamming the night spots or standing before windows full of leather shirts and sandals and teenage clothes, chatting with the cashier in the paper-book shop, walking little dogs, gawking at paintings hung behind plate-glass windows, or staring with longing at expensive but dubious antiques. Streets resounding with music from guitars and accordions played on street corners or indoors. Blaring theme songs from a movie palace. Pale girls with long streaky hair and tight black pants, pale boys with wildly uncut hair and tight black pants, kids carrying books, kids carrying musical instruments, kids carrying nothing but potential fists. Black-and-white couples were big in the Village — black men with white girls more often than the other way around. Was there a particular significance in this? I couldn't settle on any one decision except that the Village surprised me.

The boys had talked about poetry readings in beatnik espresso bars. Were the beatniks, then, today's Bohemians, one and the same phenomenon, or did they differ to an appreciable extent? I couldn't answer the question for the very good reason that I couldn't define both terms. The beatnik was easy. I had almost too many definitions for him. Everyone I met seemed eager to tell me all about the beats. But the Bohemian was something else again. Nobody seemed very sure of what a Bohemian is, or was — unless, of course, he is (or was) a kind of beatnik of the past. It was an omission in everyday thinking that startled me, because I was sure it had not always been like this. In the old days wasn't there plenty to say about Bohemia, and weren't there plenty of people to say it? What was Bohemia? What had happened to it? Had anything? I decided to look back through the years and find out.

☞ Romantic Rebels

CHAPTER 1

A Trick
of the French Language

O N AN autumn afternoon in 1856, New Yorkers enjoying a stroll along Broadway in the uptown district near Bleecker Street were shocked to observe a young lady turning in at stairs that led to a basement café known as Pfaff's. Women in New York, even disreputable ones, did not visit public taverns, and this woman looked respectable, though pretty. Remarkably, she seemed to be confident that what she was doing was all right. In the most offhand manner imaginable she lifted her skirts, though not too much, in order to descend the steps before disappearing indoors.

The sight was repeated on the following afternoon and the one after that, but occasioned less comment, for word had gone around that the young lady was Ada Clare, the poetess from South Carolina: she had recently returned from Paris after an event there too scandalous to be spoken of except in whispers. An unwed mother, no less! And Pfaff's, one learned, was the favorite haunt of a literary group that was led by Henry Clapp, Jr., the proprietor and editor of the weekly *Saturday Press*. Clapp too was a dangerous individual: he too had lived in Paris — a good deal longer than Miss Clare had, as a matter of fact — and while there had picked up a lot of Socialist ideas. He had hated to come back, and said so unblushingly: he considered his native land a hole and New York a community more dead than alive.

Henry Clapp himself must have realized that his passion for Paris was odd. He was a thorough Yankee, born in Massachusetts in 1822. He had always worked as a journalist, and before the break in his life was such an ardent crusader for temperance that more than once he landed in jail for attacking local liquor dealers in his column with excessive enthusiasm. Then he went to Paris, as secretary for Albert Brisbane, a rich American with advanced ideas on social reform, and everything was changed. Brisbane came upon the old French Socialist Fourier, working obscurely as a clerk — in the American Legation, of all places. He directed Clapp to translate some of Fourier's work into English, a task that Clapp continued even after the Socialist died. Clapp's mind was opened to the beauties of free thought. Soon he had forgotten all about the evils of drink. He had adopted the Parisian way of life, sitting at tables in boulevard cafés smoking, sipping an occasional aperitif, and, above all, talking.

After such joys it was acutely painful to be forced to come back to New York, as he was, sometime around 1850. The city seemed stale and flat. He wandered about from one café to another, nostalgically seeking a place where he might settle in and talk for happy hours, as he had done in France, but most New York cafés did not please him. The clientele had the awful American restlessness, gulping down their beer and rushing away before any discussion could even start, let alone finish. At last he happened into Charlie Pfaff's, and realized that his search was over. It was a simple, clean place run on European lines. Pfaff was not French, only Swiss, but never mind: he had lived near the rose, and his cellar was good. Clapp adopted Pfaff's. He would go over to sit awhile at lunch time and again when work was over, when he would stay for hours.

A man with a decided personality never lacks followers: Clapp's own staff came along, and so did journalists from other periodicals, and so did poets and painters who knew them, until Pfaff's became the acknowledged place in New York for an artist or literary man to be. They called themselves Bohemians. It was only a matter of time before they were joined by Ada Clare — or, as she really was, Miss Jane McElheny of South Carolina.

Miss McElheny had pulled out of the South as soon as she possibly could, when she came into an inheritance upon the death of her parents. Her native state had little, if any, use for poets, and Jane considered herself a poet, and an actress as well — an ambition for which Charleston had even less sympathy. In New York she adopted the professional name of Ada Clare, and the newspapers printed much of her verse. She was praised right and left for it — a reaction to its sweet sentiment that would not occur in our coarser age. Ada also went on the stage, but that venture was not at all successful; after one performance, her career as an actress was indefinitely postponed.

Perhaps in New York, perhaps later, in Paris, she fell in love with Louis Moreau Gottschalk, a popular pianist and composer. In Paris she gave birth to a boy, by which time Gottschalk had tired of the affair and walked out on her. When all this happened, Ada Clare did not behave in any of the conventional ways. Her career has been documented in Albert Parry's admirable exploration of the Bohemian myth, *Garrets and Pretenders*, first published in 1933, but she remains mysterious. Where, one wonders, did she find her courage? A woman of her class when "ruined" was supposed to move out of virtuous circles and become a prostitute, unless, like Hester Prynne, she meekly accepted her status of outcast. Ada Clare did not drop out of sight, nor was she an outcast: she refused to be ruined, and stayed put in the world she preferred. Nor did she suffer in silence as a lady should: through poems and open letters in the papers she called the world to witness her love and unhappiness. Ada was proud of her emotions, not ashamed. She declared that she was a Love-Philosopher. When Gottschalk made it clear that all was over between them, she used her grief as material, barely disguising the situation in short stories in which heroines berate their faithless lovers, plead with them, contemplate suicide, and resign themselves. The writing was of therapeutic value if nothing else, and by 1856, when Ada returned to New York with her little son, she had regained her characteristic vivacity. In time she evidently achieved a kind of status quo with Gottschalk. Charles Warren Stoddard, who met her in California when he was twenty years old, published in 1905 an elegiac article on her in which he repeats a conversation he had overheard between Ada and her son Aubrey.

The nine-year-old Aubrey said, "Mamma, I know who my father is."

"Who is your father?" asked Ada.

"Oh, Gottschalk's my father."

"What makes you think so?"

"Oh, don't you know that whenever we are in the same city with him he sends me tickets for all his concerts? And then he gave me a suit of soldier's clothes, just because I wanted them, and a sword and a gun and ever so many other things. I'm sure he is my father."

Ada replied, "That's a funny reason, and you are a funny boy." Stoddard appended, "He was a wise child."

Louis Gottschalk, who was to cross Ada's path only at a distance after she returned to New York, was himself a Bohemian, of American extraction, and a genius in the bargain. He was the son of an Englishman and a Creole from Santo Domingo, and was born in New Orleans in 1829. As a child he began to show great musical talent, and the Gottschalks, who had money, sent him across the Atlantic for training. This was the usual course for ambitious young artists who could afford it, it being generally (and correctly) held that the best masters were not to be found in America. When they heard the young man perform, the pundits of Europe agreed with the earlier audiences that he was good. Chopin praised his playing. He was accepted by Berlioz as a student.

Gottschalk became a concert artist who toured the Western world and won tremendous applause wherever he went, as well as the worship of women. It should be explained that musicians in those days held a special position regarding women, arrogating to themselves all the responsibility that is now shared among disc jockeys, actors and dance-band leaders. The female element was an accepted hazard of the profession — a hazard that Gottschalk, for one, found delightful. Life was particularly hectic for him and his confreres in America, where women were permitted so much freedom that European visitors raised their eyebrows and thanked God their own girls were better controlled. In Gottschalk's journal, published in 1881, he jotted down comments on most things that happened, but either he was too discreet to mention the ladies or these words were edited out. According to a story told by Robert Clairmont in private conversation, Gottschalk was forced to leave California in 1864 because Ada Clare, who was in San Francisco at that time, had captivated some local official who wanted to avenge her. A morality charge was trumped up, and the pianist, protesting in vain that he had been framed, was shipped out. The tale is probably apocryphal, but Gottschalk himself bears witness that he had little success in San Francisco, where, he claimed, concerts had never succeeded. "Ole Bill and Strakosch left it in confusion. Paul Julien, who has just passed five months

here, has not carried off one thousand dollars net. On the other
side, I regret to say it, the circus flourishes, and Miss Adah Menken, after having driven all the people crazy, has carried away
with her fifty thousand dollars. You will easily understand that
the chaste muse, sister of Apollo, can only go astray before a
public which is as enthusiastic at the nudities of Mazeppa."
Gottschalk went on to South America. Five years later he died
by violence in Rio, at the hands of an angry husband.

*   *   *

Why should all these people, obviously not denizens of the
country of that name, be called Bohemians? It was a trick of
the French language, that is all, a nickname bestowed by Balzac,
in 1840, on artists and writers of a certain type, in the story
"Prince of Bohemia." He defined the term: "Bohemia is made
up of young people, all of whom are between twenty and thirty
years of age, all men of genius in their own line, as yet almost
unknown but with the ability to become known one day, when
they will achieve real distinction. Already you can pick them
out at Carnival-time, giving rein to their superfluous high
spirits . . . The word 'bohème' is self-explanatory. Bohemia
possesses nothing, yet contrives to exist on that nothing." It is
also necessary to know, however, that the French believed that
gypsies came from Bohemia, so that "Bohemian" was used in-
terchangeably for "gypsy" or "vagabond" long before Balzac
adopted it. These young hopefuls did indeed lead a gypsy existence. The Revolution of 1830 had left Paris full of impecunious artists and writers, for whom the governments that came
and went in rapid succession made no provision. In spite of
Balzac's statement, life was not really gay for them even at Carnival-time. Most were miserably poor. The only hope of ad-
vancement for painters and sculptors was for one of their offer-

ings to be selected by the Salon committee, for the annual show. According to the inhuman rules of the time, nobody knew until the show opened if his work had been accepted or refused. On opening day, all the talent and the ragtag and bobtail of the Latin Quarter trooped across the river to the Louvre to find out their fate. "On all hands," according to a contemporary source, "were flowing locks, pointed hats, and anxious faces." When the lists were announced, those who failed had either to weep or make a joke of it.

Writers too, though they enjoyed a superior position to that of the artists in the national hierarchy, suffered from poverty. According to Malcolm Easton, who has written of the development of Bohemianism in Paris during the first half of the nineteenth century, these victims, "mainly young people of humble background," speak out in their writings in self-defense. "It is hardly surprising that, when they do, a change of accent is discernible . . . If not professing socialists themselves, such artists and writers had often absorbed the socialist ideas of the working-class from which they sprang, inheriting also the materialist viewpoint inseparable from a class-struggle against bad conditions. Though more often than not they were indifferent to politics, in France an indifference of this kind was as good as an opinion, and a seditious one at that, when couched in the violent language of the studio." Brought up on the writings of Gautier, Vigny and Musset, who never experienced their "squalid poverty," these "working-class painters and writers were forced to adapt the fashionable characteristics of emancipation — Gautier's scorn of the bourgeois, Vigny's dignified self-pity, and Musset's redemption of the soul through love — to an entirely new set of circumstances. Thus at first they strove to idealize their wretchedness, inventing for themselves a character which would rise superior to the threats of landlords and vulgar mistresses. Murger . . . was the demonstrator-in-chief of this approach."

Henri Murger, who exported the word "Bohemia" with its peculiarly French meaning to all countries in the West, was born in Paris in 1822, the same year of that other Henry's birthday in Massachusetts. As the son of a concierge who looked after an artists' lodging-house, the child saw youthful artists and students at work and play, often allied in ferocious battle against the Philistines. Childlike, he admired their "free-and-easy arrogance," and longed to be an artist himself, "even at the risk of starvation. For to be an artist was to be free. Behaving as he pleased, working or idling as the mood dictated, ill-mannered, unpunctual, he could be forgiven all," says Easton, "provided he had talent."

In pursuit of this idea Murger as a very young man lived with a number of painters and sculptors in a barn, trying to paint. At the same time he scraped a living at second-rate journalism and as a very ill-paid secretary to Count Tolstoi. It soon became apparent that he had no talent for painting. Very well, then, he would be the great poet of his generation, and the struggle continued. He was hungry and dirty and often in the public ward of the hospital, suffering from scrofula. During 1842, at the age of twenty, he nearly starved to death, as did his three best friends. Within the early months of 1844, four of his group actually did die of starvation. Murger himself had never been so down and out as he was at that time. He even lost his secretarial job. Then, as if by a miracle, a magazine, the *Corsaire*, bought an article from him — and another — and another, all of a series of humorous sketches portraying life among the artists. The public liked them and Murger wrote more. He sold all he wrote. For material he drew on his own experience, suitably watered down, for he couldn't possibly have told the truth: his readers would never swallow anything so unpalatable. Yet there was a grain of fact in all the anecdotes, glossed over to hide the squalor. Murger's friends appeared in the stories much idealized. As for himself, he would never have been recognized as his opposite number Rodolphe, the handsome, debonair poet — Murger was actually small and ugly.

The incident of Mimi was not true at the time he wrote it; he lifted much of that part of the story, including her name, from a romance by Musset. Later, however, it came all too true, when his mistress died of tuberculosis. In the meantime the public liked his work the more for this touch of sadness. As a true Bohemian Murger sometimes felt ashamed that he should be writing down to the bourgeoisie, but there was this to be said for it — he saved himself from starvation.

La Vie de Bohème, as Murger called the series, saved his life, but did not immediately make his fortune. The *Corsaire* did not pay well, and he was glad to get his job back with Count Tolstoi. The year 1848 was altogether miserable; he was often ill and his mistress, Lucille Louvet, died at the public hospital of St.-Louis, where her body, as was the custom with paupers' corpses, was confiscated for dissection. It grew more and more difficult to be amusing about *la vie de Bohème.*

Then at last came a real break, when a clerk in the Ministry of War named Barrière, who had done much playwriting, suggested that they work out something together for the stage on the basis of Murger's Bohemian pieces. The result, produced for the first time on November 22, 1849, was a great success. Murger was made, and — an even more important result from our point of view — his work at last brought Bohemia, by way of translations and, finally, the Puccini opera, into common speech everywhere. The play appeared at the height of the romantic vogue for languid, tragic, coughing ladies, and told the world that what it had always hoped was really true, that the rackety life of the artist had pathos and romance and fascination. Everyone laughed and wept over poor Mimi and Rodolphe and their friends — the same people who would have feared and scorned a real Mimi and her circle.

Thus through Murger even Henry Clapp's coterie far away in New York found their identity, or thought they had. But a concept so enthusiastically taken up by the general public was not always treated with complete gravity by artists and writers. In New York, in 1881, the Irish writer Fitz-James O'Brien took a sly poke at the new fashion, in a short story he called "The Bohemian."

"When I say I am a Bohemian, I do not wish you to understand that I am a Zingaro," says his protagonist. "I don't steal chickens, tell fortunes, or live in a camp. I am a social Bohemian, and fly at higher game . . . Have you read Henry Murger's *Scènes de la Vie de Bohéme?* . . . Well, then, you can comprehend my life. I am clever, learned, witty, and tolerably good-looking. I can write brilliant magazine articles . . . I can paint pictures, and what is more, sell the pictures I paint. I can compose songs, make comedies, and captivate women."

Nevertheless, American artists who considered themselves better than hacks were delighted with the lift Murger had given to their kind. Having suffered all their lives from neglect, they welcomed the vogue even though they realized that his picture was romanticized. They, too, needed the help. America early in the nineteenth century was not a happy place for anyone who didn't fit into the conventional pattern. A nation of farmers, builders and traders had little time for self-expression in literature or paint. They paid lip service to "culture," and few Americans would willingly have declared that they had no use for it, but few, again, really cared for music, painting or litera-ture. Only those brought up in the tradition of education and leisure, or with experience of Europe, appreciated more spe-cialized art. There was the beginning of a glimmer of hope — the country was settling down: art and literature were no longer dirty words. Still, life was not easy for artists and writers in 1850. In his study, *The Popular Book*, first published in 1950, James D. Hart lists sales figures and values of books sold in America through the years. The sum of $12,000,000, the value of books sold in 1850, compares favorably with $2,500,000 for 1820, but the books involved are for the most part poor stuff. Hawthorne, Melville and Thoreau sold slowly and couldn't put up any competition against a number of women whose names have been forgotten, such as "Fanny Fern," who wrote *Fern Leaves from Fanny's Portfolio*, and Susan Warner, who produced *The Wide, Wide World*. Only sixty copies of *Moby Dick* were bought in ten years, but *The Wide, Wide World* earned Miss Warner $4500 in six months. There were similar successes. "Publishers in the 'fifties," says Hart, "learned to wel-come any woman who turned up at their offices with a novel in bulky manuscript under her arm." This was gratifying for the scribbling ladies, but careful writers were envious and dismayed, like the serious painters who saw the public go overboard for ugly chromos when they could sell nothing. They made out as best they could. Painters and engravers and editors, Edgar Allan Poe for one, earned a little working on "gift books" — collections of poetry and pictures, printed on expensive paper and bound in luxurious material, to be kept prominently dis-played where visitors would be sure to see them.

American artists were disgruntled, and they had reason to be. The Bohemian vogue lent strength to their complaints. After Poe died in 1849 and a new generation grew up reading

Murger's book, the fashion among young artists was to speak
of him as a typical example of how badly Americans treat
genius. Poe, they said, was a martyr, a Bohemian before his
time, crushed by stupidity and provincialism just as they themselves were being crushed. Poe was their great man, the first
American Bohemian. The idea has persisted. Today Greenwich Village annalists claim that the spirit of their community
dates back to the few years Poe spent there. But when the poet
lived in that neighborhood it had no significance as an art center — it was nothing but one uptown district among others.
Nor is Poe an outstandingly Bohemian type. Not all artists are
Bohemians, any more than all Bohemians are artists, and being
a genius does not clinch the matter, since genius is not a deciding factor. Poe didn't take life in the properly careless spirit of
the Bohemian, nor was he really a rebel against society.

It may be alleged in defense of Poe's claim to Bohemianism
that he drank heavily. True, a lot of Bohemians do drink heavily. But James Gibbons Huneker's father, who was a friend of
Poe's in Philadelphia days, saw him "the worse for liquor"
only once, and then it was on a thimbleful of brandy. If this
story is to be believed, Poe seems to have been one of those unfortunate people who can't take liquor at all. If he "was not
too sullen or melancholy he would recite 'The Raven,'" says
James Gibbons Huneker. If he was not too sullen or melancholy: that is the point. Poe tended to be morose and antisocial,
which are not Bohemian traits. There is the added allegation
that he used dope. To us this sounds extremely sinful, but in
the happy-go-lucky days before the Pure Food and Drug Act
existed, a lot of people doped. A few, like FitzHugh Ludlow,
did it in the romantic desire to be wicked, but many others used
narcotics quite innocently, in patent medicines. Laudanum
was constipating but not, in the public opinion of the time, un-

conventional, and it didn't have the dignified status of a vice.

Moreover, Poe was not a nonconformist, as a Bohemian must be: he obeyed the little rules of society. He dressed as well as he could, though he found it difficult, with his insufficient means, to keep up appearances. In 1835, he wrote to tell his friend Kennedy that he couldn't come to dinner because he had no proper clothes. The elder Huneker called him "a handsome, dapper little man," and dapper is not an adjective we usually associate with Bohemians.

Poe was cross-grained and had high standards, a lethal combination in a literary critic. He said things in his reviews that the victims could not forgive. As an editorial aide he was so touchy that in spite of his remarkable talents it was almost impossible to work with him. His friend Kennedy said he was irregular, eccentric and querulous. He quarreled with almost everyone, and some people thought him possessed by a demon. "I met him two or three times," says a character in Bayard Taylor's 1876 novel, *Echo Club*, "heard him lecture once (his enunciation was exquisite) and saw him now and then on Broadway — enough to satisfy me that there were two men in him; one, a refined gentleman, an aspiring soul, an artist among those who had little sense of literary art; the other . . . built his nest with the birds of Night!"

Poe, then, was demonic, eccentric, quarrelsome and a genius, but all this does not add up to Bohemianism. In his right mind, he tried to behave like everyone else. To be sure, his parents were on the stage, following a very Bohemian profession, but he wasn't brought up by them — they died before he was out of babyhood — and his wanderings can by no stretch of the imagination be interpreted as arrant gypsy vagabondage. I cannot agree with Fitz-James O'Brien's character, Brann, or others who also call Poe a Bohemian. O'Brien himself is another matter: no genius, and forgotten today, in his time he was the most typical specimen of Bohemianism in New York.

*   *   *

Oddly enough, New York in the 1840s did not rate as one of the truly big cities of the United States. Bostonians and Philadelphians thought of her as a Johnny-come-lately, and scorned her for being commercial, noisy and comparatively new, scornful words in that young country where tradition was at a premium. New England was proud of her culture, but New York had little of it to boast. It was to Philadelphia, not New York, that Poe naturally went when he left the South, because Philadelphia was the center of magazine publishing. As a second choice he would probably have taken Boston, which had Cambridge and Harvard, Lowell and Longfellow, and Emerson with his transcendentalists — not that everyone considered these last an asset. Washington Irving was the only great name in literature that New York could claim, and the town was fully conscious of his worth. The city's chief publication was named the *Knickerbocker Magazine*. Lewis Gaylord Clark had built up the *Knickerbocker* until it reigned supreme among literary papers, and was the first to print Longfellow and Hawthorne. Even New Englanders didn't decry the *Knickerbocker* in its prime.

The literary activity of the late Thirties and early Forties in America makes pleasantly familiar reading, because it recalls the London scene of earlier decades. There are the same evenings of good talk, the characteristic enmities and friendships of writing men, the malice and wit, the making and destroying of reputations. Reports of these gatherings and gossip sound like informal groups meeting with Dr. Johnson in one of those London taverns where he loved to sit until morning, laying down the law. But in fact the New World was not like eight-

eenth-century England, and those Americans who described
it as such gave a false picture. It was rather as if ancient Britons
had written in Latin of their ceremonies, making them sound
Roman. The ambience was all wrong, but it was not the fault
of New Yorkers if they gave a misleading impression of their
city. They knew nothing else. Only a newcomer could see the
place clearly, a man whose eye was struck by details that meant
nothing to the inhabitants. Such a newcomer, Charles Dickens,
arrived in 1842.

He landed on American soil bristling with an explorer's
eagerness. With the nose of a true reporter he sniffed the air,
keen to plumb all depths and carry on the work begun by De
Tocqueville and Mrs. Trollope. As an Englishman, he had
brought with him a built-in prejudice against the ex-colonials,
but it was not strong; he was not sympathetic to imperialism.
He had an additional grievance — the vexed question of copyright and missing royalties. Nevertheless he wrote nice polite
notes on America at first, because he started out with his re-
searches in Boston — visiting Englishmen usually did like Boston. When he moved on to New York the feeling changed, and
it is at this point that we can learn from his observations. American writers didn't mention the pigs. They were used to them:
Dickens was not. He was startled by the swine that trotted or
ambled along New York streets, snorting and sniffing for food.
So should we have been, just as we are today by the cows that
walk about Indian streets. Crossing Broadway near the Tombs
— Broadway, a "wide and bustling street" four miles long, that
ran all the way from the Battery Gardens to a rural road high
up on Manhattan — Dickens had to take care not only of busy
traffic with omnibuses rolling by at least once every minute, and
hackney cabs, and coaches and gigs and carriages, but of pigs
getting in the way.

"Two portly sows are trotting up behind this carriage, and a

select party of half-a-dozen gentlemen hogs have just now turned
the corner. Here is a solitary swine, lounging homeward by
himself. He has only one ear; having parted with the other to
vagrant-dogs in the course of his city rambles . . . They are
the city scavengers, these pigs. Ugly brutes they are . . . They
are never attended upon, or fed, or driven, or caught, but
are thrown upon their own resources in early life, and become
preternaturally knowing in consequence."

In another passage of *American Notes,* he mentioned an aspect of American life that Mrs. Trollope had observed before
him — the large number of boardinghouses in the city, in which
lodged not only bachelors and spinsters, but married people.
The married couples were not transients, but made their
homes permanently in these places. Dickens was shocked by
the custom and concluded that it was due to the peculiar character of American women, who spent their time at lectures and
committee meetings, and would not take the trouble to keep
house in a normal, feminine way. In fact these families were unable, or at least unwilling, to pay the very high price of private
housing in New York, but Dickens found it hard to be fair to
American females. Like other British visitors, he was daunted
by their free, bossy manners. Even as he feared them, however,
he thought them beautiful.

He was disappointed in New York's sparse night life. There
was almost nothing to do but bowl in one of the alleys, or visit
an oyster-cellar. "But how quiet the streets are! Are there no
itinerant bands, no wind or stringed instruments? No, not one.
By day, are there no Punches, Fantoccinis, Dancing-dogs, Jug-
glers, Conjurors, Orchestrinas, or even Barrel-organs? No, not
one. Yes I remember one. One barrel-organ and a dancing-
monkey — sportive by nature, but fast fading into a dull, lump-
ish monkey, of the Utilitarian school . . .

"Are there no amusements? Yes. There is a lecture-room

across the way, from which that glare of light proceeds, and there may be evening services for the ladies thrice a week, or oftener. For the young gentlemen, there is the counting-house, the store, the bar-room: the latter, as you may see through these windows, pretty full. Hark! to the clinking sound of hammers breaking lumps of ice, and to the cool gurgling of the pounded bits, as, in the process of mixing, they are poured from glass to glass!"

"[Americans] certainly are not a humorous people," he wrote in the last pages of *American Notes*, "and their temperament always impressed me as being of a dull and gloomy character . . . I was quite oppressed by the prevailing seriousness and melancholy air of business . . ." Not surprisingly, *American Notes* raised a storm of indignation as soon as Americans got hold of their pirated editions. Everyone resented it, but New Yorkers most strongly, for their literati had honored Dickens with a banquet and generally overwhelmed him with courteous attention. Apart from their natural admiration, they had been guiltily conscious that he had ample cause for complaint in that scandalous lack of a copyright law. Publishers in America printed everything foreigners wrote without paying the authors a penny, and made fortunes. Dickens, most popular of all foreign authors, lost the most from pirating, and he was fully aware of it. No wonder that he pictures the city as a place of Yahoos whose streets were full of swine.

The scavengers were to disappear, but the memory of them evidently lingered awhile. When I was a child, seventy years after *American Notes* infuriated the country, I read somewhere the following doggerel:

> As far as I remember
> It was in the bleak December:
> I was strolling down the street in maudlin pride.

With my heart all in a flutter,
I lay down in the gutter,
And a pig came up and lay down by my side.
As I lay there in the gutter
With my heart all in a flutter,
A lady passing by was heard to say,
"You can tell a man who boozes
By the company he chooses" —
And the pig got up, and slowly walked away.

Somehow I got the idea that this little effusion referred to Edgar Allan Poe, as well as pigs, and even to Bohemians. Probably it did.

CHAPTER 2

Clapp's Crowd

THE WOUND dealt by Dickens healed in time, though a scar remained. New York grew exuberantly. There was no leisure in which to harbor old grudges, and those hateful descriptions in *American Notes* were soon outdated. Broadway stretched longer and longer; the rural road that once marked its end was swallowed under urban development, and by 1850 the thoroughfare did not end until it met Fiftieth Street, far uptown. Immigrants flowed in, a steady stream from Ireland, England and the Continent.

Though New York was now more than ever a commercial city, boys and girls of other states, ambitious to shine in artistic pursuits, were not discouraged. They kept coming. Only occasionally did one of these pilgrims opt for the superior refinement of New England. What attracted the others was just that vulgar vitality that was so deprecated by Boston. They flooded in — artists of the pencil and brush to make a living drawing labels or illustrations for picture-papers; poets and novelists clamoring for newspaper jobs or anything else that might earn them a pittance. Their spirits were supported by hopes of becoming famous, writers through publishing masterpieces, painters and sculptors by way of exhibitions — for New York, in spite of its commercial nature, also had a number of art galleries, the man-

agers of which gave prizes now and then for the best pictures
or sculpture on show. With their ambitions and their make-
shifts, New York's artists were existing in a Murger fashion, as
neo-Bohemians, before they ever heard of the French writer,
and like his characters — or, for that matter, like students anywhere in the world — they were high-spirited. There was the
artist Bellew, for example, who developed a fixation on the
duck-billed platypus. Fascinated by that strange creature whose
zoological name is *Ornithorhynchus paradoxus,* he persuaded
the proprietor of a new restaurant on Spring Street to call her
café the Ornithorhynchus Restaurant. Then he painted a sign
for the place that represented a platypus smoking a pipe and
holding a glass of beer. He and his friends adopted the Ornithorhynchus Restaurant as their pet hangout, where they
"talked, sang, joked, drank beer, and smoked church-warden
pipes." There must have been similar groups all over New York,
but the movement did not attract general attention until word
got around about Pfaff's.

Charlie Pfaff appreciated the support he got from Clapp's
crowd, especially as his place, recently started with limited
means, had nothing showy to recommend it. The basement in
which he had set up business was unusually large, and opened
out to a cavelike space directly under Broadway's sidewalk,
where stood the long table occupied every evening by the Bohemians. Pfaff's waiters and waitresses served food and drink
late into the night, and the provisions were good, but those
who wanted plushy surroundings did better at Delmonico's at
the corner of Chambers and Broadway — and paid much more.
Among the regulars of the Bohemians, or the Cave Dwellers as
they also called themselves, were Edmund Clarence Stedman,
George Arnold, William Winter and Edward G. F. Wilkins.
Occasional visitors included Bayard Taylor, Fitz-James O'Brien

and Thomas Bailey Aldrich. "Artemus Ward" dropped in, but his visit has been mentioned with such bated breath by many chroniclers that it is obvious he made only one appearance.

The regular who was to become most famous was Walt Whitman, in the 1850s a controversial figure. As yet he had only a few champions, one of them Henry Clapp. "Leaves of Grass," printed in 1855, was severely trounced in New York ("Muck and obscenity") as well as Boston ("Bombast, egotism, vulgarity, and nonsense," "Exulting audacity of Priapus-worshipping obscenity"), and if it hadn't been for Emerson's warm praise and Clapp's stubborn faith, even Whitman's self-confidence might have suffered. As it was, the staff of the *Saturday Press* made him a cause, publishing his work and declaring his genius. Of *course* the big, bearded poet clung to the Bohemians. Though not by temperament a clubbable man, during those years he behaved clubbably. Later he explained to someone that he went to the Cave "to see, talk little, and absorb," but no doubt his main absorption was badly needed comfort and encouragement. He even liked having the much-discussed girls around — such actresses as Daisy Sheppard, Jenny Danforth, and Anne Deland — though it was understood that Whitman was no womanizer. Adah Menken admired him enough to write poems in imitation of his.

Adah was new to the city when she first visited Pfaff's, and having a thin time. The story of her life has been written by Bernard Falk (*The Naked Lady*, N.Y., 1934), not without difficulty, because Miss Menken told a dozen life-stories about herself and all are different. It seems probable, however, that she was born in 1835, in New Orleans. Like Ada Clare she broke away from her native South. Like Ada she wrote poetry. Unlike Ada, she had little formal education, and her people were poor. Mr. Falk was unable to discover her real maiden name, but Adah has supplied several choices, sometimes declaring that her father was an aristocratic Sephardic Jew and at other times describing him as a Spanish bullfighter. Quite often, when it suited her, she signed her name "Dolores Adios Los Fuertes." Why not? She danced in the *corps de ballet* of the New Orleans French opera house. She acted in small-town theaters, posed for a sculptor, and did trick-riding in a circus. She learned a bit of several languages. She painted, she sang, she yearned to be a second Rachel or Lola Montez — and then, at twenty-one, she married a Cincinnati businessman named Alexander Isaac Menken. For several months they lived in Galveston, Texas; then Adah deserted her husband and went back to New Orleans.

After besieging the theater for two years or so she got a job with the Varieties Theatre in the city, but it didn't satisfy her because the management kept casting her as a man. It was the custom in show business to dress up shapely girls like this, there being no other way to display their attractions, but Adah, typically, preferred to think of herself as a great tragedienne, and nagged the management until they let her have a bash at Lady Macbeth. Unfortunately, because she hadn't studied her lines or had simply dried up from stage fright, she stood dumb on the stage until she managed to improvise enough lines and action to get her through. The management refused to repeat the experiment, and Adah and the Varieties relinquished each other. For a while after that she gave literary lectures and printed a good deal of her verse, which was even slushier than Ada Clare's, in the Cincinnati *Israelite*, under the name she used — most of the time — for the rest of her life: Adah Isaacs Menken. With indifference she received the news that her husband was divorcing her. Her mind was set on New York, and she bent all her efforts toward saving enough money for the ticket. In 1859 she got there, but found the going tough. Even when she managed now and then to get a job on the stage, her notices were bad.

Nevertheless she made friends, some of them influential. Frank Queen, editor of the *New York Clipper*, a stage journal that carried much weight, liked her and welcomed her whenever she dropped in at the office. There one day she was introduced to a rapidly rising pugilist named John C. Heenan, an ex-blacksmith from California known to the fancy as "The Benicia Boy," who at that time was challenging the world champion, Tom Sayers of England. The good-looking Benicia Boy and Adah Menken immediately fell in love, and were married within a few days. It took only a few days more for the bride to repent her hasty wedding. When Heenan wasn't getting drunk or gambling he was chasing other women. By the time he sailed for England to fight Sayers for the championship, both of the pair knew that the marriage was finished. So far so good, except that Adah now realized that she was pregnant. She was also broke. Frank Queen, heaving a patient sigh, introduced her to the drama critic on the *Sunday Mercury*, hoping that this man, Robert H. Newell, would buy some of Adah's poetry. Newell did buy her poetry regularly, and fell in love with the damsel in distress as well.

Suddenly there was appalling news for her, all over the New York papers' front pages. Alexander Menken, who had just heard of Adah's marriage to Heenan, announced to the public that she was guilty of bigamy; he himself had not yet divorced her. However, he would certainly do so now, he declared, and the petition was filed forthwith. Adah protested, no doubt truthfully, that she had been sure she was free when she married Heenan. Newell leaped to her defense and printed indignant articles on the subject — he was always a crusader, writing attacks on ramps in the War Department or government malpractice, which were signed, after the punning fashion of the day, "Orpheus C. Kerr" (office-seeker). As a seasoned battler he knew his public relations, and he gave Adah sound advice: she must brazen things out by appearing on stage in March, a good month before the Sayers-Heenan match, billed as Mrs. John C. Heenan. Adah agreed, but unwillingly. The storm of adverse criticism she suffered had cowed her for the first time in her jaunty life. When Ada Clare suggested just then that they make some outing together she replied, "No, dear! Do not be seen in public with me; you have to establish your reputation in this place, and to be seen with me might hurt it." This, to the notorious mother of Aubrey, sounds like the extreme of humility.

But Newell was right, and when "Mrs. John C. Heenan" made a public appearance, great crowds came to see her and applaud her courage. Indeed, New York paid her more attention than the Benicia Boy got from the city when, in England, he fought Tom Sayers thirty-seven rounds to a draw. Adah's spell of bad luck was not yet over, for she bore a sickly son who died soon afterwards, and she too nearly died, but she was resilient and soon went back to work. In good health she was incredibly active, performing in four or five plays a week. She would dance, play Bones in a minstrel show, imitate well-known actors, or sing, to rousing applause, "The Captain with his Whiskers gave a sly wink at me."

She was playing in Albany in the early summer of 1861 when an impresario named Captain John B. Smith approached her with an offer. He was staging *Mazeppa*, a melodrama of ancient vintage based, more or less, on a romantic poem by Byron, the story of a Cossack caught *in flagrante delicto* with a Polish lady of high degree. The climax of the drama occurred when Mazeppa was bound to the back of a fiery charger and the horse, helped on by a sharp blow from Mazeppa's captors, galloped off into the wild hills. Smith's lead having just dropped out of the cast, the impresario was inspired with the idea of putting Adah Menken in the title role. The fact that Mazeppa was a man merely made it all that much more exciting. Besides, Adah had been a circus rider; she could ride the stallion herself, where in the past they'd had to use a dummy.

Adah was lukewarm to the proposition, probably because it smacked to her of the bad old days of transvestitism in New Orleans, but Smith was so urgent that she agreed to give it a try. Things did not go well at the first rehearsal. It is one thing to ride a horse the usual way, and quite another to lie on it face upward, tied down. Adah and her stallion — a gentle mare, in truth — galloped straight off stage and fell into the orchestra pit, but no bones were broken, so they tried again. Mare and Mazeppa learned to get along with each other. *Mazeppa* opened in Albany on June 7 and won a triumph that is still remembered. From that night on, Adah Isaacs Menken, no matter what she did, was a smash hit.

The secret of her success, if the word "secret" is appropriate, was that she wore flesh-colored tights for the part. Admittedly, the tights were not all. She wore a tunic as well which covered her down to the thighs, and in the many pictures that survive of Adah as Mazeppa she looks, to the modern eye, pretty well bundled up. There is more nakedness to be seen today on any beach of America or Europe, even in prudish Portugal. But this was in the Sixties, when men stood around on windy street corners all afternoon in hope of stealing one glimpse of a feminine ankle. Seeing Adah's legs gave people a tremendous thrill. She became known as "The Naked Lady," and this made her more thrilling then ever. People came from miles around to look at her, even when she was playing some other part than Mazeppa: wickedness and glamor still clung to her when she was clothed.

Adah loved it all. She earned money and she spent money, or gave it away, at a great rate. The Heenan scandal had no terrors for her now. She divorced Heenan, against his counterclaim that she couldn't divorce him because they hadn't been married. In 1862 she managed, between stage appearances and tours, to marry the faithful Robert Newell. From the rich mining center of Virginia City, Nevada, came urgent offers. Adah thought them over and decided that a tour of the Golden West was indicated. She packed, and with the unresisting Orpheus C. Kerr in tow set out for new pastures. Pfaff's was to see no more of Adah Menken, but her sojourn among the literary Bohemians of the Cave beneath Broadway had left an indelible stamp on her. In spirit she would always be one of them.

*   *   *

Everyone at Pfaff's was proud of Ada Clare for her rebellious principles, her beauty and her spirit. Many of the unattached Bohemians fell in love with her and wrote poems about their passion, until people outside whispered scandalous rumors about the café. Drink! Women! Orgies! They shuddered in delighted horror, but the stories were untrue, and showed gross ignorance of the habits of intellectuals. Pfaff's was not in the least orgiastic. The prevailing vice of a crowd like that is conversation. Though Ada had love affairs she was no *devidasi*. Her function at Pfaff's was more that of a socially prominent clubwoman in some small town: she organized literary contests, reminded the members of each other's birthdays, and when money was needed for such community celebrations it was Ada who passed around the hat. When the circle was not tearing some recent publication to pieces, or making clever puns, it sometimes discussed the nature of the Bohemian, and Ada wrote out her personal definition of the animal:

"The Bohemian is by nature, if not by habit, a cosmopolite, with a general sympathy for the fine arts, and for all things above and beyond convention. The Bohemian is not, like the creature of society, a victim of rules and customs; he steps over them all with an easy, graceful, joyous unconsciousness, guided by the principles of good taste and feeling. Above all others, essentially, the Bohemian must not be narrow-minded; if he be, he is degraded back to the position of a mere worldling."

Yet, with due respect to Ada, not *all* the Bohemians at Pfaff's were joyous *all* the time. Unremitting joy would have been out of character, just as Poe's somber gloom, unrelieved, strikes a wrong note at the other extreme. The young Englishman William North was an early tragedy in the group's annals — a writer who quarreled bitterly with Fitz-James O'Brien, accusing him of plagiarism, and in revenge wrote him up as a burlesque figure in a novel. In 1854, when North was only twenty-eight, he drank prussic acid and died, an action his friends attributed to unhappiness over a love affair. In an envelope on his desk he left twelve cents and a note saying that this was all he had to show for a life's work.

*   *   *

Pfaff's Bohemia stimulated comment, a good deal of which was adverse. As a result, the public began going there to see the sights. The more lurid the rumors, the more they came. A number of youthful malcontents, feeling that Pfaff's crowd represented what they were looking for, moved into the neighborhood, taking rooms in adjacent boardinghouses. This

aroused and alarmed the Philistines. Newspapers printed
editorial denunciations of Bohemia. Respectable Americans
preferred to forget how much they had enjoyed that book of
Murger's that started the whole thing, seeing now that such
ideas, though all very well in France, could not be allowed to
flourish at home. Some Cave habitués defended themselves,
wrote solemn expositions of their creed, and attempted to de-
flate the wilder rumors of what Bohemia really was, but as an
early example of public relations the attempt was ineffective.
It is to be doubted if the Cavemen's hearts were in the work,
anyway. Ada Clare, for one, would not be inclined to abandon
her favorite pastime of shocking the middle class. The bad
press went on, but Pfaff's Bohemia enlisted friendly spirits too,
like William Winter.

He was a young newspaperman of Boston who grew impatient with the smug spirit of the "modern Athens" and went
to New York. There Henry Clapp took him on as a sub-editor
of the *Saturday Press*. Winter loved the work and the evenings
at Pfaff's and considered himself a thoroughgoing Bohemian.
One feels that in this he was mistaken, though it is not easy to
say why — perhaps it is because his Bohemianism was so obviously a mere phase of youth. At any rate he was an ardent
member of the Clapp crowd and has left us warm words about
its leader. Because of Clapp's gray beard and general appearance the others called him the Oldest Man, though in 1858 he
was only forty-six. He was small and slight, with a thin, in-
cisive voice; he had a brilliant mind, was impatient of the commonplace and intolerant of "smug, ponderous, empty, obstruc-
tive respectability." He was reckless of public opinion and loved
to shock "the commonplace mind." Withered, bitter, a good
fighter and a kind heart — "he was the Prince of our Bohemian
circle," said Winter. And the *Saturday Press* was a fine, stimu-

lating paper, added the writer; piquant and pugnacious and full of jibes at unworthy — and, alas, occasionally worthy — reputations. Clapp was belligerent and hasty, but he was witty, too. Probably the most famous of his jibes is that on Horace Greeley — "a self-made man who worships his creator." When asked what a certain smug clergyman was doing at the time, Clapp said, "Waiting for a vacancy in the Trinity." The *Press* suspended publication at the start of the Civil War when satire seemed to have no place in the scheme of things, but Clapp re-suscitated it, though only for a short time, in 1865, explaining in his first issue, "This paper was stopped in 1860, for want of means; it is now started again for the same reason."

In 1900, years after Clapp's death, William Dean Howells published a section of his memoirs in a book with the title *Literary Friends and Acquaintances*, in which he described how in 1860, as a young man who had contributed a few things to Eastern magazines, he came on a pilgrimage to the Atlantic seaboard from his home town of Columbus, Ohio. His first port of call was Boston; he had decided even before seeing the modern Athens that here, and not New York, was his spiritual home. "I suppose there is no question but our literary centre was then in Boston, wherever it is, or is not, at present," he said. There, every meeting with great minds left him more starry-eyed, more convinced that he was right in his preference. It was part of his plan to visit New York and the office of the *Saturday Press* nevertheless; he had sold to the *Press* and had heard of Pfaff's and Ada Clare. But he knew from the beginning that he wouldn't care for the city as he did for Boston. Oliver Wendell Holmes forewarned him against what he might read in the *Press* about Boston, which, said Holmes, was "the New York bohemian view." (Naturally the New England connotation of that adjective was pejorative.)

Howells visited the *Press* in Spruce Street and learned immediately that Holmes was right, for Clapp lost no time in violently attacking Boston's fair name. The editor walked up and down the room as he talked, shocking William Dean Howells the more with every statement, though, admittedly, it was never difficult to shock Howells. Even in retrospect Howells was scathing about New York's Bohemia: "a sickly colony, transplanted from the mother asphalt of Paris, and never really striking root in the pavements of New York; it was a colony of ideas, of theories, which had perhaps never had any deep roots anywhere."

Howells could not condemn the *Saturday Press*, a clever, witty paper in which young writers were eager to appear even though they were seldom paid. Still, Clapp had said dreadful things, and the young man came away seething with retorts he had been too refined to utter. Just who were these so-called Bohemians anyway? What made them so special? He determined to give them a last chance to prove their quality by visiting Pfaff's that very night. He did so, and found the Cave company dull and disappointing. Everything "went but slow for an orgy," he declared, though two men who came in late declared that they had hangovers after a fearful debauch. If this is Bohemia, said Howells to himself, I have had enough of it. He says that he got up to go, but was hailed on his way out by an acquaintance who presented him to Walt Whitman. Heretofore, says Howells, he had disapproved of Whitman, accepting the dictum that he was eccentric, immoral and vulgar: besides, the *Press* supported the poet and that was condemnation in itself. But Howells found Whitman, surprisingly, perfectly charming. "The apostle of the rough, the uncouth, was the gentlest person; his barbaric yawp, translated into the terms of social encounter, was an address of singular quiet."

It took William Winter eight years to publish a retort to

Howells in his memoirs, but when he got around to it he assailed the other elderly man with as much vigor and ferocity
as if they were still youths. Howells's account of that meeting
with Whitman, said Winter, was twisted: in fact, the man from
Ohio had gone to Pfaff's with the one idea of being presented
to Whitman, and it was all arranged beforehand. "Walt, at
that time, affected the Pompadour style of shirt and jacket —
making no secret of his brawny anatomy — and his hirsute
chest and complacent visage were, as usual, on liberal exhibition." In fact, Winter did not share the other Cavemen's admiration for Whitman. He says he once asked Whitman to define "the Poet," and got the answer, "A poet is a Maker."

"But Walt, what does he make?"

"He gazed upon me for a moment, with that bovine air of
omniscience for which he was remarkable, and then he said:
'He makes Poems.' "

Whitman apart, said Winter, Howells's reference to hangovers was the unfairest thing of all, for Pfaff's Bohemians didn't
go in for debauches. Even at Clapp's birthday party that year
they pledged his health in simple beer. "Those old comrades
of mine were not sots, nor were they given to 'debauchery.'
Most of them were poor, and they were poorly paid . . . Rev-
elry requires money."

Certainly they were poor. War was on the way; the
economy was disrupted. The artist's or writer's income, un-
certain at the best of times, was at its lowest. "A precarious
vocation," recalled Winter, looking back on those days from a
more prosperous time. Still, he remembered that he was happy.
The high point of his Bohemian days was his friendship with
the Irishman Fitz-James O'Brien, who had inherited a fortune
in his native land, then squandered it within two years in
London. In 1852 the twenty-four-year-old O'Brien came to

America. He started out living high: because of his good looks and charm he was a great social success, but soon he had spent every penny of the remains of the Irish money, and started to write for a living. Clapp took him on the *Saturday Press* staff, but regular jobs were not to Fitz's taste, and he soon went back to free-lancing. He published a good deal, but could never hold on to his earnings. A hard drinker, in his cups he would become recklessly pugnacious, and his beauty was ruined by a pugilist he challenged in a bar, who flattened his nose.

When William Winter met him in 1859, Fitz was on bad terms with most of the world and often hadn't the means to pay for a room. One day he asked if he could come home with Winter for the afternoon to do a spot of work. Winter did better than that, and fixed up a bedroom for the visitor in his flat on Varick Street. There O'Brien stayed, working hard, for thirty-six hours on end, during which time he refused to eat or drink, and slept four hours at most. On the third morning, waking early, Winter found his guest standing by the bed, a roll of manuscript in his hand. Frigidly polite, O'Brien said, "I wish you good-morning," and walked out of the house. That afternoon at four o'clock, Winter dropped in at Delmonico's and found Fitz transformed, in new clothes, uproariously standing treat to everyone in the place. He had sold the poem written at Varick Street, "The Sewing Bird," to *Harper's* magazine for the staggering sum of $150, and all was sweetness and light once more. Noisily, he insisted on lending money to Winter.

There were plenty of stories about Fitz. Once he came bustling into Pfaff's with a new poem and a black eye. Brushing off all reference, however jocular, to the mouse, he sat down at the table, brought out a small bottle from which he extracted a leech, applied the leech to the bruised eye, unrolled the script, and began declaiming his poem.

In later days, Thomas Bailey Aldrich wrote to Winter, "I

half smile as I recall how hurt I was on an occasion when O'Brien borrowed $35.00 from me to pay a pressing bill, and, instead of paying the bill, gave a little dinner at Delmonico's to which he did *not* invite *me!* Arnold and Clapp were there, and perhaps you. *I gave that dinner!*"

Of course Fitz enlisted in the army as soon as war was declared; he and Thomas Bailey Aldrich happened to apply for the same post on the staff of one General Lander. The General got Aldrich's letter first, and telegraphed to say that he had been accepted, but Aldrich didn't get the telegram. After waiting vainly for the reply, the General appointed Fitz-James O'Brien instead. Soon afterwards Fitz was wounded in the shoulder, the wound went septic, and the Irishman died of lockjaw.

"Aldrich was shot in O'Brien's shoulder," said Clapp.

*   *   *

After the war Pfaff's Cave was never the same. The *Saturday Press,* its mainspring, limped along for only a short time, then died for good, and Clapp resorted to writing for other papers. He was drinking, more and more heavily, but unlike most drunks he refused to sponge on friends when he needed money, and was often in want. At least once he entered a home for inebriates, but the cure did not last. By 1875, when he died, the old crowd had long since come apart. Some of them became successful and automatically stopped being Bohemian. Others died young. Walt Whitman served as a nurse during the war, and afterwards got a government job in Washington. Slowly, step by step, with many a disappointment on the way, he achieved recognition in the great world. He never reassumed a café existence, and this seems reasonable, for it had always been incongruous for him.

Charlie Pfaff prospered, though his first clients were gone.

He moved his place up to Twenty-Fourth Street, where it acquired a conventional elegance unknown to it in the Bleecker Street days. Now and then a survivor from Clapp's crowd dropped in for a visit, but Ada Clare was not among them. Her income stopped when the South was vanquished, and in 1864 she took little Aubrey to San Francisco, to make a new life in the West. There she hoped to meet Adah Menken, supposedly still on a western tour, but in this she was disappointed, for Adah had already moved on to fresh triumphs in England. Still, there was a ready market for Ada Clare's writing in the *Golden Era,* a literary weekly edited by Bret Harte, and, as always, she quickly became the center of a group of admirers, with Charles Warren Stoddard at their head. Stoddard, still dizzy from the heady effects of Adah Menken, was completely bowled over by Ada Clare — "in my eyes a remarkable woman." Trailed by this adoring youth Ada moved about the city, visited Hawaii, returned, and, disastrously, decided to star in a play at one of the local theaters. Worse: unabashed by the fact that she had flopped in New York, years earlier, she chose for a start to play the title role in *Camille.* Many experienced actresses have come to grief as Camille, and Ada was only an amateur. She was booed off the stage.

San Francisco, then, was finished for her, and she packed her bags and sailed to New York, determined to make money by writing a novel. *Only a Woman's Heart* appeared in 1866, and was greeted on all sides by hostile reviews. The historian Albert Parry thinks the critics were against Ada because she had so often dealt out harsh reviews to other writers, but it is possible that they simply thought it a bad novel, that America had outgrown her style. Deeply hurt, she made up her mind to cut her losses. She changed her name and went away again, this time to Memphis, Tennessee, where she joined a stock company as an actress. No more did she insist on starting at the top of the ladder: she took whatever part she was offered, and learned to act the hard way. Like Adah Menken, she was annoyed at being given male roles, but it couldn't be helped. She married a man named Noyes who was in the same troupe, and after that the couple toured and worked as a team, with reasonable success. Noyes adopted Aubrey, and Ada gave birth to another son, but he died in infancy.

One day when she was visiting friends, sitting on the porch, their pet dog suddenly jumped at her and bit her in the face. Nobody realized how grave the situation was. Ada's preoccupation was with her appearance; for a while she was afraid that she would be too badly scarred to go on with her work. She was happy when the wound healed and she wasn't disfigured. Then the disease struck: the dog had been rabid. It was far too late to do anything for the poor woman, even if the doctors had known what preventive measures to take. After suffering for several days, alternately delirious and lucid, Ada Clare died raving mad.

"The queen is dead; but who shall cry 'Long live the Queen!' in her stead?" wrote Stoddard in mournful retrospect. "Are there no more queens of Bohemia, I wonder, and is the Bohemia of that day a thing of the past, dead and gone forever? Of course it is gone . . ."

*   *   *

For the rest of his life William Winter spoke proudly of his Bohemian days, but long after Clapp's crowd was dispersed the prejudice of alarmed Philistines survived. Bayard Taylor, when he was an elderly, honored man of letters, felt compelled to protest that he hadn't gone to Pfaff's so *very* much. Charles Godfrey Leland went further and became quite agitated when

someone mentioned him as an habitué of Pfaff's in the old days.
In 1893 he published a disclaimer in his *Memoirs:*

"There was . . . in the city a kind of irregular club known
as the Bohemians, who had been inspired by Murger's novel
of that name to imitate the life of its heroes. They met every
evening at a lager-beer restaurant kept by a German named
Pfaff. For a year or two they made a great sensation in New
York . . . Now I must here specify, for good reasons, that
I held myself very strictly aloof from the Bohemians, save
in business affairs. This was partly because I was married, and
I never saw the day in my life when to be regarded as a real
Bohemian vagabond, or shiftless person, would not have given
me the horrors." This sounds strange, considering it was written by a man who devoted a large part of his life to following,
living with, and writing about gypsies, and who became, as Van
Wyck Brooks said, "something more than a second Borrow."
Moreover, in his youth Leland, who referred to his birthplace
Philadelphia as "pleasant sunny Philistia," had written a novel
in French that was so shocking that no Parisian editor would
publish it. That such a man should be afraid of the appellation
"bohemian" shows what had happened to it in the public mind.

"The gypsy camp is broken," said Winter sorrowfully. "The
music is hushed. The fires are put out. The gypsies are all
gone. There is no Bohemia any more, nor ever will be except
in luxury's lap or imagination's dream."

Like Stoddard, Winter was growing old: his own Bohemia
had long since vanished. And yet, even before Clapp died, new
campfires caught and began to smolder.

CHAPTER 3

Foils, Philistines
and Fugitives

C LAPP'S GROUP saw themselves as an extension of Murger's
Left Bank in Paris, but they were mistaken. Pfaff's had
its own character, which was by no means Parisian. There was
a different emphasis: when we think of Murger's characters,
painters and poets come first to mind, but most of Clapp's
followers were of a separate order of literary men: journalists.
Painters, poets, sculptors, actors and musicians by the very nature of their work could not immortalize themselves like these
gentry, who in obedience to their nature gave publicity to their
own sort at the expense of the plastic artists. Clapp himself
was no moody, creative type like Murger's Rodolphe, but a
practical man — or, at least, a man who tried to run a paper in
a practical way. Though he championed poets, he was one
stage removed from the waterhole of Pegasus, and that much
farther away from the other arts.

Still, painters and sculptors and actors were very much a
part of the New York Bohemian scene, their style surviving the
natural demise of the Ornithorhynchus Restaurant. A book entitled *The Physiology of the New York Boarding-Houses,* published in 1857, describes at some length the lodgings and living
habits of actors and artists. They tended to herd together.
There were special theatrical boardinghouses where the acting

folk could have late suppers, and where in festive mood they played cards, pounded the piano-forte, and sang choruses. Their ladies smoked cigars, drank hot brandy-and-water, and were rather casual in bringing up their children. At a boardinghouse patronized by painters, the studios and offices were full of "all the heterogeneous medley of articles only to be seen in such places: plaster casts, boxing gloves, easels, squares of canvas, skulls, portfolios, pipes, armor, weapons, sketches, and fencing foils."

For some reason, foils used to fascinate artists, or at least writers about artists. Again and again they are mentioned as an essential part of a studio's decoration. One wonders why. Was fencing a popular sort of exercise? Did hearty painters wield the foils to keep fit, as men today swing golf clubs? Whatever the explanation, there they are in the ateliers, as firmly part of the scene as the inevitable easel. One instance is in William Dean Howells's *The Coast of Bohemia,* set in the New York of the mid-Eighties. Charmian, a Bohemia-struck young lady of means who attends art school, fits up a special room in her mother's fashionable Fifth Avenue flat where she can relax in a truly Bohemian atmosphere. There is a tiger-skin on the floor, rich rugs hanging on the walls, and a false ceiling of gray canvas to hide the genuine spaciousness of the room. Cigarettes, cigars and pipes are waiting in handy places, not that Charmian smokes, but she intends to learn. "Bernhardt does," she explains. She says that the studio is not quite ready as yet: "I'm going to have foils and masks over the chimney."

The old gentleman of Henry Harland's *Bohemian Girl,* an all-round Bohemian in Paris, keeps a home away from home in a café. "There he dined, wrote his letters, dispensed his hospitalities; he had his own piano there, if you can believe me, his foils and boxing-gloves." And of course there was *Trilby,*

George du Maurier's novel of 1894, the book that swept the board and made more people cry, in more parts of the world, than any other romance of the decade. During *Trilby*'s vogue Murger was swamped and forgotten, not to be resurrected until the end of the century when Puccini put the book to music. Yet the minute we enter that Paris studio on the first page of *Trilby* we have the eerie sensation of *déjà vu*. There are the plaster casts, the easels, the lay figures and weapons and boxing gloves, and there are the fencing foils. But research has lured us beyond our period, to the Eighties and Nineties when girls like Charmian were cashing in on the revival. Actually, in the late Sixties and Seventies Bohemia was in the doldrums. Ada Clare had been forgotten long before she died. The day Walt Whitman thought she heralded, that of the New Woman, was still a long way off.

It will be recalled that our old friend William Winter — "Weeping Willie," as he was called in later days, because he wrote such gushy obituaries of old friends — said that pre-war days were precarious for hard-up artists and writers. Now the artists and writers faced a different sort of hazard: prosperous times. During the post-war boom many a once rebellious soul softened and lost his chief motivation. It was in the Seventies that James Laurens Ford, a young newspaperman, dropped in at Pfaff's much as we might spend a few minutes in a museum, and stared at a few survivors of Clapp's once turbulent crowd as they sat around in listless silence. Pondering the mutability of human affairs, he finished his drink and continued to stroll up Broadway, where a moment later he encountered an omen of the Future: one of his friends whizzed by on a wooden velocipede.

When Ford and his friends went out to dine they had a choice of restaurants that would have confounded Dickens. Swelling immigration brought to New York foreigners who wanted to eat their own sorts of food, and other foreigners willing to supply it. Though German cuisine was still the easiest to find, Francophiles too could eat what they liked at quite a number of places, Martin's being the best known. Those who favored honest meat and no nonsensical fancy sauces went to English chophouses as they had always done, but the latest rage was Italian cookery. Moretti's, at the corner of Third Avenue and Fourteenth Street, the pioneer Italian restaurant, was already there during Pfaff's heyday. Its owner introduced, for the special benefit of compatriot opera singers adrift in the New World, the Italian table d'hôte, spaghetti, olives, and Chianti, all unknown to New Yorkers before he took the plunge. Next came Martinelli, and then more Italians, and more. They flourished, for the New Yorkers liked the food and it was not expensive: fifty cents was the usual price of an Italian meal.

Thirty years and an intervening war had also jollied up the night life of which Dickens complained. The double standard of morality waved shamelessly in the breeze. Near Houston Street was a thriving red-light district with a selection of callhouses. Not far off were the dance halls — Harry Hill's Dance House, The House of Lords, the House of Commons. Here also was Harry Clifton's, a kind of American café-chantant where the clients joined in glee-singing and men gave solo renditions. Those who wanted to feel wicked could go slumming in Chinatown and enjoy a pipe in an opium joint. Opium, being an indulgence of the criminal classes, was considered romantic by the bourgeoisie. The bourgeoisie were a romantic lot altogether, if always finding wickedness is a sign of it. The new apartment houses, for example, were at first considered immoral: people called them "French flats."

Brazen hussies in tights cavorted on the stage where "The

Black Crook" was performed, untroubled by the broadcasts launched at the production from the city's pulpits. It paid to cavort. According to the charming custom of the day, stage-door Johnnies sent their favorite chorus girls jewelry hidden in bouquets: these were presented in the usual way onstage, and frenzied activity ensued. Showers of petals and mangled blossoms filled the air as the girls tore their nosegays to pieces to find the pretty things.

It was the Tweed era, when the city was at once colorful and extraordinarily vulgar. Serious artists found themselves less and less able to stay in touch, to sympathize, with "top people." Men like the sybaritic James Fiske, Jr., who liked to drive down Fifth Avenue in a four-in-hand brake full of "gaudily bedizened and painted women," as James Lauren Ford called them, were not the type to stand patron to any painters and poets except those of the simplest, most debased style. Dramatists must have been bitter when they reflected that the favorite stage attraction of the day was Dolly Adams the Water Queen, who, says Ford, "spent much of her time in a glass tank eating bananas and smoking cigars under water." Though she *would* have been well worth seeing, at that.

This is not to say that there was a total eclipse of the arts, only that the temper of the times led to a sharp division between them and what was considered ordinary, or normal.

*   *   *

Then the pendulum took a backward swing. Those scenes of "extravagance and vulgarity, open immorality and thievery" (as Ford piously called them) came to a sudden halt when the country was overtaken by the financial panic of 1873. Fortunes were lost overnight, the Tweeds and the Fiskes toppled from their thrones, and New York plunged into gloom. For the next few years almost everyone found life real, earnest and dull, but there was one happy exception — the acting fraternity. In search of escape from sad reality, people went to see the comedy team of Harrigan and Hart, who put on programs of short sketches depicting the life of the Irish either as peasants in the Old Country or as immigrants in America. Harrigan wrote and stage-managed, and Hart acted the chief parts, old or young, male or female. Through the series ran, in continuity, the characters of Dan Mulligan and his family. Harrigan and Hart were fun-makers, and though in their own way they were social commentators as well, entertainment was their aim and achievement. What they produced was not exactly music hall or vaudeville, nor drama in the usual sense. It was something individual, a kind of feature journalism of the stage, flexible and adaptable, which solidified, unwieldy, costly, conventional theater can never be. Modern Off-Broadway reviews are aiming at a similar target.

But conventional theater, too, was changing. Producers had always been prejudiced against contemporary playwrights, chiefly because they had to be paid. When you could satisfy people with Shakespeare and the other classics, not to mention improve their minds, why bother with anything modern? But the moment came when they had to bother, when the public wanted something fresh. Stock-company managers therefore added to their repertoires the works of living English and Irish playwrights, and translated and "adapted" — a euphemistic term for pirated — the latest hits from Germany and France. *The Two Orphans* started out as a French play, but in American guise it far outlasted the original. Even American dramatists got a chance occasionally, though the producers, who resented having to pay royalties, claimed that foreign plays had a superior snob attraction. American painters could bitterly attest that this attitude was not confined to the theater.

Movements in society behave much like laboratory cultures, yeast for example. From the nucleus, an idea spreads out and covers an area that grows wider and wider. In the meantime the nucleus develops and changes. In time the same changes occur in the spread-out area, but as organisms there get their start progressively later and later, the changes are delayed accordingly. Fresh beginnings are at once younger and more old-fashioned than their sources. So it was with Bohemia in America. By the time New York's first colony grew mature, aged, and died, the concept of Bohemia had caught on in the provinces, where it started up with new youth and vigor. In small towns in the Middle West and South were a few ardent souls who formed tiny enclaves of Latin Quarter country. In larger communities the groups were sometimes of a size to assert themselves openly.

It was a fashion among Bohemians to condemn the nation for being solidly Philistine, but the facts prove them wrong. The public of the later nineteenth century had begun to want more than daily bread, and though their yearning for hyacinths often led them astray, so that housewives bought ugly ornaments and perpetrated such hideous things as decorative poker-work, these efforts were born of the same aesthetic urge that motivated accomplished artists. In Howells's *Coast of Bohemia*, a novel beginning in the Eighties, he depicts a county fair in Ohio where, among cattle and pigs and prize ears of corn, stands a tent labeled "Fine Arts Department" that shelters an exhibit of needlework, painted china, and "medley paintings" put together much like the collages of today. A prize has been offered for the best work of art. The hero, a successful painter from New York, warns a small-town girl who wants to go to the city to study art: "New York is swarming with girl art-students." The girl goes anyway. If she never seems to arrive in New York's Bohemia, it is not because the colony wasn't there, but that her creator was incapable of portraying it. As Winter said, Howells was a prig, and he knew nothing of Bohemia. But he knew his native Middle West. He had felt the hunger suffered by young people in Ohio and Illinois and Indiana: that same hunger had uprooted him and carried him to his destiny in the East. He thought that this restlessness was a peculiarity of the Mississippi basin, a disease that could be cured by geographical change.

But easterners too were discontented, and complained bitterly. For a Bohemian, the parental home, no matter where it is, invariably falls short of the ideal. Bohemians want the land of Somewhere Else, and Leland's epithet for Philadelphia, "pleasant sunny Philistia," is mild compared with what another native son, James Gibbons Huneker, called it. He saw himself in Philadelphia as a grub entrapped in a cocoon, struggling to get free and spread his butterfly wings. This was unfair — few other Americans of his time got as much encouragement to develop their aesthetic sensibilities. Huneker, born in 1857, came of a family that loved music, painting and literature. Though his father was a house-painter by trade, his ideas were wide. Young James wanted to work in the railway shops? Very well. But when James changed his mind and quit the railways, that was all right too. The elder Huneker became mildly exasperated by his son's impractical behavior: he said once that James's specialty was working for other people at reduced rates. But Father Huneker was no unlettered boor. He collected etchings and engravings, knew music, and — as we have seen — belonged to a circle that included Edgar Allan Poe. His wife was an ex-schoolteacher, educated in a convent, and had considerable knowledge of languages.

In 1876 Philadelphia celebrated her centennial with a great Exposition. Contemporary European paintings were shown for the first time in America, and the nineteen-year-old James heard Offenbach conduct his own works. A panorama, "Paris by Night," sharpened James's discontent and filled him with desire to visit Paris. That Paris was soon to have her own Exposition gave him a deadline and incentive. Two years later James and his newly acquired wife arrived in the City of Light, where he managed to subsist for nine months on a small allowance from home and an occasional five dollars paid for articles he wrote for the Philadelphia *Evening Bulletin*. His choice of subjects for these is striking — Prussian music, art collections, architecture, *haute couture* — but the paper did print them, and one is bound to reflect that a city willing to read such essays should not be condemned as wholly Philistine. Huneker no doubt felt oppressed at home not so much because Philadelphia lacked culture as that even those residents who cared for art and literature were conservative in their tastes. In Van Wyck Brooks's words, they "belonged to an Anglo-Saxon world, still dominant in the Eastern states, that retained in certain respects a colonial stamp." It is fruitless to argue that young artists like Huneker should not feel crowded at home; one might as well tell chicks not to break out of their shells when the time comes. The artist wants out. He's got to find somewhere else and create his own country, even though, when he gets old, he cannot understand the young squirt who criticizes that creation, and wants to get away in his own turn. "What an unreasonable young squirt!" marvels the old one.

"We might have been bohemians but we did not know it, though we dined at table d'hôtes in a manner that nowadays imparts the true touch of bohemianism to every one sufficiently sophisticated to call the wine 'red ink,'" wrote James Ford. The professional Bohemian, he adds, was unknown then, but old men forget. In *Bohemia Invaded* (1895) Ford uses the term unashamedly, applying it to himself — as narrator — and friends of the past who had frequented a "snug little basement" café below Washington Square: artists, writers, stage people, explorers, and "illustrious exiles" who were playing an increasingly large role on the stage of the Latin Quarter. Americans in general welcomed fugitives from the political battlefields of Europe out of a feeling that there, but for the grace of God and their own ancestors, went themselves, but such refugees had a special appeal for Bohemians. Rebel sides with rebel, and whatever the object of one's protest — academicism in art, heavy parents or political despotism — it's all injustice, and must be downed. Since opinions differed among various exiles as to what constituted tyranny, there were occasions when Europeans of violently opposed political convictions found themselves cheek by jowl in some American basement or attic gathering, being solaced and cosseted together. It didn't matter to the Bohemian hosts, happy in their expression of protest, but the situation must have flummoxed a lot of fugitives.

*   *   *

The California gold rush had calmed down, but some gold mines were still being worked, and secondary industry was developing along the West Coast. In the war Californians had searched their hearts and finally plumped for the union. Now the territory was a full-fledged state, distant and romantic in the minds of many eastern Americans who dreamed of the mountains and Indians and grizzly bears of the West, and then set out to find them. San Francisco had become famous — a beautiful city among the hills, with a bay always full of ships from South America, Asia, and the South Seas. San Francisco, seemingly as far off as China yet part of America, was enchanting, and this exotic quality was reflected in her Bohemia. Isolated by the difficulties of communication with the East, California's artistic dissidents worked out their own nonconformist conventions. They were always a little behind the eastern Bohemians, always a little different. The word itself came late to the West Coast. Possibly Bret Harte brought it when he came out with his family in 1854.

Harte was born in Albany in 1836, so at eighteen he had certainly heard of Henry Clapp and Pfaff's. Francis Brett Harte was his full name before he shortened it for literary purposes; the family called him Frank. For a few years he batted around the West Coast, earning his living in a variety of ways. He taught school, drove a stagecoach, clerked in a drugstore, and learned to set type and write for a newspaper in a little Humboldt County town. In 1857 he returned to San Francisco, where one of his sisters was writing for the *Golden Era,* a popular literary weekly: she got him a job on the paper as type-setter, and soon he won promotion to the editorial room. From these precincts his first stories were published.

Cheerfully informal, the *Era's* headquarters served as a gathering-place for writers, artists and visiting firemen of all descriptions. Wandering Pfaffians in the West thought of the *Era* as a sister of their own *Saturday Press,* and made a bee-line for it as soon as they got to San Francisco, where Bret Harte welcomed them and asked them to do something for the journal. Adah Menken with her husband came on from her triumphal tour of the West and a protracted season at Virginia City. Soon Newell was writing Orpheus C. Kerr pieces for Harte. When Mark Twain walked in there was a happy reunion, for the Newells had known him well in Virginia City, where he spent two years on the *Territorial Enterprise.* Mark had witnessed Adah's conquest of the miners and given her enthusiastic reviews. Ada Clare wrote for Bret Harte, and when her book, *Only a Woman's Heart,* was a flop, what distressed her most of all was the rumor that Bret Harte had roasted it.

Harte left the *Era* about that time, 1864, to help in launching a new weekly, the *Californian.* Charles Henry Webb, who provided the money, was one of five — Harte, Mark Twain, Charles Warren Stoddard and Prentice Mulford being the others — who wrote practically everything in the paper except the padding, which consisted of paragraphs and poems by famous writers who had not been asked for permission to reprint and hadn't a hope in hell of collecting payment. This was nothing new in the *Californian:* all journals did it until the law was tightened up.

The relationship between Mark Twain and Bret Harte was then a close one, though later they quarreled. "Bret Harte was one of the pleasantest men I have ever known": said Twain after the quarrel: "he was also one of the unpleasantest men I have ever known." But he gave full credit to Harte's technique, saying that he himself had been "trimmed and trained and schooled . . . patiently" by the editor. Stoddard said the same, in effect — that Harte was always a careful, stimulating editor — and Harte must have found Stoddard an apt pupil, for when in 1866 he embarked on a more ambitious enterprise — a full-dress magazine, the *Overland Monthly,* financed by a San Francisco bookseller — Stoddard and Ina Coolbrith worked with him as the editorial board. They came to be known as the "Golden Gate Trinity."

Bret Harte was a hard worker. It was his nature to be, but he was egged on to extra effort and longer hours by the peculiar temperament of his wife. He was twenty-five when he married Anna, and she was some years older. A concert singer, she felt trapped in the marriage, especially as they promptly had a baby and were very poor. By the time Harte began making more money, complaints had become a habit with Anna. She grew more and more shrewish. We might think there were extenuating circumstances for a woman who had tasted independence — in those days a rare flavor for a female — only to have the cup dashed from her lips. Sweet-tempered wives accepted such a fate as inevitable, but Anna was not sweet-tempered. She bossed little Harte, and the more meekly he obeyed her commands the worse she got. He tried to plan the day so that when he had done his stint of editing at the office he could write two hours every evening at home after supper, but Anna wouldn't have it. Why should that man sit quietly at his desk enjoying himself, when she'd had to spend the day drearily running his house and looking after his children? She would order him to get up and paper the walls or paint the porch, and when he did the chores badly — as he usually did — she berated him at the top of her voice. Harte tried waiting until the rest of the household had gone to bed, hoping he could then write in peace, but Anna would outfox him by saying she couldn't sleep as long as a light burned.

At first glance, we might wonder why Bret Harte in San Francisco should consider himself a Bohemian, since he followed a routine of bourgeois respectability, with regular hours and almost aggressive virtue. He was as finicky as Poe about his appearance, being particularly careful with his cravats, around which the rest of the costume was arranged. He loved cravats of bright, glowing, block colors. Nevertheless Harte *was* eccentric in his way. About money he was definitely Murgerish, and so was Anna: the Hartes were chronically in debt, and though one of Bret's biographers puts all the blame on Anna as a bad manager, there is not much on the record to prove that her husband was a better one. About his work, however, Harte was never slipshod. He had a strong sense of the artistic values that shows up in the incident of the magazine's second number and Bret

Harte's story "The Luck of Roaring Camp." He included
"Luck" in the *Overland* that month rather than using some
other piece, because it was an important point in his policy
that each issue should contain at least one article or story with
a western subject. Everything had gone off to the printer, when
suddenly he — the printer — announced that he couldn't possibly be responsible for putting "The Luck of Roaring Camp"
into type, or publishing it in the magazine: that it was indecent,
irreligious, and improper, in that order. He said that his
young lady assistant had only with difficulty been prevailed
upon to read it through. This fuss perturbed the bookseller
whose money supported the *Overland,* and he decided that he
agreed with the printer.

Bret Harte had to fight, therefore, on two fronts, but he
did it, and he won. First he managed to get the bookseller back
on his side, and then he went out and found another printer,
presumably one with a less impressionable assistant. It was a
tense period, but when the *Overland* came out, "Luck" was in
it. However, the troubles of the author-editor were not over,
for local readers now declared themselves as horrified and disgusted as the first printer had been. Bret Harte was impugning
their sacred state, they said. He was fouling his nest and biting
the hand that fed him. Righteous resentment increased in
its customary way, and trouncing Bret Harte was the season's
favorite sport, until word arrived from the East that everybody
over there was of another mind entirely and thought "Luck"
a splendid story. Even the *Atlantic Monthly* — its editor had
written to Harte from Boston, that citadel of good taste, asking
him for another of his stories. This was the accolade, and
California critics had to calm down. But they continued to
resent Harte and showed it in a dozen little ways, picking
holes in his work and criticizing whatever the magazine did,
until he got tired of the struggle. The bookseller sold the

Overland to another man, which made the situation worse. In 1871 Harte finally broke with the owner, pulled up stakes, and took Anna and the children east.

They went cross-country and paused in Chicago, where there occurred a *contretemps* that has remained rather mysterious. For months before his migration, Harte had corresponded with a group of Chicagoans who were starting a magazine, the *Lakeside Monthly*. They wanted Bret Harte to edit it and had already offered him terms that included part ownership of the journal: he had expressed interest in the proposition. It was arranged — still by letter — that the proposers give a dinner for Harte as soon as he arrived in Chicago, where he would meet everybody involved and the matter could be settled. The famous man and his family got to Chicago according to schedule. So far so good. Everybody came to the dinner as agreed — except Bret Harte. The next the hosts heard of their guest of honor he had moved on to New York, without sending one word of apology or explanation.

Officially there was never a sequel, but of course word got around, and at last a friend asked Harte just what had happened. He replied carelessly, as if to a question of no importance, that he hadn't attended the dinner because no one had called to escort him to the restaurant and he couldn't have found his way around Chicago alone. The gossips said Anna had made him stay at home because she hadn't been asked to come along.

In Cambridge the Hartes visited Howells, at that time assistant editor on the *Atlantic*. Howells liked them both, but he could see that Bret might be a problem, socially speaking — he was invariably late for appointments, and would never have started out at all if the family had not dressed him, tied his tie, and pushed him off in the right direction.

For seven years Harte made New York his center, trying his hand at various ways of making a living and failing at all of them. He went on lecture tours, but his delivery was too mild to suit the robust taste of the times. He wrote plays; all but one were hopeless. He edited a newspaper in Washington and it folded. When at last he got an appointment to a diplomatic post in Prussia, there was not enough money to pay the family's passage, and he went alone. It was in fact the end of the marriage, though he and Anna were never divorced and he continued to send money to her. When the administration changed in 1885, Bret Harte, who had been Consul in Glasgow for some time, found himself out of a job, but his success as a writer was sufficient to keep him — and Anna and the children — going. He had fallen in love with England, and now he retired to London. Life began all over for him at forty-eight. London was full of literary American pilgrims, as Van Wyck Brooks called them. Most American writers still felt that they needed a term in England for polishing, just as American painters aimed to spend a year, at least, in Paris, but Harte's desire was no mere pilgrimage. Like Henry James, he went to England for good and settled in London. (Not that these two were friends. They hated each other.)

In London Harte made a comfortable place for himself. A devoted friend kept house for him. He had his circle, called on hostesses in their drawing rooms, and took to wearing a monocle. Bohemians are adaptable, and Bret Harte took in his stride the transition from the rootin', tootin' Wild West to this sedate existence. But some part of America followed him at last, in the person of his son Francis, who himself settled down in the English countryside, with wife and children. In due course Anna came to visit Francis. Bret did the proper thing and called on her, but she made a scene and screamed abuse at him, so he went away. This was their last encounter. Bret Harte died in England, wifeless and at peace, in 1902.

CHAPTER 4

The Westerners

INA COOLBRITH, an important figure in San Francisco's early Bohemia, was the daughter of Carlos Smith and a niece of Joseph Smith, the Mormon leader. Her real name was Josephine Smith. She was born in 1843 in Illinois, where her father died soon after her birth. At that time Mormonism was one of the most scandalous topics of the day, and Josephine's mother was heartily sick of it, and of Illinois. She married again, but was careful to choose a husband from outside the flock, and must have been glad to take her little girl and go with him, by emigrant train, to settle in Los Angeles. Josephine grew up knowing that Joseph Smith was not a relative to boast of, so she changed her name to Ina Coolbrith; "Ina" was a form of Josephine, she argued, and Coolbrith was her mother's maiden name.

Ina married young and was soon divorced; it was a period in her life that she never talked about later. Whatever the trouble was, she determined to get out of Los Angeles. Still in her early twenties, she moved to San Francisco, and as a poet and a literary critic she joined the city's group of artists and writers — a pretty girl with thick dark-red hair and delicate profile. When Bret Harte admitted her to the circle of the *Overland* editorial board the gossips talked, just as they talked of her relations with

Stoddard and Mark Twain, but if Ina was distressed by this circumstance she gave no sign of her feelings. Without Harte the *Overland* deteriorated, so Ina left it to become librarian at the Oakland Public Library. A librarian can be as important to young literary aspirants as a schoolteacher — perhaps more so. Ina filled the role admirably. In her long life she served as listener, adviser and general all-round nursemaid to many writers in Bohemia, but it is safe to say that she never had a noisier charge than Joaquin Miller, who is thought to have been her lover.

Miller inspired a huge number of legends about himself. He was a most inventive liar, but even without lies his life story is not dull, though in recounting it we ought to pause at almost every comma, to distinguish between his version and the true one. He was born in 1837 — not 1842, as he said — on his father's farm in Indiana. He claimed to have been born in a covered wagon, pointed west. The wagon bit came fifteen years late, but the Miller family did go west in '52. His name was Cincinnatus Hiner Miller: "Cincinnatus" because his father came from Cincinnati, and "Hiner" because it was a family name — unimportant facts that gain a certain slight significance only because he himself claimed to have been named after the noble Roman and the poet Heine. But it is no use running after Joaquin Miller and picking up every little piece of the shattered truth.

When the Millers trekked west it was to homestead in Oregon, and there the elder Miller settled his family. At seventeen, Cincinnatus found himself bored with farm life and ran away to make his fortune in the gold-diggings of California. Going broke before he got very far, he took a job as cook for a mining camp on the Klamath River. Cincinnatus was not a good cook, and the Klamath job ended when he got scurvy. Moving on, he reached another camp on Shasta, and there became cook again. The miners called him "Crazy Miller" and suspected him, with some reason, of writing poetry in the kitchen. He managed at last to attain the status of a regular miner, but the work proved too hard for his immature frame, and when he found himself involved in gambling debts, he sneaked out of camp and headed for home. In the Squaw Valley, falling in with an Indian girl, he postponed the homecoming. Paquita, as he called her, was willing to keep him, and he was quite happy as a squaw man until she bore him a daughter, Cali-Shasta. Then Cincinnatus resumed his journey, arriving home on the farm in 1857.

Out of this ignoble adventure he later spun wonderful yarns that became legendary. Paquita in his version was a noble Modoc maiden: actually she was of the lowly Digger tribe. Cincinnatus said he had fought on the Indian side in the Modoc Wars, for which he was run out of the state as a renegade. In fact he fought on the white men's side. He also claimed to have founded a Utopian Republic for Indians on Mount Shasta; and Van Wyck Brooks believed it — though he realized what a liar Miller was on other points — but there was not a word of truth in that tale either. Cincinnatus was eloquent as to his part in the expedition the filibuster Walker led into Nicaragua. In "Songs of the Sierras" he wrote of witnessing Walker's death. He was not there at all, but he had a good answer for the skeptic who asked if he had been. "Was Milton ever in Hell?" retorted Miller.

Yet the man was something more than a mere confidence trickster. During the years that followed that escapade until his renascence as poet in San Francisco, he acquired a training of sorts in law, edited a newspaper that got itself suppressed for its Secession sentiments, rode for the Pony Express, and was actually appointed Judge for three years in a small Oregon town. He continued trying to write poetry. When he met and married Minnie Myrtle, the Sweet Singer of Coquille, a girl who actually published verse in the newspaper, it was the most important thing that ever happened to him — not the marriage, but the fact that Minnie taught him to use a rhyming dictionary. During the one military adventure that reflects genuine credit on Cincinnatus — a campaign against Utah and Nevada Indians who were carrying on a scalping program — he led the town's volunteer brigade with courage and resource. Strangely, he never boasted about this afterward. Was it because the truth, however favorable, couldn't possibly attract Cincinnatus?

Though as Judge he now rode high in Canyon City, poetry was not forgotten. He organized a Literary Society of which he was president. He published, privately, two collections of his verse, sending at least one of them to the *Overland* in San Francisco for review, and was charmed, though not surprised, when it actually got a notice in the magazine that was not *absolutely* discouraging. That man Bret Harte seemed to have possibilities, reflected Cincinnatus, and he resolved to go to San Francisco himself some day, even though Harte always turned down his direct contributions. (In truth Harte had flayed Miller's book, but tender-hearted Ina Coolbrith rewrote the review. She believed in the gentle approach.) Hopefully, Cincinnatus then wrote to Charles Warren Stoddard and asked him for a good word on his work. Away on a South Sea tour when the letter arrived in San Francisco, Stoddard didn't get it for nearly a year. Then, overcome with guilt, he replied more cordially than he might otherwise have done — even as you or I might — though he didn't know Cincinnatus Hiner Miller from Adam. The letter came just when Cincinnatus was undergoing a crisis in his family affairs. The Sweet Singer, losing patience with her husband for good and all, had taken their three sons and gone away from Canyon City to her mother's house, where she issued a series of wrathful statements about Cincinnatus's character and general habits. It couldn't have happened at a worse time for Miller: the three years of his judgeship had just ended and he was campaigning for reappointment. He realized he hadn't a hope now of getting it, for every wife in Canyon City would be on Minnie's side. Fortunately, as he told himself, he had other resources. He was a poet, wasn't he? Every good American poet ought to see and be seen by London, and Cincinnatus decided to go there on a lecture tour. First, however, he must visit San Francisco, where people seemed to appreciate him properly.

It was 1870 when an amazed Stoddard in San Francisco received a letter from that odd man in Oregon, stating that the writer was accepting Stoddard's kind invitation — what invitation, for Heaven's sake? — and would soon be in San Francisco to visit him. The writer apologized because the visit would be short, as he was on his way to England, and ended the letter with the time of arrival of his boat. Fearful yet fascinated, Stoddard was there at the gangplank. His protégé proved to be a tall, rawboned, backwoods type in a ten-gallon hat, very tight Levis, beaded moccasins and a white linen dust-coat that reached almost to the ground. The two men spoke. They shook hands. Miller looked around as if expecting others. He said, "Well, let us go and talk to the poets."

Apparently he thought poets habitually went everywhere together in a jolly little group, like Robin Hood's men, eating together, singing their Bohemian songs together, and writing poems together. Stoddard explained that it was not quite like that, at least not in San Francisco. Swallowing his disappointment, Cincinnatus handed Stoddard, in lieu of all the others, a manuscript, then stood back in proud silence, expecting the other man to read it on the spot. The mesmerized Stoddard did just that. It was a poem entitled "The Bards of San Francisco Bay," beginning:

> I am as one unlearned, uncouth
> From country come to join the youth
> Of some sweet town in quest of truth:
> A skilless northern Nazarene . . .

Though Cincinnatus Miller was soon the favorite joke of the season in San Francisco, not everyone was charmed by his naïveté. Bret Harte, for one, disliked him then and always. But Ina Coolbrith took an interest in him, tucked him under her wing, and set to work grooming him for the London venture. She gave him poetry to read — he already knew Byron, but Ina showed him the verses of Swinburne and Rossetti. She corrected his spelling and made him rewrite his doggerel. Shrewdly she counseled him to show the English what they expected to see in a man from the Wildest West — an uncouth, picturesque cowboy with long hair, high-heeled boots and a big hat. Cincinnatus wouldn't believe her. Certainly he had been dressed rather like that when he arrived from Oregon, but not because he didn't know better; they were his only clothes. When, weeks later, he arrived in London, he went to expense he couldn't afford to fix himself up like a man of the town, only to find that Ina had been perfectly right. Cincinnatus was equally refractory at first about another piece of her advice — that he change his name to "Joaquin Miller." The name "Joaquin" she took from one of his titles, which in turn derived from Joaquin Valley, but Cincinnatus Hiner couldn't see the change as at all necessary. In the end, after much rebellious muttering, he yielded, and the new name turned out to be such an asset that after a while he wouldn't admit it had not been his own idea.

Ina had her way again when she told Miller that he must do something for his daughter by the Digger woman. The girl Cali-Shasta was now fourteen, still living with her mother in the Squaw Valley. Reluctantly, Joaquin fetched her to San Francisco, where she was installed in Ina's house, and Ina bore the expense and responsibility of the charge without complaint for the next seven years. Cali-Shasta was a beautiful girl, but her life proved short and tragic. She married at twenty-one, took to drink, and her husband walked out on her. She then moved in with her father, and there remained until she died of alcoholism. Her mother Paquita had a better time of it. Joaquin had killed her off in one of his flights of fancy, saying that she sacrificed her life to save him from some great peril or other, but when in 1908 he himself died, she was still alive and healthy. Her name by then, incidentally, was Mrs. Amanda Brock.

In London, Joaquin found things hard at first. No publisher was interested in his poetry, and his borrowed money was running out when he met Thomas Hood, son of the poet and editor of *Fun*, a humor magazine. Hood had romantic ideas about the Wild West in America, and the swashbuckling Joaquin seems to have impressed him in spite of affording amusement. Before long he was giving the American much the same advice Ina had proffered in San Francisco. The hard-won city clothes must be discarded, Hood said firmly, and he was adamant when Joaquin, who now possessed calling cards printed with the words "Byron of the Rockies," pleaded to be permitted an open, Byronic collar. He didn't get it. Hood persuaded him to let his hair grow down to his shoulders and to grow an Imperial beard and long mustache. He said Joaquin must always wear a sombrero, a red shirt with blue bandana neckerchief, cowboy boots with spurs, and chaps. He coached the frustrated Byron, telling him to swagger and always tell tall stories — as if Joaquin needed this advice — and at last, when his protégé looked the part even down to his rawhide quirt, Hood introduced him to Rossetti and the other Pre-Raphaelites. They simply loved Joaquin, and took him everywhere. One introduction led to another, until the American was being invited to call on Duchesses and Countesses. There was no difficulty now in finding a publisher; soon Joaquin's books were reprinted in England. They were well reviewed by a lot of people who should have known better, and had a good sale.

Joaquin's bubble burst later, but it is a mystery that it ever managed to be blown at all. One can only suppose that the savants who spoke well of "Songs of the Sierras" were so snobbish that Joaquin Miller's social success blinded them. Or perhaps the British made allowances because he was an untutored American. But in time all allowances come to an end. Joaquin outstayed his welcome, or, rather, went back when he shouldn't have, on a second visit. In the meantime his eccentricities had increased until, in the eyes of once delighted hostesses, he became too boorish even for a quaint frontiersman from the American West, and when he published again, the reviews were corrosive.

America, on the other hand, was never fooled about Miller. Bayard Taylor, in *The Echo Club,* wrote: "Much of Joaquin Miller's work is itself a travesty of poetry . . . he is an Indianized copy of Byron, made up of shrieks and war-paint, and the life he describes is too brutal, selfish, and insane ever to have existed anywhere."

If this sounds harsh, read Joaquin's romance *The Baroness of New York* (1877). Swinburne, not Byron, seems to have been his model here, but the change is not necessarily for the better. It begins:

> In a land so far that you wonder whether
>   The God would know it should you fall dead,
> In a land so far thro' the wilds and weather
>   That the sun falls weary and flushed and red —
> That the sea and the sky seem coming together,
>   Seem closing together as a book that is read: . . .

Joaquin really hit his stride in the Prelude to Part Two, apostrophizing Fifth Avenue in New York — "O Avenue, splendid Fifth Avenue! . . ."

> Dear and delicious, loved Avenue!
> I have had my day in the Bois de Boulogne,
> I have stood very near the first steps of a throne,
> I have roamed all cities of splendor thro' . . .
> On gay Rotten Row I have galloped the rounds,
> And, too, have made one of a long line of hounds,
> But nothing 'neath sun or tide-guiding moor
> Approaches thine populus afternoon.

Once one has begun, it is difficult to stop quoting Joaquin, so let us have one more stanza on the subject of Central Park:

> 'Tis said this park is proud Manhattan's pride;
> It is, indeed, a most capacious park.
> It looks as long as all the plains, as wide;
> That is, if you behold it in the dark.

*　　*　　*

After he became a grand old character in San Francisco Joaquin added to his legend, like a caddis decorating its case. Of course he had heard much of Adah Menken and her stay in the Bay City; everybody heard about Adah, especially when she became notorious in Europe. So Joaquin took her and incorporated her in his saga, much as he used William Walker of Nicaragua and a host of others. Actually he was never in San Francisco at the same time as Adah, but one can understand why he wanted to claim her scalp — few other Bohemians had made as much of a splash. The rest of her life, after the Newells left San Francisco, was even wilder than what had gone before.

It was to fulfill an engagement in London that Adah went east from the Coast at the end of 1863. En route to New York, in spite of Newell's presence, she managed to acquire a rich follower, James Paul Barkley, and when she sailed from New York — having paused there only long enough to drop off her husband, much as a deep-sea liner, outward bound, stops to drop the pilot — Barkley was still with her. "Mazeppa" set London on its ear, with perhaps the biggest impact Adah had yet made. Part of the press attacked her but the remaining papers came staunchly to her defense, until all London was discussing the quarrel and taking sides on the question of Adah Menken's taste, talent and decency, if any. All was grist, as Adah and her manager knew. The more the Naked Lady was talked about, the more the preachers thundered at her from their pulpits, the more people would flock to look at her and judge those flesh-colored tights for themselves. She — and Barkley — lived at a smart hotel where she kept open house. People of the highest rank came to her parties. She enjoyed her social success, but Adah was a Bohemian above all, and it seemed to her far more satisfactory to meet leading poets than be complimented by princes. After all, she took her own poetry very seriously. She was delighted, therefore, when one night Dante Gabriel Rossetti, whom she already knew, brought Algernon Charles Swinburne backstage and presented him. Swinburne's reputation was at its height. Adah didn't mind his being so odd-looking, with a tiny body and huge head of flaming hair. He was *Swinburne*.

At the end of 1864, when Barkley had to go back to New York and attend to his business affairs, Adah was left free to get into fresh mischief, and promptly did. Rossetti, far from being the bloodless aesthete his works imply, had an earthy side and was addicted to practical jokes, of which presenting Swinburne to the Naked Lady was a sample — for little Swinburne, in spite of his burning, passionate poems, was a virgin. All his friends knew it, and discussed the problem in a cheerfully unabashed manner that might surprise today's moderns with their set ideas of Victorian prudery. Swinburne was a sado-masochist. Rossetti thought it exquisitely funny to egg on Adah Menken, hearty, extrovert wench that she was, to seduce Algernon. Adah was more than ready to comply. No doubt she too found the idea amusing, but she had great admiration for Swinburne as a poet, and thousands of people can testify to the catnip effect of versification on women, which runs music a very close second.

So Adah stalked Swinburne. Something came of it, though exactly what is not easy to sort out. Nobody involved in the business can be accused of reticence, but the various reports do not agree. In cheerful letters to friends, Swinburne proudly referred to Adah as his mistress. Adah, on the other hand, told Rossetti that her encounters with Swinburne were frustrating, as she could not seem to make the poet understand that mere biting was no use. Nevertheless — though she did not put it quite that way — she profited from the relationship; she got Swinburne to read proof on a book of poetry she was getting ready for publication under the title *Infelicia* — an apt name, since most of Adah's verses were sorrowful. Later, Swinburne told a friend that he had not only looked over the book but thought he had improved some of the lines considerably. "Considerably" was an appropriate word: when *Infelicia* appeared in 1868 it carried passages so very like Swinburne's work that readers thought she had swiped them from him without permission. One quatrain in particular, they said, bore out the theory:

> Leaves pallid and sombre and ruddy,
>   Dead fruits of the fugitive years;
> Some stained as with wine and made bloody,
>   And some as with tears.

Not Swinburne at his best, perhaps, said the gossips, but indubitably Swinburne. Other lines of Adah's unimproved by the poet, can be compared:

> Look at these tear-drops.
> See how they quiver and die on your open hands.

Those who expected Swinburne to share their indignation were disappointed. The British Museum copy of *Infelicia* bears on the flyleaf the following inscription in Swinburne's own hand: *Lo! This is she that was the World's delight.*

However, when after Adah's death someone asked Swinburne if she had really been such a good poet, the little Lion of Putney replied with blunt honesty, "How can you ask me? A girl may be admired as 'Mazeppa' without being admired as a poet. I think it the greatest rot ever published." In extenuation we should remember that Joaquin Miller's work had yet to appear.

Adah returned to New York in 1866, broke. This was the normal state of affairs for her; she spent money faster than she earned it. Her reappearance on the New York stage raised fresh hullaballoo, and once again the old abusive terms were trotted out. While the air reverberated, Adah's divorce from Robert

Newell was arranged, and he moved out of the limelight, no doubt still wondering just what had happened. This was the third broken marriage for Adah, and she would have preferred to remain single, but she soon discovered herself pregnant by Barkley. So they married, and Adah moved into his house on Seventh Avenue — for two days, which was enough respectability for incorrigible Mazeppa. On the third morning she set sail for Europe. Barkley's son was born in Paris but died shortly afterward, and Adah went back to work on the stage, this time making Mazeppa's hair-raising dash for liberty before French audiences, accompanied by the customary outcry in the press.

The last scandal featuring Adah Menken involved another literary figure, Dumas the elder. They would walk along the boulevards together, Adah on the arm of the big fat novelist, his mustache curled, his top hat at a jaunty angle, his old face beaming with pride in his fascinating companion. Paris looked on and tittered. Dumas *père* was too old to be suspected of immorality, Parisians told each other merrily, but he was not too old to be made a fool of, and that is what happened when he was cajoled into permitting photographs to be made of Adah and himself. In one pose he looked sentimentally into her eyes; in another she balanced precariously on his knee; in another he was wearing only his underwear. The Dumas family was furious and the publicity tremendous. But scandal, anger and laughter all came to an abrupt end when Adah suddenly died of pneumonia. It was 1868. Dead at thirty-three, she had come a long way from New Orleans.

*   *   *

Adah Isaacs Menken, Ada Clare, Joaquin Miller — no one could call them ordinary. I have named them more or less at random, because they had in common considerable experience of California, and that is a state of peculiar interest to the student of American nonconformism. In her toleration of these three, particularly the outrageous Joaquin Miller, nineteenth-century California proves to have started early to earn the name she sometimes bears today; the state of crackpots. But that is an unfair 'name, because it is pejorative. Tolerance is still a rare virtue, and was rarer then than now. Besides, in California as elsewhere, there have always been good, solid Bohemians among the crackpots. Ambrose Bierce was one. He was more than that; he was perhaps the first of America's literary men to express opinions about public events, war in particular, that were likely to make him unpopular. After all, unpopularity was the least of "Bitter Bierce's" worries.

It should be mentioned that he was not California born, but this was nothing to set him apart in those times. Born in Ohio in 1842, at a prayer meeting, he was to carry through life a hatred of the Middle West, of his parents and of the evangelical religion they practiced. That his birth year and his native state were those of William Dean Howells was a coincidence that must have displeased him if called to his attention, for everything about "Miss Nancy Howells" displeased him. (It was not easy, offhand, to think of things that pleased him, but Howells, like "Miss Nancy James," he singled out for particular disfavor.)

The Bierces were poor, and Ambrose was given little schooling. He was born, he said later, "to work as a peasant in the fields." In fact he worked as handyman in a general store, printer's devil with the local newspaper, laborer — often for sixteen hours a day — in a brickyard, while rebellion, an angry coal, glowed in his heart. When war was declared he exulted as he enlisted in the Union Army to fight against slavery. He found "no hint of glory" in war, and his original fervor was quenched, but the army did serve him as an escape-hatch, for it was there that he learned the profession of topographical engineering and campaign strategy. Before the end he had been twice wounded and was commissioned a first lieutenant. Some of his acquaintances in later life attributed his sour temper to a head wound, but this does not necessarily follow.

During the era of reconstruction he joined a government expedition and crossed the plains to San Francisco, arriving there in 1866. At this time Bret Harte's group was going strong, and Bierce began to write for the local journals. He was still untrained and scarcely literate, but such disadvantages were not uncommon in the West, and his work had vigor and originality. He attempted marriage, and it seemed to work for a while; there were three children. But in the end the couple broke up. Van Wyck Brooks points out that the attitude of men toward their wives in Bierce's fiction always gives the impression of cold dislike and forbearance rather than affection, as does the attitude between parents and children.

Then, like other American journalists before him, Bierce decided to look at England. He went to London in 1871, and for the first time found himself in congenial surroundings. He loved Grub Street, the libraries, the smoke-blackened buildings and the taverns. Tom Hood gave him work on *Fun,* but the visitor's most important task was to teach himself proper English, and this he did, reading and studying until he had acquired a vocabulary and the habit of discipline. He loved to use the long words he now knew — as Brooks observes, his tardy discovery of good English rather went to his head — but usually he employed them deliberately, in order to give a humorous effect. He rewrote his old articles and stories, and published three books of them while he was in England.

Returning to California, he found the transition painful and made no secret of it. He castigated his public, snarled at America, and generally made himself known as a terror, but people respected him for it. He had great talent for succinct condemnation. Writers lived in fear of his book reviews, and he seldom gave them reassurance. It was he who wrote the classic nine-word critique: "The covers of this book are too far apart." But he did not remain within the confines of the literary world: he wrote columns attacking politicians, railway magnates and the courts, three classes which he declared corrupt in California. For twenty years he held a top position in San Francisco bullying everybody.

Bierce's eccentricities were many. He loved graveyards, sometimes sleeping all night on a tombstone. He hated dogs and cats, but kept pet lizards. Once he threatened to kill his chief disciple, George Sterling, if Sterling should dare to appear in a bathing suit before Bierce's niece. His opinions were delivered with such arrogance that only a brave man would venture to take issue with them, and the poet George Sterling was not brave enough. He always showed what he wrote to Bierce, who had constituted himself Sterling's mentor, and took for gospel whatever the great man decreed. This serfhood did not cease until 1899, when Bierce was sent by his paper to Washington to live.

There he carried on a crusade against the railway men who had grabbed tracts of land in California in the days when the lines were being built, and who held most of the state's affairs in their hands. Bierce was a sort of Socialist, and his attacks were fierce and unremitting. He was given much credit for his part in vanquishing the vested interests. He disapproved of the expansionist spirit that furthered the outbreak of the Spanish-American War, declared himself discontented with Washington, and called the first decade of the 1900s "weak and fluffy."

Brooks describes him in that period as a bored old man, despondent and cynical, waiting for death, who passed his time talking with other old soldiers. He kept the skull of a friend on his desk and used to ask it questions. In 1912, because, he said, he wanted to get the smell of his country out of his nostrils, he went to Mexico to report on the current revolution. He was seventy years old. He sent a few reports back from across the border, and then there was silence. Nobody knows exactly what happened to Ambrose Bierce.

*   *   *

Through his journalism Bierce brought an amount of glory to California, as had many other Bohemians before him, and the natives of that state naturally started to feel proud of themselves for their record in producing, or at least fostering, artistic talent. Inevitably some of them decided to do more of the good work. When Americans go into public-spirited action like this, ten to one they form a club. That is what happened in California, and that is how the Bohemian Club of San Francisco — a contradiction in terms if ever there was one — came to be born.

According to its *Annals*, the Club was founded "for the promotion of good fellowship among journalists and the elevation of journalism to that place in the popular estimation to which it is entitled," which seems to imply that the journalists of the Bay City felt inferior to creative artists and were trying to climb into place beside them. In fact it did not happen quite like that. As Albert Parry tells it, James F. Bowman of the *Chronicle* started the whole thing when he and his wife took to inviting friends in for breakfast every Sunday. These breakfasts, doubtless so-called because they started at noon and continued until evening, were first attended only by newspaper people. But

newspaper people are a gregarious lot, and soon the regular
guest-list included artists of all sorts, talking and drinking
and — sometimes — illustrating arguments by drawing on
the tablecloth. In the early days Mrs. Bowman didn't mind pictures on her tablecloths, because they were drawn by well-
known artists: indeed, she liked them, and put away the cloths
to keep as souvenirs. But in time the parties grew too large
and unmanageable for any hostess, however appreciative of
pen-and-ink sketches. Mrs. Bowman ran out of clean table-
linen and patience. Her husband, sympathizing, realized that
the only way out of the difficulty was to organize an official
club that would hold its meetings in some public, or at least
communal, location. This was done, and the Bohemian Club
was born. Among the charter members a few objected to the
name "Bohemian," which they thought had a disreputable
sound, but the majority favored it.

For a few years the Bohemian Club had fun. The flavor of
its amusements does not carry over in the minutes, but that
doesn't mean the members failed to find enjoyment, even on
Ladies' Night, the last Saturday of every month, when members would recite poetry, or the party discussed some "serious
topic of the day," or everyone joined in a singsong. No doubt
the wits kept things light, and the spirit was gay. It seems right
that the Club should have taken in Joaquin Miller when he returned from Europe, so that he enjoyed, at last, the company
of that group of poets he had once imagined clustered in a
kind of Valhalla. Mark Twain and Bret Harte were elected *in
absentia*. Even the antisocial Ambrose Bierce belonged. Out
of Ladies' Night grew the institution of "High Jinks," and, later,
"Low Jinks," when theatricals were the order of the day, and
in summer the Bohemians went camping for a fortnight, sixty
miles out of town in a wood they named the Bohemian Grove,

on the Russian River. The Jinks grew more and more elaborate, until the committee needed funds. Without doing violence to the spirit of Bohemia, they felt, they could invite professors from San Francisco's universities to join, thereby increasing the take from dues. This was done — a logical enough move, considering how many professors are genuine Bohemians. Everything was still all right. It was a later move that really altered things, when the committee began accepting rich businessmen as members. These millionaires first took a simple, harmless pleasure in being close to clever chaps who painted or wrote for a living, but ultimately they could not help behaving like the captains of industry they were. Soon they were changing the Club's customs, bringing it nearer their hearts' desire and ever farther from Bohemia. Within a decade of its first meeting the Bohemian Club had become as stuffy an institution as you could find.

Doubtless another reason for this swift downfall was the difference between eastern and western notions of the nature of Bohemia. Even today San Franciscans consider *all* artists Bohemian, by the very virtue of their craft, as if a man's habits and outlook did not have a good deal more than his art to do with the question. The trouble is that once you accept that thesis you open the door to elements that have nothing whatever to do with Bohemia and are even inimical to it. A man might be a sculptor or a composer and yet belong wholeheartedly to the world of squares, with never so much as an hour of genuine Bohemianism in his life. But the innocent businessmen of the Bohemian Club did not realize this. They judged artists, as they judged each other, by material success. The more popular a painter's pictures, they felt, the better and more Bohemian the painter must be. Soon the Club was taking it as a solemn duty to entertain any distinguished visitor to the city who had some connection with the arts, and that word "distinguished" sums up the whole situation. "In their entertainment of such guests members spared no pains to make the events memorable ones," wrote Oscar Lewis in *Bay Window Bohemia,* a state of affairs so like the Rotarian outlook that it is pleasant to think of what Oscar Wilde did in 1882, when some of the Club members invited him to dinner and planned to drink him under the table. He outdrank them instead, and left them insensible.

The Club rules got more and more rigid. Members were snubbed for telling dirty stories. Members began to dress for dinner. An Italian opera singer who was a member in 1887 got drunk one night — though not, presumably, within Club precincts — and had a fight with his servant which got into the papers. There was only one thing for a gentleman to do, he felt, and he did it: he offered his resignation to the Bohemian Club. And it was accepted! Jack London was made a member in 1904, *after* he became famous, of course: the newspapers had a field day, and were full of witty comment on political radicals who make the grade socially. Yet it was barely more than three decades since the Club's charter members had scribbled and drawn on Mrs. Bowman's tablecloth.

The moral seems to be: it is not that Bohemia dies — in spite of what the oldsters say — but that it doesn't stay put. You cannot nail it down. Such as it is, the Bohemian Club of San Francisco is still going strong. Indeed, Helen Hayes, the first woman ever to be so honored, was entertained in November, 1962, in its main dining room, where it is to be hoped that she behaved herself.

CHAPTER 5

Lone Wolf

Was the prejudice against Bohemia dying down? For a while it seemed to be in abeyance, at least. The Irish-born John Boyle O'Reilly, of the Boston *Pilot,* the soul of respectability, came out in favor of Bohemia in the most telling manner possible — he wrote a poem, "In Bohemia," that became a popular piece for party recitations in middle-class houses all over the country.

> I'd rather live in Bohemia than in any other land;
> For only there are the values true,
> And the laurels gathered in all men's view . . .

If anyone had asked John Boyle O'Reilly, co-owner with the Archbishop of Boston of the *Pilot,* what he could know about Bohemia, he would have been indignant. Wasn't he a rebel of long standing? Hadn't he been tried in England and convicted of conspiracy against the Crown, and escaped from Australia to make his way to America? Yes, he had; it is a matter of history. What is more, he organized a society for his cronies, the Papyrus Club, in 1870, the members meeting at a tavern every night to smoke at each other, drink moderately, and discuss topics of the day. They may have been Boston politicians and newspaper poets, but they called themselves Bohemian. Some Bohemians,

O'Reilly would have explained, are good, decent Bohemians. Well, the belief made him happy.

Besides, he had part of it right: Bohemians are rebels, and many of them enjoy a good fight. But there are those who don't seek strife and are surprised when it overtakes them: a man of this stamp follows his particular star with such rapt concentration that he isn't aware of the boundaries of convention until he has overstepped them. He is the born Bohemian, the Bohemian without consciousness of being one. Lafcadio Hearn was of this company, and was the last person in the world to have sought a barricade on which to die, but he stumbled into a cause nevertheless. Well ahead of his time he challenged race prejudice — and made a mess of his gesture. It is a strange story.

He was born in 1850, not in America, but on the Ionian island Leucadia, where his parents — Charles Hearn, an Anglo-Irish army surgeon, and Rosa, his Maltese wife — were on a tour of military duty. They christened the child Patrick Lafcadio, the second name being the Greek form of Leucadia: Lafcadio always referred to his mother's family as Greek. He was three years old when Rosa took the children to Ireland, where she had not yet been, to live with her widowed mother-in-law while her husband served a tour in India. It was a disastrous move. She hated the North for its climate and customs, and made no attempt to adapt herself or the children. She wouldn't learn English. Patrick, undersized, swarthy and near-sighted, ran around Dublin like a Leucadian child, in petticoats and earrings. The hearty Irish children teased him brutally. It is no wonder that he became shy and withdrawn.

By the time Charles Hearn returned to Ireland his wife was definitely unstable. Soon afterwards she ran out on the family to return to her people on the Mediterranean, and Charles's

widowed aunt, a Mrs. Brehane, offered to adopt Patrick. His
father was glad to hand him over. The Hearns were Prot-
estants, but Mrs. Brehane was a Catholic convert with a convert's
proverbial fervor: Rosa was Catholic, and Mrs. Brehane was determined to bring up this child, at least, in the truth faith. In
fact, she meant him for the priesthood. While he was a small
boy the old lady did the best she could with him according to
her lights, but she had strange theories. Because he was terrified of the dark and imagined his room full of bogies and
"haunters," she insisted that he sleep without a night-light, to
toughen his spirit. There were always friends who fomented
trouble for the boy, hoping to turn his grand-aunt against him
so that they could get her money for the church.

Patrick outgrew his childish prettiness, and any appeal he
held for the old lady vanished. Then, while playing with some
other boys, he injured his eye and lost the use of it. As an adolescent he made it clear that he would not become a priest, after
which good relations were finished between them. Mrs. Brehane
neglected Patrick. The boy would run away for days at a time,
scratching out his living like an accomplished vagabond, until
she sent him off to school in France, where he quickly learned
the language. He was nineteen when he had a letter from his
aunt sending him enough money for a steerage passage to New
York and directing him curtly to proceed to Cincinnati when
he got there. She had done what she could for him, she said:
from now on he must look after himself. Patrick's feelings were
wounded, and he took the only revenge in his power by dropping his first name — thus, symbolically, forswearing Irish
blood and the Catholic religion. He would be Lafcadio Hearn
from that time on, he resolved, a Greek and a pagan.

In America, his attempt to defy Mrs. Brehane's authority by
remaining in New York was frustrated. He was only one among

thousands of poor immigrants there, looking for work. Even as a day-laborer he could find nothing, being too small and light to compete. After some days of near starvation he did what he had been told to do, and moved on to Cincinnati where Mrs. Brehane told him someone was waiting to help "give him a start in life." In fact this surly character was no help at all, beyond arranging for Lafcadio to peddle small goods for a Syrian merchant. Lafcadio went out with a tray hanging around his neck, but no one bought any of his wares, and he and the Syrian agreed to give up the project. He existed as best he could, sleeping in haylofts or in a rusty boiler he found on a vacant lot. For some time he was janitor and waiter at a boarding-house. He spent a lot of time reading in the public library, where a librarian noticed the studious little tramp, talked to him, and gave him secretarial work.

Now that he was being paid, Lafcadio found a room in a boardinghouse in the slum district where Negroes and poor whites lived. Alethea Foley, a handsome colored girl, was the cook, and Lafcadio spent much time with her in the kitchen, leading her on to talk about her life. He was always attracted by other races and unfamiliar cultures, and Alethea's story fascinated him: she was born a slave in the South and trained as a lady's maid. After the liberation she made her way to Cincinnati, taking help wherever a pretty girl would naturally find it. She had a four-year-old son, Willie, by a white man.

When the library work came to an end, Lafcadio found a job with Henry Watkin, an Englishman who owned a printing press. Watkin hired him as an errand-boy, but soon he discovered that Lafcadio was a good proofreader and put him to work in the editorial department, so that Hearn became a printer's apprentice. Through Watkin he got a job on a little trade paper, and then found even better work. There came a time when

Lafcadio felt familiar enough with journalism's ways to submit an article to the editor of the Cincinnati *Enquirer*, and the editor bought it. Lafcadio went on writing and the *Enquirer* bought more. He wrote a long book review of Tennyson's "Idylls of the King" that impressed the editor with its erudition, a quality in short supply in Cincinnati at the time. The review ran in two installments, and Cincinnati readers began talking about the young genius in their midst. He was now a regular contributor at staff rates, enjoying the dignity of a desk in the newspaper office. In 1874 he became a salaried reporter. The boy who shuddered at the thought of ghosts and goblins in the dark had grown into a man preoccupied with the occult and the horrible: his nature gave him just the right touch for the sensational journalism of the 1870s. All seemed fair sailing.

And then he spoiled it by marrying Alethea Foley. Worse, he broke the law in doing so, for he would not have been able to get the license if he hadn't suppressed the fact, on the application, that she was colored. Alethea knew this and tried to talk him out of the project, but Lafcadio was determined. After a long hunt for a minister, a Negro clergyman consented to officiate, and the wedding ceremony took place.

The couple set up housekeeping in a shabby cottage next to a livery stable, where Lafcadio spent his days teaching the child Willie and writing vivid stories for the *Enquirer* about life among the Negroes. Soon, however, he was troubled. Never in close touch with reality, he was surprised and distressed by his white friends' disapproval of the match, and as people continued to snub him he grew increasingly resentful. The editor and his colleagues were tolerant at first, but Lafcadio dragged so much anger into his work and wrote so bitterly about Cincinnati's stuffy citizens that he became impossible to work with. Always a difficult writer to edit, he now picked quarrels with the

editor whenever such passages were excised, until, after an un-
comfortable year, he lost his job. This development took him
by surprise. He plunged into depression and came close to suicide until a staunch friend found him another place with the
Cincinnati *Commercial.*

Back on the payroll, Lafcadio cheered up and resumed what
had become his favorite leisure-time occupation, translating
French writers into English. But the marriage that had cost
him so much was no longer happy. Lafcadio treated Alethea
badly, taking revenge on the unfortunate girl for all his mis-
fortune. Once he referred to the wedding as "a certain
escapade," in correspondence with another woman who was
in love with him. Women did fall in love with Lafcadio,
though he always considered himself too ugly to attract them.
Nothing came of this Cincinnati admirer's passion, because he
did not find himself aroused by her, but Lafcadio had no objection to sexual indulgence. On the contrary, he believed in sen-
ual pleasure and said so openly — an attitude that shocked his
contemporaries, who were used to conventional silence on sexual
matters.

H. E. Krehbiel, a colleague on the *Commercial* who later became a leading music critic in New York, was a friend of
Lafcadio's, but he could never accept the little man's code of
morality. They often quarreled about such matters. On one
occasion they worked together on a news item concerning a prostitute who had been arrested and was being held at the police
station pending further inquiries. Krehbiel referred to her in
the story as "the notorious cyprian." Lafcadio protested against
what he considered an unduly harsh epithet, but the story came
out as Krehbiel had written it, at least in the first edition. The
men were still arguing when word reached the office that the
girl had hanged herself with her own shawl. Krehbiel must

have felt a little compunction after all, since in the second edition he changed his sentence and called the dead woman "an unfortunate cyprian."

Not long afterwards Krehbiel was thoroughly disgusted by an anecdote concerning Lafcadio that was going the rounds of the newspaper world. According to this, Lafcadio and a colleague went out together and visited a brothel, agreeing to meet in the parlor when their separate amatory affairs had been concluded. The other reporter went down to the parlor as arranged, but Lafcadio did not come down for such a long time that he became uneasy and began snooping around the place, fearing that the little man might have been mugged. Seeing a door slightly open, he peeped in. There stood one of the girls, stark naked and motionless under a bright light, and there was little Lafcadio walking circles around her, inspecting her as if she had been a statue, his near-sighted eye so close to her body that his nose almost brushed her skin. As the friend watched, Lafcadio stepped back, heaved a sigh, and said raptly, "Yes, indeed. The Greeks were right! No line in nature is as beautiful as a woman's hip!"

Lafcadio, then, was doing as well as could be expected, but for his wife Alethea things were going from bad to worse. The poor girl could do nothing to suit Hearn. He complained that she didn't iron his clothes properly, and often he would refuse to eat what she had cooked, so that she had to go out and buy his meal at a restaurant. In short, his temper became impossible, so that it must have been a relief to her, though she would not have admitted such a thing, when one day he walked out of the house for good. It was 1877: three years had been enough to extinguish his spark of revolt against social injustice. Alethea tried for a time to persuade him to return; it was no use, and she took Willie and moved away from Cincinnati.

"I think I can redeem myself socially here," wrote Lafcadio to Krehbiel that winter from New Orleans.

His early biographers evidently found his mixed-race marriage so embarrassing that they accepted with relief his own explanation for leaving Cincinnati — a longing for a warmer climate. Undoubtedly, however, he simply found it easier to go away than to stay on, listening to people saying "I told you so." As a refuge New Orleans sounded attractive not only for its warmth but because of its mixed population of Negro, Mexican, Indian, Spanish and French origin. Lafcadio dreamed of what he would see — ruined plantation houses, colorful markets, and the blue Gulf of Mexico, which he thought must be like his lost Mediterranean.

The *Commercial* editor helped him out when it came to planning his livelihood. Politically the South was interesting: still suffering from the carpetbagger era, Southerners were deeply suspicious of Washington, and when Hayes won the Presidential election of 1876 he got only one vote south of the Mason-Dixon line, detected by recount. Any article Lafcadio Hearn wrote on the political situation would be paid for, the editor assured him, though naturally his formal connection with the paper was severed as soon as he left.

Lafcadio arrived in New Orleans late in the autumn. He found himself enthralled by the city's strange atmosphere, Negroes singing as they worked on the waterfront, the Creole patois, the color and life of the Vieux Carré, and he sent back to the *Commercial* floods of text. Unfortunately it was all atmosphere, with never a word of politics. The editor was not pleased and wrote to say so, but Lafcadio paid no attention. Similar letters followed: still he paid no attention. He didn't care about politics. It was far more interesting to gather strange songs for Krehbiel's collection of songs, to take walks, to explore. At last the editor's patience was exhausted and he wrote to tell Lafcadio that they wanted no more of his work. As in his experience with the *Enquirer,* Lafcadio should not have been surprised by this, but he was.

He was also strapped. It was impossible to find work on a local paper; this was March, 1878, and New Orleans was suffering a depression. Managing editors could not keep on as much staff as they already had, let alone hire a new hand. Lafcadio went hungry. He sold everything he owned, and slept on park benches. Yet when he did at last succeed in selling an article to a newspaper for ten dollars, he went into a passion of rage at the editor's temerity in daring to alter it, though the alteration was slight. He walked into the editorial office, threw the money down on the desk, and stalked out. For a while he subsisted on a five-cent meal every other day, but even that much became impossible. He was a dreadful sight when on a last throw, a final appeal to Providence before drowning himself, he visited the office of the *Republican.* Major Robinson, the editor, had long since turned away the little man just as all the other newspaper bigwigs had done, but when he saw Lafcadio standing there, ragged and dirty and starving and silent, his eyes filled with tears of shock. He was able — when he could speak — to tell the ragamuffin that there actually *was* a job going at last, not on his paper but on a little periodical, the *Item,* and he grabbed it on Lafcadio's behalf before taking him out to eat.

Now, with ten dollars a week and plenty of free time, Lafcadio's luck changed. Modest though the salary was, he could live on it, and with a free conscience he spent hours at his favorite pastime translating the French writers he admired — Gautier, Pierre Loti, Huysmans, De Maupassant. As the months and years passed, Lafcadio Hearn published quite a few articles in national magazines, and even an occasional book. There was a novella, *Chita,* laid in Louisiana. Never a popular writer, he gained a special audience.

In New Orleans he sometimes met George Washington Cable and other local literati, but his most fervent friendships were carried on by letter. Even for pen pals it was better not to depend too heavily on one's friendship with Lafcadio Hearn: he had a way of suddenly dropping you. One of his erstwhile acquaintances explained this pattern charitably, saying that Lafcadio was such an idealist, people couldn't live up to his expectations and so he was forced to give them up. Others were not so kind about it. The inevitable break with Krehbiel was belated, but it took place at last when Lafcadio got angry at some fancied slight from the music critic, and Krehbiel told him to go to the devil.

After ten years of New Orleans Lafcadio had had enough of it, and was glad to accept a suggestion made by *Harper's* that he move to the Antilles and write of the Caribbean. But perfection finally failed him in the Antilles too, and he began to think longingly of Japan. And so, in 1890, *Harper's* agreed to his going to the Orient to write a series for them.

When he reached Japan he was helped by friends to get work teaching English. His first post was in so remote a town that few other Westerners would willingly have undertaken it, but Hearn was delighted. His new life was not unalloyed bliss, for Lafcadio carried with him a built-in discontent, but he adapted himself to arduous conditions of cold and poverty, and remained in Japan for the rest of his life. So readily and deliberately did he slip into Japanese custom that he married, a member of a Samurai family that had come down in the world, just as a Japanese would have done: that is, by an arrangement that was made before the two met. His wife's relatives moved in with them, and it was from her old father that Lafcadio heard many of the tales he wrote. At the beginning he spoke only a few words of Japanese, but he persisted until he had at his command a kind of broken Japanese, or "Hearn language," as his in-laws and children called it. It was through the articles and books he produced during this last phase of his life that Lafcadio became a figure in American literary history. Consistently he deplored the Westernization of Japan, and would praise the old ways so exaggeratedly that even his wife did not always agree with him.

No twinge of conscience on Alethea's account seems to have troubled Hearn, though he had never been divorced from her. Probably he told himself that it wasn't a binding ceremony because he had lied to get the license. Indirectly, however, he did refer at least once to that incident in his life; when writing a little moral homily for one of his Japanese students, he said that young people are wrong to think that they always know everything. In obscure terms he cited his own example as proof of how a young man can make mistakes. In defying a convention, he had brought trouble on himself. Ergo, older people know better.

Shortly before his death in 1904, Lafcadio at last found the religion that suited him; the man who in his youth had renounced Christianity became a Buddhist.

CHAPTER 6

Real Wolf

LAFCADIO HEARN was terrified of New York's clamor and bustle. Once he planned to stay there for a season and see something of friends, but after only a couple of days he fled to Philadelphia, where it was calm and he could nurse his bruised soul back to health. Hearn was neurotic, but there is no doubt that New York was stunningly noisy: some other people loved it for that very reason. Huneker, who ran away from Philadelphia, reveled in Manhattan's din, and loved the vigor that seemed to be brought in anew with every immigrant ship.

Of the masses of European newcomers who poured into New York, the majority had no desire to pass through the city and make for the hinterland. They sought out compatriots and settled into communities, often slummy, where they could pretend that they were back in their native lands. The illusion was not too difficult. In New York, immigrants ate the food they were used to, talked their own language, and strongly, if unconsciously, resisted the process of assimilation as long as they could. It was an ever-fresh battle, constantly renewed, and New York was a varicolored chart of foreigners' districts: Irish, German, Italian, French, and — especially in the 1880s — Russian Jewish fugitives from the pogroms.

Here Bohemians found the variety and cross-fertilization that

their restless souls craved. Among America's writers it may well
have been that non-Bohemian, William Dean Howells, who
first tried to describe the assimilation process with serious intention. In the middle of the Eighties, owing to the fate that
had shifted literature's center from his adored Boston to New
York, Howells followed it to Manhattan. He described the experience in a novel, *A Hazard of New Fortunes,* in which he also
came to grips with the question of immigration and labor.

The central character in the novel is an editor named
March. March and his wife, down from Boston, look all over
New York for a place to live. They want a furnished apartment
— for apartments have now become respectable — of ten rooms,
preferably near Washington Square and certainly not above
Twentieth Street. They consider New York streets in general
ill-paved and dirty compared to Boston's, though here and there
they see a poshed-up house, bricks reddened and picked out
with white, brass doorknob shining, and they fall in love with
"the L." "Those bends in the L that you get in the corner of
Washington Square, or just below the Cooper Institute
— they're the gayest things in the world." All in all, New York
is not as bad as the Marches had expected, until one day, driving
along in a hired coupé, they find themselves in a tenement district. It is a shocking slum. Iron fire escapes cover the house-
fronts, children swarm over sidewalk and roadway, ashbarrels
and garbage heaps are everywhere. Slatternly women lean over
every windowsill, and the basement shops are mean and dirty.
In Naples such a sight would be picturesque, says March, but in
America it shocks him.

In *Hazard* Howells, an admirer of Tolstoi, grapples with a
few more sociological ideas. One of the characters is a German
immigrant, Lindau, embittered to the point of insanity by his
troubles, which he attributes to capitalism. Lindau earns a liv-

ing sitting as an artist's model and translating an occasional article. Because he is an intellectual, the modern reader cannot see him as a fair representative of the working classes, but that is the role he plays in the novel. The New York horsecar employees go on strike, and Lindau takes their side. In a riot instigated by him, another character is killed. All of this is merely part of the subsidiary plot, and it would be exaggerating to call *Hazard* a novel of social awareness, but even so it is one of the earliest attempts made in American literature to treat the subject. Bohemia is present too, in the person of a clever young artist named Beaton, a villain of sorts — heartless, selfish, climbing; he is not violently villainous because Howells's characters are never violent, but one can see that the old resentment Beaton's creator acquired at Pfaff's never wore off.

*   *   *

To go from *A Hazard of New Fortunes* to James Gibbons Huneker's reminiscent pieces about New York is enough to make one wonder if the two men could possibly be speaking of the same place. To some extent the disparity is natural; though they refer to the same city, they are of different times. Howells's first appearance in the East, when he came from Ohio, must have coincided with Huneker's third birthday.

Huneker was an oddity — another like him might not be seen for more than the space of a generation. Alone and with sheer zest for his subjects, he pushed forward American appreciation of the arts by several considerable paces. Not in the ordinary sense a rebel — he thought highly of Howells, for example — he was outstandingly erratic in his own way. Though music was his first passion, and he tried for years to be a pianist of concert stature, his true work was criticism. All art was his province — painting, literature, drama, even architecture, and music of course.

Huneker's first venture abroad to Paris, in 1878, to visit the Paris Exposition, was not quite the bachelor adventure he describes in *Steeplejack*: a wife, Lizzie, went with him. The Hunekers had to return to Philadelphia before a year was out, and for the following six years James lived unhappily in his native city, teaching piano for a living but depending in part on his parents and money Lizzie made by dressmaking. Philadelphia was not exactly a cultural desert. There James met musicians who came to give concerts in the city, and enjoyed a friendship with Walt Whitman, who had settled down in Camden. Nevertheless he suffered. Philadelphia seemed to him maddeningly smug and placid, and married life was a thorn.

One project above all kept Huneker busy. In Paris he had become aware of lacunae in his education. Now he drew up a list of books he resolved to read, a staggering five hundred authors "of major works in history, art, music, painting, and sculpture as well as belles lettres" and textbooks on astronomy, poetry, chemistry, natural philosophy, mythology, and modern languages. According to his biographer, Arnold T. Schwab, it was Huneker's hopeful idea to read all this in five years. As far as the timetable was concerned, he failed, but he finished the list before he died in 1921, and with his remarkable memory he retained most of what he read.

Etude was a monthly magazine on musical subjects, first published in Philadelphia in 1885, for which Huneker became a regular contributor. He went to New York in 1886 to review several important concerts, and when he returned, Philadelphia seemed so awful that at last he came to a decision and walked out on it, Lizzie and all. This was a significant break: he was, after all, no slip of a lad but a man of twenty-nine. He lodged for a time in a boardinghouse on Seventh Avenue near Thirteenth, handy for the cafés in the neighborhood — Luchow's was one. Fourteenth Street was then the center of concert halls

and theaters, though a few playhouses had begun to appear farther north, as far up as the new Metropolitan at Thirty-ninth
and Broadway. Huneker had only his small *Etude* job to begin
with, and for a few months it was hard sledding, but he soon followed up contacts and got an additional job writing for the
Musical Courier. His career was launched. It was not an overnight success, but Huneker climbed, slowly and steadily, until
he was in the top rank among the critics. His comments were
witty and excited. Every day he would meet other critics in
some café, where he usually sat up half the night drinking
enormously, and talking to his heart's content. One of his colleagues was Krehbiel, Lafcadio Hearn's acquaintance of Cincinnati days, now an elderly music pundit with the *Tribune*.
Huneker paid due respect to Krehbiel, but considered him
something of a fogy. For himself, Huneker never let his tastes
and opinions atrophy: he was always ready to hear or see something new.

The love of women that had sent him headlong into his relationship with Lizzie, and then headlong out of it, was to com-
plicate his whole life. Huneker's affairs were of a candor that
amazed the age, but even he usually practiced restraint when
he wrote about his amatory adventures, and little of the story
can be found in his books. Soon after he reached New York he
got mixed up with an attractive red-haired young woman who
lived with her husband in the same boardinghouse, Mrs. Josephine Laski. One night Mr. Laski came home earlier than his
wife expected him, and James had to climb out of her bedroom
window stark naked and scale the wall to his own room, a story
above. After that feat the management asked him to leave, so
he moved to Werle's Hotel on Irving Place but kept on seeing
Josephine.

On the whole, James enjoyed the change. At Werle's he met

the famous Red Countess, Helene von Schewitsch, the original unheroic heroine of George Meredith's *Tragic Comedians*. She was now too old and fat to stir Huneker's amorous propensities, but he was thrilled at knowing her. Helene had figured, more than twenty years earlier, in a great scandal in Europe, when her lover, the Socialist leader Ferdinand Lassalle, was killed in a duel with her fiancé, Prince Racowitz. Helene then married the Prince, and Meredith wrote his book, painting an unflattering portrait of the girl. According to Huneker, she felt that the English novelist had been unfair to her, and Huneker was ready to believe anything she said, for he was fascinated by her career. She had married twice since Racowitz's death; her present husband, Schewitsch, had been kicked out of Russia for his radical politics, and now the pair were busy in New York, leading a group of refugees and forming a political Bohemia. Helene wrote fiction, acted in German plays, and wrote dramatic criticism for the New York *Volkszeitung*.

Happily James wandered about the East Side where such people as the Schewitsches spent their time. He knew the German district well, where, according to his biographer, he "hobnobbed with French communards, Spanish and Italian refugees, German socialists, and Russian politicals." He thought more and more about European music, writing and art; he read Nietzsche and Schopenhauer. He took up French literature — Flaubert, Stendhal, Huysmans, Baudelaire. Music was his first but not his only passion: he became a stimulating critic of stage, architecture and painting, defending George Luks, Cézanne, Gauguin, Matisse, Ibsen, Shaw — much that was new and, in many cases, unknown in America until he wrote of it. As he educated himself, so to a lesser extent did he educate his readers. "In a day of 'uncritical parochialism' that made American criticism a 'cemetery of clichés,' as Huneker put it, he widened its consciousness of the great world outside," says Van Wyck Brooks. "He left it broad awake to modernity elsewhere, rambler and prowler that he was, leisurely and curious, with an all but incomparable feeling for the romance of art."

Huneker was not a Murger type of Bohemian. Perhaps it is impossible for any discerning critic to be one. He was fundamentally an observer, not a producer. He was creative — it is doubtful if the nation has ever produced a more creative man, in his way — but when he wrote a novel, as he did at last, it was strangely flat, something several degrees removed from direct storytelling. His Bohemianism was his own, and cannot be pigeon-holed. The same is true of his love-life, which makes an incredible story. Josephine, the lady for whose honor he climbed the front wall of the boardinghouse, left her husband for Huneker, and Laski shot himself dead. Now she was free to marry, but James was not. His wife Lizzie was a Catholic, like James himself, and though he was perfectly willing to lapse from the church's law and get a divorce, Lizzie would not. So Josephine and James lived together without benefit of clergy, peacefully enough, for several years. He was not faithful, and Josephine knew this, but she was wise enough never to let it spoil their relationship. She took care of him and cooked for him — Huneker, who loved Jewish cuisine, declared that she was the best cook in the world. But when he married another girl, even Josephine's good nature was ruffled.

The other lady was Clio Hinton, a talented sculptor, beautiful and in 1891 only twenty-two to Josephine's twenty-six. Huneker was so much in love with her that he was determined this time to persuade Lizzie to let him go. In pursuit of this end he took Clio to Philadelphia so that Lizzie might see for herself what a nice girl he had selected. Josephine came along as well, uninvited: she even moved into Huneker's room at the hotel, and he didn't push her out because he never pushed Josephine out: he loved her. Lizzie did approve of Clio, and divorced James accordingly. The wedding posed a difficulty, a Catholic priest being out of the question and Huneker flatly refusing to apply to a Protestant. But Clio's father, the journalist Howard Hinton, came to the rescue. He was an anti-cleric and a freethinker, and he performed the service himself in the family living room.

Clio got pregnant. Before the pregnancy was over she knew that she could not possibly live happily ever after with James Huneker, a man who drank at least twelve bottles of beer a day and often stayed away from home for several days on end without explanation. Nor would he give up Josephine. "Sometimes a man's wife won't let him marry the girl he likes (women are so unreasonable)," he wrote irritably in *Steeplejack*; possibly he was thinking of Lizzie, but perhaps he meant Clio instead. When his son Erik was born, in 1894, the proud father stayed away from the house for a week, explaining that he couldn't bear to see people in pain. After that Clio gave up: she took Erik and went off to Paris to study sculpture. Huneker did not take this act as final. On his way to cover the Wagner Festival at Bayreuth in 1896 he stopped off in Paris to see Clio, because he had missed her, and they were temporarily reconciled. Very soon afterwards, in Bayreuth, he had a love affair with the handsome singer Olive Fremstad, but on his return journey he stopped off in Paris again to beg Clio to come back with him to America. She refused, and he returned to the comforts provided by Josephine. It was not long before he was involved with another singer, Georgiana Carhart. Huneker at the time was living at the Maison Felix and so was Georgie, who at first knew nothing about Josephine. One day Huneker broke a date with her: she got suspicious and tracked him down to Josephine's apartment, walking in on the pair in the bedroom.

"Well, thank God you two have met at last!" said Huneker.

Georgie stayed on for dinner with James and Josephine. For two years the amazing man managed to live with one or the other of his dear charmers, presumably untroubled by tantrums. Then Clio, who wished to marry again, got a divorce, and Huneker suggested that he and Georgiana marry, and that Josephine live with them. Both of the ladies showed such a marked lack of enthusiasm for this idea, however, that he let it drop.

It was Josephine who won out. She always claimed, through the years that passed after James died, that they were actually married, and perhaps they were. Georgie went to Germany to study singing. After that, Josephine and Huneker lived happily ever after, or at least until James's kidneys gave out. He died in February, 1921. "The greatest of American critics," said George Jean Nathan in his public address at the memorial service. ". . . Good-bye, dear Jim . . . God rest your splendid soul."

CHAPTER 7

Gaudy Aesthetes
and Boy Socialists

AMERICANS HAD a sweet tooth. Not only did they like jelly with their meat; they demanded plenty of sugar-coating on the arts. There was usually some odd intellectual around who deprecated the pouring of sentimental prettiness over painting and literature, but it was not until the Eighties that a change in general public taste can be discerned. Possibly it is true, as certain sociologists opine, that the shift toward realism was the reflection of trouble in industrial affairs — the 1880s were stormy with the birth of unions — and that people were now ready, even willing, to read such astringent literature as *The Adventures of Huckleberry Finn,* published in 1884, because they were quaking with fear of anarchy. Other sociologists maintain just as convincingly that the public, wishing to escape from their worries, bought thousands of copies of Rider Haggard's *King Solomon's Mines,* published the following year. Whichever theory is correct — or if neither can be said to hold true — the fact remains that a lot of people read both books. Possibly it was merely because they are both so readable.

In more rarefied atmosphere, however, there was a genuine movement toward realism. We have seen how William Dean Howells tried his hand at it, and though he was not the man to break through, he knew enough to appreciate the attempts of others and to sympathize with and encourage them. He supported Hamlin Garland when Garland produced grim stories "exposing" the drabness of Middle West life, and did it all the more strongly, no doubt, because of his Ohio background: Howells never ceased congratulating himself on having got out of Ohio. Another member of the anti-sweetness brigade, Henry Harland, was so fascinated by the atmosphere of New York's East Side that he created an *alter ego*, and as a Russian Jew named Sidney Luska wrote novels about the Jewish community. There were a few painters, too, who broke away from the calendar type of art; best known and most execrated of them were George Luks and Arthur B. Davies. In all, however, these pioneers were few, nearly swamped by the rest. Even those who wrote about life among the artists dipped their pens in syrup. For example, take Thomas A. Janvier, whose *Color Studies,* a collection of whimsical little stories about painters, came out in 1885. His characters lived in Greenwich Village, as we feel that painters should, though Janvier indicates that the name of the vicinity as we know it was not generally used in his day, for he refers to "Fourth Street and the old Greenwich road — quite the court end of what used to be Greenwich Village three score years or so ago." There are French and Italian shopkeepers round about, but no Mimis, no grisettes at all — just nice respectable girls to whom the quaintly impecunious artists pay court when they aren't trying to get pictures into exhibitions sponsored by the Society of American Artists. It is Murger as he might be interpreted by Walt Disney.

Still, change *was* under way, and as the world moved into what Thomas Beer called the Mauve Decade, even conventional Americans demanded stronger stuff. In Europe realism was an

old story, and the wistful *boulevardiers* of Union Square
thought it high time their compatriots should catch up. They
longed for the enlightened atmosphere of the Old World, and
felt great respect for friends and colleagues who actually knew
something about it at first hand. Huneker, for one, could preen
himself on nine months' residence in Paris (and often did).
But Huneker himself yielded the palm to the far more sophisticated and picturesque Edgar Saltus, who had not merely
visited, but dwelt in the Promised Land for several years at a
stretch, going and coming whenever the fancy took him. In the
eyes of the Luchow crowd, Saltus's career was altogether fascinating. It is true that at first his elder brother Francis out-
shone him: Frank Saltus was a poet and a lush, who drank
absinthe in the romantic tradition and sat up all night in cafés,
just like a true Parisian Bohemian. But though Frank died
young, he was already supplanted in his public's imagination
by the tougher, gaudier Edgar, born in 1855.

The Saltuses were a New York family with money. Edgar
had just completed his freshman year at Yale when his parents
divorced, and Mrs. Saltus whisked the boy off to Europe, where
for the following years he attended universities in Germany
and France and Switzerland — anywhere his mother went. He
acquired a certain grounding in philosophy, but in his own
opinion the icing on the cake was Paris. There he made friends
with Stuart Merrill, who had grown up in France — his father
was an American attached to the diplomatic service — and
wrote poetry in either language. Howells had tried to persuade
young Merrill to stay in America, but the poet, feeling that
his native culture fell short of what he needed, opted for Paris,
the same decision most young American artists would have
made unhesitatingly, given the chance. Merrill introduced
young Edgar to the stars of the Parisian literary firmament:

Verlaine, Lecomte de Lisle, and Oscar Wilde, with whom Edgar was to remain on friendly terms until Wilde's death, and whose style was to influence his own.

By the time Edgar returned to New York for more than a brief visit, in 1880, his mind was made up: he would be a writer. Four years later he brought out a biography of Balzac, declaring in the preface his sympathy for atheism. Robert J. Ingersoll, the "parish-pump atheist," had just visited New York and thrown people into turmoil, so Saltus's statement made the book mildly notorious. This, as he fully realized, was no bad thing for an aspiring man of letters. His model Wilde often went out of his way to shock the world, and Saltus followed his example. The biography was followed by two works on philosophy, and then came a stream of novels, dealing with the idle, epigrammatic rich. In Van Wyck Brooks's opinion Edgar Saltus was the cleverest novelist of the 1890s, and in life aped his own characters as "the typical 'Reggie' or 'Clarence' of *Puck* with his waxed moustache and boutonniere . . ." "A woman who marries a second time does not deserve to have lost her first husband," declares one of his creations.

But in Saltus's own opinion, writing was not a frivolous pastime: when it came to prose he was dead serious, saying that only three things matter — style, style polished, and style repolished. He reveled in the unusual word and the fresh turn of phrase. *Imperial Purple*, his best-known book, a history of Rome pegged on the lives of the emperors, gave him a chance to indulge these preferences to the utmost. The *Dictionary of American Biography* says that it is "distinguished for its unusual vocabulary, bizarre mode of expression, and skill in innuendo" — all virtues of which, we must admit, there was no surplus in contemporary American literature, and for a little time at least Edgar Saltus became the toast of New York salons.

As the *DAB* comments, rather waspishly, "Merely because he was a rebel, he attracted the attention of a small and rather esoteric group, counting among his admirers James Huneker and Elbert Hubbard." If this means, as it seems to, that Elbert Hubbard was esoteric, we need not give any more consideration to the *DAB*'s editorial opinion, but the facts are dependable. Huneker did admire Saltus. He had thought well of him from the beginning, but with *Imperial Purple* the Philadelphian's esteem increased, and added to it was a little good-natured envy. The book possessed qualities Huneker tried to attain in his own work — unusual vocabulary, bizarre mode, and no self-consciousness whatever. A few Saltus comments give the flavor.

On Julius Caesar: "A phantom in a ballad was not swifter than he. Simultaneously his sword flashed in Germany, on the banks of the Adriatic, in that Ultima Thule where the Britons lived."

On Mark Antony: "A splendid, an impudent bandit, first and foremost a soldier, calling himself a descendant of Hercules whom he resembled, hailed at Ephesus as Bacchus, in Egypt as Osiris; Asiatic in lavishness, and Teuton in his capacity for drink; vomiting in the open Forum, and making and unmaking kings; weaving with that viper of the Nile a romance which is history; passing initiate into the inimitable life, it would have been curious to have watched him that last night when the silence was stirred by the hum of harps, the cries of bacchantes bearing his tutelary god back to the Roman camp, while he said farewell to love, to empire and to life." Yes, it's strong stuff.

Slight and dark, Edgar did not have his brother Frank's battered good looks, but he possessed great attraction for women in his own way. They loved his large brown eyes and his carefully maintained air of helplessness which turned out to be no pose after all. Helen Sturges Read, his first wife, who married him in 1883, learned about this the hard way. She was prone to neuralgic attacks, and when she had one soon after the wedding she expected Edgar to administer to her comfort by applying hot and cold compresses, or at least sitting at her side and holding her hand while she suffered. Not a bit of it: the minute she announced that she was having a twinge, her husband explained calmly that he couldn't bear illness in others or himself, then left the house and stayed away until he was sure she had recovered. It was enough to take all the fun out of neuralgia.

Moreover, she was commanded to stay out of his workroom during a certain number of clearly defined hours every day. When she disregarded his orders, as any independent American wife might be expected to do, and walked in during the forbidden time, there was hell to pay. Edgar pulled out his hair, and screamed, and batted his head against the wall. He even tore up his manuscript. It need hardly be said that after a certain amount of this sort of behavior Helen left Edgar and the couple were divorced. She claimed that he was spoiled, eccentric, and incredibly selfish — complaints which the second Mrs. Saltus was to echo heartily when her turn came, and which are strikingly similar to Clio Huneker's allegations against her James. It looks as if these two Bohemian males were speaking up for their whole sex when they defied convention and treated their wives as they did. No doubt both of them had taken to heart the criticisms of American customs that they heard on all sides when they were abroad — that American women ought not to get away with what they did.

The second bride, married in 1895, was named Elsie Walsh Smith. They went to Europe for the honeymoon. There, somehow or other, the bridegroom broke his ankle, and while the bone was being set he fainted, not once but three times. As a matter of fact, Edgar fainted very easily. At the dentist's he invariably did so, and nobody there thought the worse of him for it. But the dentist was used to it, and Elsie was not. She took a poor view of the thing, considering it a sign of weakness, and made no allowances for artistic temperament. This marriage, too, foundered, but the Saltuses did not get divorced, possibly because Elsie was pregnant when they agreed to separate. In 1897, only two years after that second wedding, Saltus fell in love again, with Marie Giles. She was very young, but as he habitually claimed to be thirteen years younger than he really was, the discrepancy didn't seem to matter. Theirs was a long, tempestuous affair that ranged over a good deal of the world: they would quarrel and dash off in opposite directions, remain apart long enough to simmer down, and catch up with each other at last in California, or England, or France. The second Mrs. Saltus died in 1911 and the lovers were at last able to make it legal, in which state they remained, presumably happy, until Edgar's death in 1921. They used to communicate in baby-talk, not only verbally but by letter and telegram. Did the ardent stylist realize that one day his wife would record this special language in his biography? He couldn't have, but she did.

*   *   *

Saltus was in a special position among America's rebels, and was able to assert his protests in an equally special way. His lilies and languors, his airs and graces, were aimed at the money-grubbers of his country, as were those sudden darts across the Atlantic in pursuit of a richer, better life among people who could appreciate the finer things. Obviously, he could not have used this way of expressing himself if his forefathers hadn't been efficient money-grubbers themselves: he would not, indeed, have acquired a European education, but he was not the first or the last aesthete to overlook this consideration.

The antisocial behavior of his contemporary Stephen Crane

was necessarily of a very different kind, and this was fortunate for American literature. Crane didn't turn away from America for the sake of beauty; beauty as an aim in itself seems not to have occurred to him. He didn't actually reject America at all, though he was violently opposed to certain aspects of it. Other reasons led to his self-imposed exile in England.

The Cranes lived in Newark, where Stephen was born, the youngest son in a large family. His father was a Methodist minister and his mother, between lyings-in, was also a preacher. They were not rich, and Stephen worked in the summer while going to college in Syracuse. Through one of his brothers who owned a press bureau he slipped into newspaper work, and was writing for the New York *Herald* even before he graduated. In 1891 he went to New York as a regular reporter.

Middle-class life in the big city bored Stephen and perhaps intimidated him too. He was shy of nice girls, and scornful of the average New Yorker's tastes. "A young writer in New York may be given tea and a bun by his publisher's wife but the city is not hospitable to talents unless they come from Europe," he later wrote to an English friend. ". . . You asked me last year what the rich New Yorker reads. He reads the newspapers." Some of the severity of this dictum was no doubt due to the struggle he had getting his first book published. For Stephen plunged straight into novel-writing, and within a year of his arrival in New York, when he was only twenty-one, had finished *Maggie, A Girl of the Streets.*

The subject of Maggie is a prostitute's life and death, and Stephen got his material from his chosen sphere in the city, where he spent all his spare time — the Bowery, with its criminals and outcasts. His style was, as always, deceptively plain and surprisingly telling, but these virtues were not enough to overcome the editorial prejudices of the time. When the author submitted the book to Gilder of the *Century Magazine*, the editor was profoundly shocked. It was not only the young man's choice of subject, he felt, that was so bad — though it was bad enough — but the words he used. One of the characters in *Maggie* says, "God damn!" outright. Gilder sent the book straight back, and so did the other editors Stephen tried, until after a year he gave up hope of publication through ordinary channels and himself paid to have it printed. He was already hard up, and this expense left him with nothing to cushion the blow when the *Herald*, tired of a reporter who hardly ever turned up in the office, who spent most of the day sitting on benches among the down-and-outs, and seldom wrote a story that wasn't merely atmospheric stuff about poor people, fired him. After that, Stephen was more than ever one with the Bowery bums. He knew what it meant to be hungry and homeless, but he didn't quite lose his grip, and now and then he got an odd job. His own publication of *Maggie* had sold one hundred copies at most: now he tried once again to find someone else to issue it properly. He knew Hamlin Garland and consulted him. Garland saw the true merit of the work, and told him to send a copy to William Dean Howells, which Stephen did. That would-be realist, fired with enthusiasm for *Maggie*, took up the cause and tried to make *Harper's* reconsider. *Harper's* would not, but under the stimulus of Howells's generous praise, Crane finished another novel, *The Red Badge of Courage*. It was this work, published first as a syndicated serial in newspapers and then, in 1895, as a book, that brought success to the writer.

He was still only twenty-three when the serialized pieces appeared in the newspapers, and by the time *Badge* came out in book form everyone in New York who read at all had at least heard of it, and was asking how it came about that a youth who had never been to war — had not in fact been born while the

Civil War was going on — could know so much about a private soldier's feelings under fire. One story has it that Stephen started to write it because he had just read Zola's *Débacle*, and declared that he could do the same thing better. Whatever started him on the idea, he went to work systematically to learn something of the period, studying Winslow Homer's vivid war sketches. Moreover, as A. J. Liebling pointed out in a piece published in *The New Yorker*, Crane could hardly have grown up at the time he did without having listened raptly in Newark, hour after hour, to the stories told by veterans of the war who were still young and in their prime in the Seventies. He wrote the whole thing in ten days, and it must have been boiling and bubbling in his mind for some time before that.

Now that he was successful, Appleton's, who published *Badge,* were delighted to do the same with *Maggie* the following year. It was a fine time for Stephen. He could pick and choose his assignments, and because the editors had got into the way of thinking of him as a war correspondent — though he wasn't one as yet — the offers he received were usually to go to the likeliest front available and write stories about it. For this reason he went to Mexico for the *Journal*, to report on one of the local flare-ups, following this with a trip through the western states. He also continued to write novels and stories. In *The Third Violet*, a novel published in 1897, is a scene in an artists' lodging-house in New York — a room the description of which will not be unfamiliar to students of Bohemia:

"Pennoyer threw down his pen, and tossed his drawing over on the wonderful heap of stuff that hid the table.

" 'It's too dark to work.' . . .

"The flood of orange light showed clearly the dull wall lined with sketches, the tousled bed in one corner, the masses of boxes and trunks in another, a little dead stove, and the wonderful table. Moreover, there were wine-colored draperies flung in some places, and on a shelf, high up, there were plaster casts, with dust in the creases. A long stove-pipe wandered off in the wrong direction, and then turned impulsively toward a hole in the wall. There were some elaborate cobwebs on the ceiling."

The novel has little plot: Crane never went in for plottiness. A young painter named Hawker, the son of a poor farmer, goes home to spend the summer and meets and falls in love with a girl who is staying at a nearby resort inn. She is rich, he is just beginning to make a name. He feels inadequate, is jealous of a rival, tries to give up his hopes of her, and realizes at last that she loves him too. That is all, but Crane makes what happens so real that the work is memorable.

Late in 1896 when the Cuban insurrection against Spain was growing hot, Stephen was sent by the *Journal* to get a story on the filibustering American ships that were carrying contraband arms and Cuban insurrectionists from Florida to the troubled island. Most leading war correspondents in the States were headed in the same direction; when Crane got to Jacksonville in November he probably exchanged greetings with half a dozen colleagues before he checked in at his hotel. Like the rest of them, he had to cool his heels for some weeks, waiting for a story: filibustering vessels were so much in demand that none that he could ship on were in the harbor. In New York, Stephen in idleness would have gone straight to the Bowery, and now in Jacksonville he sought out its nearest equivalent, the red light district, or "down the line." Success had not given him any new fondness for the social graces: he still avoided nice ladies. In the Hotel de Dream, a place that was not, technically speaking, a bordello but rather a call-house, he met the proprietress, Cora Taylor as she was called. Now, Crane was romantic, in a cock-eyed way, about prostitutes; he was evidently already on cordial terms with one of Cora's competitors, Lyda de Camp who ran "Lyda's," for he gave her an inscribed copy of *Maggie*. But it was Cora who got him, and remained his devoted consort for the rest of his short life. It was Cora who grieved when his ship went down and he was given up for lost, and she who rejoiced at his return. No doubt she lavished warm praise on the story he wrote later about the adventure, "The Open Boat": she was already a Crane fan before they ever met and was reading one of his novels when he first walked into the hotel.

She was small and plump, with a pugnacious, snub-nosed face and red-gold hair. Lillian Gilkes's recent biography, *Cora Crane,* has several good photographs of this spirited woman, who at the age of thirty-one, when Stephen met her, had left her Boston home to strike out for herself and — after various adventures, which she never detailed, and two marriages — found herself flourishing as a madam in Jacksonville. She and Crane wanted to marry, but her second husband, an English officer named Stewart, refused to divorce her. Stephen could not contemplate facing the storm that would arise if they attempted to set up a household anywhere within reach of his Methodist relatives, so they reverted to a stratagem popular in those days among irregular couples, and went abroad to make a fresh start.

England, where they settled as Mr. and Mrs. Crane, was already aware of Stephen's work, and he had many admirers there. Before finding a house and settling in, however, he accepted a commission to report on the war that was just breaking out between Greece and Turkey, and Cora accompanied him with a commission in her own right, to send dispatches to the New York *Journal.* They sailed across the Black Sea from Varna in Bulgaria to Constantinople, in a ship she described as a terrible old tub, and were assailed by so fierce a storm that for a while it looked as if Stephen's experience in Florida waters, when he had to take to an open boat, might be repeated for both of them. However, it wasn't, and all ended well. From Athens and Crete Cora sent home articles above the byline "Imogene Carter," thus becoming, as Miss Gilkes says, the first woman war correspondent, the Marguerite Higgins of her time. The Cranes had plenty of adventures and thoroughly enjoyed the Balkans, though toward the end Stephen fell ill with dysentery, and Richard Harding Davis, who recognized Cora from her Jacksonville days, snubbed her. He wrote home, cattily, of one "Lady Stuart," traveling around with Stephen — "a commonplace dull woman old enough to have been his mother — and with dyed yellow hair." Poor Cora! She could not have been more than thirty-two at the time, and Miss Gilkes insists that the golden color of her hair was natural.

Stephen recovered, though his health was always to be rather shaky after that, and the Cranes moved into an English country house near another American couple who, like themselves, could not marry. Harold Frederic, author of the best-selling *Damnation of Theron Ware* — a novel on the controversial subject of a Methodist minister who breaks away from the church — was married to a woman who refused to divorce him so that he might marry his girl, Kate. He had a job with the New York *Times* in London, and he and Kate were raising a family. Through this couple the Cranes met Edward and Constance Garnett, Ford Madox Hueffer, and many others. As time went on they made more friends: Henry James often dropped in, and they were on cordial terms with H. G. Wells and his wife.

Stephen's work was more highly thought of in England than it was at home — doubtless, as A. J. Liebling says, because his contemporaries in America resented his quick rise and his

abandonment of his native country. " 'The Red Badge' had
been received in America with the equivalent of a pat on the
head for an exceptional child," wrote Liebling. "The crashing
acclaim of the British critics, who constituted a higher court,
had promoted him over the heads of his older compatriots, who
never forgave him." The English liked Cora, too, most of them,
though she startled some by her habit of wearing simple, loose
wrap-around garments and sandals when she was at home,
and often let her hair hang down her back if only a few friends
were there. She explained the odd hairdo, saying it was good
for hair to be unpinned and aired occasionally, but the English
weren't at all sure about that, nor would they admit that the
theory made up for such outlandish habits. Still, women admitted that when Mrs. Crane tried, she could look very smart:
there was no doubt, they said, that she knew how to dress. They
usually added that she was much too outspoken. A few ladies
were badly shocked when they asked politely after Stephen's
health and Cora replied in casual tones that it had never been
very good since he'd had dysentery in Greece. Straight out she
said it: whatever next? — of course one had to make allowances
for writers and such.

Little by little the Cranes' entertaining increased, especially
after they took on long lease a large, dilapidated, Elizabethan
manor house in Surrey — Brede Place. They had never been
ahead of the game financially: now they fell very definitely behind. Neither Cora nor Stephen could believe that his fortunes
wouldn't be repaired soon. Wasn't he famous and successful?
Weren't editors clamoring for his work? So Stephen wrote
faster and faster, and Cora urged his agent more and more often
to send them a bit of money in advance, until everything slipped
from control all at once. Christmas week in 1899 brought a
tremendous bustle at Brede, where the Cranes were entertain-

ing sixty guests. Every room in the house was full of beds. Stephen and some friends had written a humorous play about the Brede Place ghost, and this was acted out. Then there was a grand ball on the night of December 29th. In the small hours of the morning, H. G. Wells cycled at furious pace in to Rye to fetch a doctor: Stephen was hemorrhaging.

In the five months that followed, Cora tried frantically to scrape together enough money to take her husband away, to this place or that, wherever the doctors said he must live if he was to have a chance. (Stephen's tuberculosis, though evidently of long standing, had not been discovered until the preceding year.) Liebling points out that TB is aggravated by worry and strain: no doubt Crane, therefore, died of his finances and bad doctoring as much as the disease itself. In the final throes of the disease, he was dragged by slow and painful stages to the Black Forest, where the doctor had thought the air would do him good. There he took his last breath early in June, 1900. He was twenty-nine.

As Cora wasn't his legal wife she had no claim on the estate, which anyway was worth less than nothing: Stephen died in debt for $5000. There could be no question of her staying on in England, though it must have been a wrench to leave the country where she had been happy: where her respectability had reached such a pitch that she was an honorary member of the Society of American Women in London, her name having been put forward by Mrs. Moreton Frewen, sister of Lady Randolph Churchill, and where she had for fellow members the Duchess of Manchester, Mrs. Cavendish-Bentinck, and Lady Paget. It was hard for Cora to go back to America, but she had to do it: there was no way out. She tried for a little while to make a living by writing, but it was no use. Finally she went once more to Jacksonville, bought a new house, and became a

madam, even more committed to the trade than she had been
when she met Stephen. She was doing well enough, but her romantic proclivities played her false when she chose another
mate, a good-looking but unbalanced young man named Ham-
mond McNeil. His family had money, but McNeil himself was
tending bar in the red-light district when he met Cora. They
were married, but he was a drunk, and Cora soon threw him
out. Not long afterwards he shot and killed a seventeen-year-old
boy he accused of enjoying Cora's favors, and she went abroad,
revisiting England, to avoid having to give evidence at the trial.
When she returned to Jacksonville once more, she resumed the
old life at her house. She died in 1910 of a stroke.

*   *   *

Until the last years of the nineteenth century most Bohemians were close to the pattern drawn by Murger. Their eccentricities varied — Bret Harte and his haphazard ways with
money, Huneker's passion for sitting up all night in cafés, Ambrose Bierce's lizard pets — but in one important rebellion
they agreed: they were against the tyranny of convention over
sex. The demand for freedom in private life was their chief
assertion against Society, and for most of Bohemia it was to continue to be for several decades more. Now, however, came the
first departure, a man ahead of his time in this one respect —
Jack London. Where his contemporary, Crane, assailed Mrs.
Grundy, London turned his youthful energy against the ogre
Capital.

His passion for the political rights of man was a natural reflection of the times and the place he lived in. Born in San
Francisco in 1876, he grew up in California's most troubled
years, when the new railways were having a disastrous effect
on the state's economy. As a child he heard much talk of strikes

and protests; San Francisco was full of unemployed laborers who stayed there simply because they had no better place to go. And his personal background was unsettled beyond this. Flora, his mother, had been deserted before Jack was born, by his father, an itinerant preacher of astrology named William Chaney. She attempted suicide but survived, and Jack was farmed out in the country while Flora earned his keep with needlework. Fortunately this stage didn't last long; she soon married a contractor, John London, who adopted the boy and gave him his own name. John's business did badly, and finally he gave it up, taking his family — including two daughters by his first wife — out of town to a farm across the bay, where he tried to earn a living on the land. This venture too failed, after which the Londons moved from farm to farm until they surrendered to fate, moved to Oakland, and bought a lodging-house which Flora operated.

Before meeting Chaney she had practiced as a spiritualist. Now she resumed this part-time occupation, and sometimes maintained a kindergarten as well. The Londons didn't starve, but what with constant parental anxiety and the frequent changes of address, Jack learned early in life to fend for himself. He grew up tough, working through the school vacations at a local canning factory, but he found the time to read whatever books he could get hold of. Ships fascinated him. He saved money and managed, at fifteen, to buy an old oyster sloop, in which he and his gang poached from oyster beds at night and sold their booty early next morning to dealers in San Francisco. He played truant more and more often, until there seemed no point in going to school at all, and when he was seventeen he stopped pretending. He signed on as ordinary seaman with a sealing vessel and spent nearly a year off Japan and in the Bering Sea.

After this adventure he had various jobs. He worked in a jute mill, and as a school janitor, stoking furnaces. But always when he had time he visited the Oakland Public Library, where Ina Coolbrith was still working as she had done since the departure of Bret Harte from California. Her eye was as sharp as ever for budding talent, and she took an interest in Jack. She had known many young people who used the library for a while and then, as they grew older, stopped coming, but Jack was different. He continued to call for books, and to discuss them with her. Now he began to bring to her stories he had written, asking Miss Coolbrith for her opinions, and she was impressed by his talent and encouraged him to go on. In 1893 the local newspaper, the *Morning Call*, announced a story contest. Flora London urged her seventeen-year-old son to send in one of his pieces, about a typhoon off the coast of Japan, and it won the prize.

After that little triumph, Ina as a self-appointed teacher probably urged him gently to settle down and put in some hard work at the desk, but Jack was not ready to abandon a life of physical action: he felt himself committed to the cause of the working-man. It was a burning topic. The depression that had long darkened California now clouded the whole country. The unions were fighting for their right to exist, and Eugene Debs had been sentenced to jail. There were fiery speeches on the San Francisco street corners, and Jack made up his mind to join "Kelly's Army," a group of unemployed men who proposed to march from Omaha to Washington, D. C., as Coxey's Army was doing from Ohio, to register their protest. With a number of other angry men he climbed into a freight car and rode away. They got as far as Omaha by rail, but nobody in the company was permitted to ride trains farther east, so Kelly's Army set out on foot to cover the rest of the journey.

They were an ill-disciplined crew, and their idea of living on the land as they moved did not please the farmers whose chickens and crops were pillaged. In Des Moines, where nearly thirteen hundred of the army, including Jack, stayed a long time, the citizens took active measures to get them out, loading them aboard riverboats and sending them down to Mississippi. Even after that setback some of the army carried on toward Washington. Jack, however, had long since lost his early fervor, and now he deserted. For some weeks he wandered around by himself, sleeping in barns, and seeing a large part of the eastern country in the process. He got into New York, but hated the city and got out again as fast as he could. In Buffalo he was picked up as a vagrant and given a thirty-day sentence. He was still locked up when the great Railway Union strike began.

This journey was the act of a restless youth in search of excitement rather than a planned gesture of social protest, but Jack London had plenty of time to think as he sat in the Buffalo jail, and when he got back to Oakland he saw his path clear before him. He would be a rebel with a plan of action, a reformer of the labor laws, a Socialist. He realized that a youth of eighteen was at a disadvantage, even more so if he had no education, so he went back to high school in Oakland and worked at high speed so that he might get into college and finish the course as quickly as possible. He toiled at his books, often as much as nineteen hours a day, and passed the entrance examinations for the university. But the effort had so bored and exasperated him that he stayed only a year at his higher studies before dropping out for good in 1897. The Socialist Party, which he had joined the year before, furnished much more amusement. Jack spoke for the cause at street corners, exhorting his fellowman to be up and doing for reform, until he was arrested and jailed for the second time. The newspapers featured him as "the Boy Socialist," though he was now twenty-one.

After he was freed, time hung heavily on his hands. Writing

did not attract him just then. His ambition was to strike a blow for mankind and make the world a fit place for the underprivileged. The old panacea, manual labor, did not fill the bill either, and it seemed a heaven-sent chance that there should be a gold rush in the Klondike. Hundreds of people were sailing to Alaska. Even Joaquin Miller was going, as a reporter for one of the journals. Jack London went too. He didn't make a fortune there: on the contrary, he lost the money he took with him, and found himself stuck and frozen in when winter came. By the time spring released him he was weak with scurvy, and stone broke. Bad news met him: John London was dead, and Flora needed his help. He hurried home. Now the necessary apprenticeship had been obtained: he had something to write about, and he needed money for the family, so he began to write in earnest of the Klondike and people he had seen there. He was immediately successful at selling his stories, and within five months they were appearing in magazines.

It might be supposed that "the Boy Socialist" would fit straight into an honored place among San Francisco's Bohemians. There were plenty of them around, not only the old guard but a lively new lot which included the founders of *The Lark*, California's lively if short-lasting little magazine, but young Jack was indifferent toward any group save that of his working-class friends downtown. The indifference did not last: he learned to enjoy the company of other writers and even, as we have seen, joined the Bohemian Club when this honor was offered to him. In fact, he became too gregarious for the good of his health, but all this came a few years later, and his first standoffishness offended many San Franciscans. Ambrose Bierce, as the self-appointed doyen of California writers, never forgave London for making his way without first getting the green light from Bierce, but his was not the only voice raised against him.

There was probably an element of resentment because of his socialism, too.

In *Footloose in Arcadia*, Joseph Noel says that in 1901 it was common knowledge around town that Ambrose Bierce had written to his brother Albert asking if he knew anything about a young Oakland man named London, "who wrote in the *Overland Monthly* as if his digestion, like his politics and rhetoric, was out of order." Noel describes the conversation at a picnic attended by a number of painters, musicians, writers and their female relatives — Albert Bierce was there, and so was the poet George Sterling — when many of the party were loudly critical of Jack's writing. George Sterling, however, had never met the author, and when Noel defended him Sterling asked to be introduced. He got his wish and became one of London's most intimate friends, though it was unusual in him to defy his master, Bierce, to such an extent. Jack didn't care how close Sterling might be to Bierce: he took issue with the poet over the fact that he worked in the office of a family connection named Havens, a prominent businessman who had recently consolidated the streetcar system of Alameda County. Speaking as a good Socialist, Jack declared that the operation was a swindle.

"Jack was successful; George, failing, found refuge in Bohemia," explains Jack's daughter Joan London, in *Jack London and His Times*. "It was a charming, old-fashioned sort of bohemianism that George assumed, and consisted chiefly of flouting social and moral conventions and behaving, when not working at his white-collar job, as if he were still a youth. Tall, slender and graceful, with a sensitively modeled face . . . George was well suited physically to his role of poet-playboy."

Jack himself was a good-looking man with boyish features, a strong body and a smile that was the more charming, perhaps, since his irregular teeth had gone bad and been replaced by decorative false ones. He got into the habit of attending parties on the campus of Stanford University, where he met a young Russian student, Anna Strunsky. The two became close friends. Anna and Jack exchanged letters with the idea of publishing them as a book, and the volume duly appeared under the title *The Kempton-Wace Letters.*

In 1900 Jack married Bessie Maddern, and they had two daughters. At the time he met Sterling the family was living in an Italian house — that is, a house that had been built by an Italian, a wildly elaborate building on the side of a steep hill in Piedmont. His plan was to stay there, writing books, but the plan didn't work out. In that age of the roving war correspondent, as soon as a man made a name in print, especially if he wrote adventure stories, newspaper editors thought of trips for him to take, and Jack was no exception. He went to England for the American Press Association, intending to move on to the Boer War in South Africa, but before he could leave Europe the Boers surrendered, so he remained, roaming the Continent and writing in England, until he had produced three more books. He came back to California in 1903, but was off again the next year to report the Japanese-Russian War in Korea. By this time he was an outstanding figure, and when he got a divorce the news was announced in headlines. Anna Strunsky was named as corespondent, but Jack was in love with someone else, and after the divorce he married Charmian Kittredge, his "Mate Woman," as Charmian in her book *Jack London* says that he called her. (More and more as one reads biographies prepared by fond widows, it becomes evident that censorship is not always a totally bad thing.)

Coinciding with London's matrimonial rearrangements was a certain amount of upheaval in the political circles he frequented. Other Socialists were lining up as extreme leftists or moderates, but Jack had never committed himself to either side. A conference in Chicago in 1904 produced the organization of the Independent Workers of the World, the IWW, commonly called the Wobblies. Conservatives spoke jeeringly of the Wobblies, saying that the initials stood for "I Won't Work," or "I Want Whisky," but they felt that it was all going beyond a joke really, and did not like it when London spoke of his political convictions. The fellow was a menace. During the time immediately preceding his divorce he went on an extensive lecture tour through the States, giving talks on his adventures, literature, and Socialism. He must have had a naïve character, for he was surprised when newspapers pounced on the story of the divorce with undisguised malice, and he was outraged when dozens of lecture engagements were promptly canceled because, as it was said, Jack London had abandoned his poor wife and babies for another woman. This version does seem unfair, since according to his daughter Joan's cool account of the proceedings, Bessie felt little rancor. It is clear that Joan herself bore Charmian no ill will, but the truth did not matter: Jack's critics had waited a long time to get the upper hand over the impertinent radical, and the chance was too good to miss.

Much more distressing, he felt, were similar attacks from the other side, his own hitherto loyal mates, who were asking in ever louder voices how a writer who made such a lot of money could honestly claim to be on the side of the poor, exploited workingman. Wasn't London doing himself pretty well for a Socialist? He liked the fleshpots too much. He enjoyed his food and had taken to riding everywhere in Pullmans. He even brought back a Korean valet from the East, and took him with him on his trips — what was a Socialist doing with a valet? On all sides the clamor increased. A library in Connecticut banned

London's works: people demanded that magazines stop printing stories by Jack London and threatened to boycott any periodical that wouldn't listen to their protests. Some editors were
intimidated, and for a while London's sales fell off. Mrs.
Grundy and the ogre Capital had got together, and a formida-
ble foe they made.

In defiant reply to all this, Jack wrote and published *The Iron
Heel*, a book with more "social significance" than any he had
hitherto produced. Radicals at least were silenced. *The Iron
Heel* did not sell well, but Jack had made his point. Trotsky
was later to praise it: "The book surprised me with the audacity
and independence of its historical foresight." But in Joan London's opinion, it was the swan song of Jack's political passion.
After that experience he changed — in his work, his interests
and himself. Joan says sadly that his devotion to the cause became "merely a nostalgic sentiment," though he never admitted this. He would back down rather than anger his readers, and
when Alexander Berkman asked him to write an introduction
to Berkman's *Prison Memoirs of an Anarchist*, Jack went to
great lengths to state in the article that he had no sympathy
whatever for anarchism.

Of course Berkman didn't use the introduction, but Jack had
no time to worry about such questions: with Charmian he had
moved to a ranch in the country where he planted eucalypti
for the market and was building a yacht to his own specifica-
tions. The yacht cost a lot of money — the great earthquake of
1906 had sent the prices of everything skyrocketing — but he
had always wanted it, and he went ahead. He planned to sail
the South Seas, an announcement that brought a fresh chorus
of protests from his old friends in the Party. A yacht? Whatever next, Comrade?

Jack London sailed off in spite of the protesting voices, but the minute he was away everything went wrong. The bottom fell out of the eucalyptus market. The new ranch house, not yet finished, was eating up his money, and when he got back, after pouring $75,000 into it, it burned down. He was charged with plagiarism in his book *Love of Life* and had to admit that he *had* lifted the plot from another author's story. Nevertheless he continued to plagiarize when he couldn't think of anything new for himself, until he hit on a less dangerous means of getting fresh material, buying plots ready-made from Sinclair Lewis and George Sterling. All this happened within a relatively short space of time: it was 1910 and London was still young, only thirty-four, when he made that arrangement with Lewis.

"I feel that I have done my part," he said to a youthful radical journalist in the course of an interview. "Socialism has cost me hundreds of thousands of dollars."

Vengefully or with sorrow, the radicals watched the steady decline of their old comrade. They noted, and commented fiercely upon, his remarks after he returned from a visit to Mexico to report the revolution there for *Collier's*, in 1914. He had been unable to find the war, and caught dysentery in Vera Cruz. Joan says severely that his reactions to Mexico were altogether those of a provincial middle-class American: he had no use for the revolution or the peons, to whom he referred as "breeds," and said disgustedly that America ought to take over the whole country and settle matters. "The way he lived was destroying him," says his daughter.

Listed as the highest-paid writer in the country, he ground out four books in 1913. His health was bad. The boyish features were islanded in an expanse of flesh. Not a tall man, he weighed nearly two hundred pounds, and his nature had changed for the worse; he had become "domineering, ungracious, rude," says Joan. But he did not formally cut himself off from the Socialist Party until after the First World War was under way. In March, 1916, he resigned because, he said, Socialists were against fighting, and "I am with the Allies, life and death. Germany today is a paranoiac."

Society had no reason now to fear Jack London. He was forty years old, tubby of figure and red of face. It was generally assumed that his problem was drinking, but in fact it was his eating habits that ruined his health — he was fond of raw meat, fish and fowl. Doctors warned him against this indulgence, but he laughed off their words, saying that he had a cast-iron stomach. He liked to eat two underdone wild ducks a day.

In November, 1916, Jack London made the headlines once more: he was dead. He had taken poison by mistake, said the newspapers, during an attack of stomach trouble, but in spite of all Charmian could do to change the record, the world soon learned that there was no mistake about it.

By the time Jack London died, nobody could have called him a rebel. Yet he was the pioneer: he had started something, and though he dropped by the wayside long before his death, Bohemia was heading for a rapprochement with the forces of political revolution.

CHAPTER 8

Several Magazines,
One Legend

FEW BOHEMIANS followed Jack London's early venture into the Socialist struggle, or blamed him when he abandoned it. What had economics or politics to do with them? They were not interested in unemployment figures: any topic that did not come under the heading of art, literature or music bored them.

Besides, the depression was abating and everyone felt more cheerful, with towns no longer choked by woeful derelicts looking for work. The Philistines prospered, and if the Bohemians did not, at least they could satisfy their rebellious urges with small, individual attacks on the enemy — authority, or Mrs. Grundy, or bad taste, or whatever constituted the artist's particular irritation. Art for art's sake was still their battle-cry, and few noticed, much less discussed, the death of Karl Marx. Fewer spoke of the struggle between capitalism and labor: what really excited them was the old double-headed monster, Ugliness and Materialism. In the 1890s, seething Bohemians found new opportunities to express themselves on all these grievances — or, to be exact, found new opportunities merely to express themselves — in the recent invention, the little magazine.

The adjective "little" in this connotation has a special meaning, as it has when we refer to a little dressmaker or the little butcher around the corner. Like the dressmaker and the butcher, a little magazine is not necessarily wee in dimension: *Broom*, a little magazine of the 1930s, was a fairly big book, but if it had been even bigger — if it had been the same size as today's Sunday New York *Times* — it would probably still have been called, quite correctly, a little magazine. The reason these periodicals are so persistently miscalled is that the parent of them all, *Chap-Book*, actually *was* diminutive.

Little magazines were and are — for there are more now than there ever were before — unlike the *Saturday Evening Post* or *Redbook* or the dead-and-gone *Youth's Companion* or any other popular trade magazine, because they are intended for people with unpopular tastes, who want something that isn't everyone's cup of tea. They are not meant to make money, and most are so unprofitable that they soon pack up and disappear. Yet during their short lives they usually do tremendous service, to some hitherto mute poet or some artist whose work is chronically refused by all the galleries. It is a long, difficult road the aspiring artist treads before he makes the grade; the little magazine helps him on his way. The editor of a little magazine pays little, if he pays anything at all, for contributions, but he seldom goes begging for material: dozens of people are willing to give him their work. For all this, the odd fact is that *Chap-Book*, which started the whole thing, was conceived for a commercial reason. It was meant to be merely a small magazine, but quite by accident it turned into a little one.

Its creators were two young Harvard seniors, Herbert E. Stone and Ingalls Kimball. Stone came naturally by his interest in the printed word from his father, Melville E. Stone, founder of the Chicago *Daily News* and manager of the Associated Press. These enterprising youths formed a company, Stone & Kimball, while they were still at Harvard, with which they meant to publish books and fill orders for printing. They probably got the idea for *Chap-Book* from England's new *Yellow Book*, just then rapidly gaining favor among the literati, but they saw their projected magazine as something rather different — a house-organ and advertising sample in one package. They used the best paper available and took care to have the text beautifully printed. Quite aware that their firm would not break even on such a de luxe job, they figured that it would more than pay for itself indirectly. Once the public had seen their handsome *Chap-Book*, the office would be crowded with customers clamoring to have printing jobs done.

The first number appeared in May, 1894. Four and a half inches by seven and a half, selling for five cents, it carried among other features a self-portrait of Aubrey Beardsley and an article about Francis Thompson by Bliss Carman, associate editor of *Chap-Book*. Both these subjects, it will be observed, were British; and *Chap-Book* was to use many contributions from Europe before it folded. The newcomer was received with an acclaim that surprised as much as it delighted its creators. Everyone, it seemed, was reading *Chap-Book* and praising it: everyone, that is, except for those Harvard faculty members who took a dim view of undergraduates going into business before leaving the Yard — but this difficulty was solved when Herbert and Ingalls finished their last year and took themselves, and *Chap-Book*, to Chicago. There, under the eye of the famous printer Goudy, the little magazine became even prettier. It was never financially solvent — in spite of its popularity the circulation averaged only twenty thousand, and even when the price went up to ten cents it lost money — but the standard of contributions remained excellent. In its four years of life *Chap-Book* published Hamlin Garland, Henry James ("What Maisie Knew"), Andrew Lang, Max Beerbohm, whose caricatures were featured, Richard Burton, Stephen Crane, Edmund

Gosse, Thomas Hardy, Mallarmé, Quiller-Couch, R. L. Stevenson, Verlaine, Yeats, and many other well-known names. John Sloan was one of the artists who illustrated its pages.

Most eloquent witness of its success was the large number of other little magazines that made their appearance in imitation of *Chap-Book*. At the time of its death, said *Publisher's Weekly* soon afterwards, there were one hundred and fifty of them, but five years later this number was corrected: according to the bibliographer F. W. Faxon, it was two hundred and twenty. Most successful, though again not in the commercial sense, were *The Lark* of San Francisco and *M'lle New York*. Both were born in 1895, a year after *Chap-Book*'s appearance, but neither could in fairness be called slavish imitations.

The Lark, as its name implies, was a light-hearted little book, owing its origin to a group of talented young people in San Francisco who called themselves "Les Jeunes." They thought it might be fun to run a magazine for a few issues. Its moving spirit — for these projects must have one firm hand to direct the others — was Gelett Burgess, a civil engineer teaching at the University of California, who often amused himself outside the lecture room by drawing and making up jingles. Browsing in Chinatown, he happened to find a bale of attractive brown paper made of bamboo, which could be printed successfully on only one side, and it was this paper that "Les Jeunes" used for their *Lark*. Burgess and a mural painter, Bruce Porter, did all the work for the first number and invested one hundred dollars to get it on the road, though later associates and contributors included Carolyn Wells, Willis Polk, Yoni Noguchi and Ernest Peixotto. The first issue contained the famous quatrain, "The Purple Cow," but its author wrote other lines for the magazine that were to become nearly as well-known and illustrated them in his characteristic style — hard, clean outlines

and boneless limbs that he incorporated, later, in "The Goops."
One of his *Lark* limericks is this classic:

> I wish that this house had a floor.
> I don't really care for a door,
>   But this walking around
>   Without touching the ground
> Is getting to be quite a bore.

The Lark did not die after the first few numbers, as "Les
Jeunes" had expected it would: enough people were charmed
with it to give a regular publisher the idea of backing the editors in their project. In all it lasted an imposing two years, and
even then didn't simply disappear or starve to death in the
usual way of little magazines. Though Gelett Burgess could
have kept it going longer, he killed it in cold blood, saying that
he wanted it to die young and in its full freshness.

The Lark made no attempt to bring Old World culture to its
readers in the fashion of *Chap-Book* and *Chap-Book*'s imitators
in Eastern cities. It was truly Californian in spirit — sturdy, independent — almost, one might say, self-satisfied. At least it
was more satisfied with its native city, where it was evidently
joy enough for artists to be young and ambitious, than other
little magazines that seemed to have been started for the sole
purpose of expressing their creators' fretful feelings toward
their surroundings in a world they never made.

The Lark left a mark on the city that may well be permanent;
it founded a little magazine tradition. Today such periodicals
are born in great number every year in San Francisco, to live
briefly and, presumably, happily, before they vanish like May-
flies. The shortest tenure of all was that of a contemporary of
The Lark, *Le Petit Journal des Refusées*, which consisted of one
single number, printed on wallpaper. The longest-lived may

well be *Laughing Horse*. Started by undergraduates at the University of California in 1922, *Horse* recorded a higher temperature of social indignation than *The Lark*'s. Like the rest of America, the young in California were by that time becoming interested in politics. Before the turn of the century Jack London and Ambrose Bierce were the only ones who cared, but in 1922 everybody was doing it. *Laughing Horse* soon ran afoul of the authorities for criticizing local politicos and the University Board of Governors, and one of the editors, Spud Johnson, had to shift the magazine to New Mexico when the going got too rough in California. *Horse* survived until 1938. But Spud's is another era, to be studied later. Let us return to the 1890s and *The Lark*'s contemporary, *M'lle New York*.

Vance Thompson, drama, music and literary critic for the New York *Commercial Advertiser,* fathered this one. Like Edgar Saltus he had spent several years studying in Europe, and his reactions on coming back early in the decade to the fatherland were also like Saltus's — horror, a strong sense of superiority, and homesickness for the Old World. Good heavens, what Philistines these Americans were! How could any man of true culture bear to live among them? Thompson declared that New Yorkers were years behind Europe in intellectual interests, and that even the liberals were pathetically backward. He was amazed and scornful when a Columbia professor, who already had a bad reputation for free thinking, got into fresh trouble because he defended Zola. Other free spirits rushed to his defense and had a good time, as such champions always do, but Vance Thompson scoffed at the whole tempest. Zola? Why, nobody in Paris ever mentioned Zola any more, he said: Zola was old hat. As for American magazines, they didn't bear discussion: hadn't Gilder of the *Century* recently rejected a story because there was in it mention of a boy's nipple?

Thompson cut a swathe in his circle, not only with his shattering opinions but because he was married to an actress and wore an English coat, yellow gloves, top hat and monocle. There was much pleased excitement when it became known in the newspaper and literary sets that he intended to start a little magazine, a spicy, amusing journal like those he had enjoyed in Paris. His great friend James Huneker was asked to help in the project, and enthusiastically assented. There was a natural sympathy between Thompson and Huneker: Huneker vastly admired Thompson's writing, for he was, as Arnold Schwab observes, a "practitioner of gorgeous prose" whose fondness for the unusual or foreign in phrases was, once again, like Saltus's. "This hollow-eyed woman is the hasheesh of the stage," Thompson once declared of Duse.

The first issue of *M'lle New York,* with a colored cover depicting a pretty lady sitting in a café, appeared in August, 1895. Incidentally, it was not particularly small. It was lavishly illustrated by Thomas Fleming and Thomas Powers, friends of Thompson and Huneker. The inevitable preface, or manifesto, in which all magazine-starters used to set forth their intentions, was written by Thompson:

> The public . . . corrupts the language it has inherited from the mob and the poets; it has debauched the stage to the level of Mr. Richard Watson Gilder's poetry and looks upon the drama merely as a help to digestion, a peptic or aperitive . . . This grotesque aggregation of foolish individuals pretends to literary taste; it has its painters, its playwrights, its authors; that part of it which reads the male blue-stocking, William Dean Howells, looks down upon that part of it which reads the female blue-stocking, Richard Harding Davis; that part which reads Richard Harding Davis looks down upon the part which reads Laura Jean Libbey, (why, in Heaven's name?), and the

readers of Miss Libbey look down in turn upon the readers of
the *Police Gazette*.

M'LLE NEW YORK is not concerned with the public. Her
only ambition is to disintegrate some small portion of the public into its original component parts — the aristocracies of
birth, wit, learning and art and the joyously vulgar mob.

"M'lle New York is a free lance, and even in this first number draws blood," commented Huneker approvingly in another
paper, as if he had had no hand whatever in planning the venture.

There are more ways than the surgeon's of drawing blood:
Vance Thompson's instrument was like a sledgehammer. Sub-
sequent numbers, however, showed more talent for editing and
less rancor. Huneker did some of his best writing for *M'lle,*
while Thompson contributed criticism of foreign artists and
writers, many of whom had not been heard of previously by his
readers. "More Parisian than either the *Chap-Book* or *The
Lark,"* says Schwab, *"M'lle New York* was advanced and daring
for its time. The colored illustrations, wide margins, tiny pictures across the letter-press, and impertinent marginal comments widened the eyes of editors and layout men, while
Powers' mildly bawdy, Beardsleyan drawings might have offended Anthony Comstock if the 'precious' prose surrounding
them had not given the magazine a certain highbrow dignity."
Huneker and Thompson carried on in its pages a carefully nur-
tured argument about women, for and against: Thompson
waxed furious over the American worship of females, while
Huneker defended the popular attitude. The idea of Thompson's waging what Thurber later named The War Between
Men and Women was as funny as Huneker's defense, because
Thompson's actress wife henpecked him to the ultimate degree,
and Huneker handled his girl friends cavalierly.

In other articles Thompson attacked similarly cherished national ideals. America was not a democracy, he asserted — the whole thing was ruled by the dollar. Hoaxes apart, Huneker usually agreed on these matters with his friend, but they never saw eye to eye on Jews: Thompson was violently anti-Semitic and the attitude is obvious in the pages of *M'lle New York*.

Although none of the contributors was paid, the editors were chronically short of funds. Often there occurred a hiatus in publication until Thompson managed to dig up enough money to pay the printer. Finally he was unable to meet any more bills and in 1897 *M'lle New York* closed down for good, it was thought, until one of the Jews he so hated came to his rescue. Marc Blumenberg, owner of the *Musical Courier,* made an offer of support in 1898, and thanks to him, *M'lle* was revived. For four new issues she breathed again, but then died completely, having enjoyed, all in all, a reasonable run for the kind of magazine she represented. In a post mortem Schwab credits *M'lle* with several firsts: "It printed far more works by modern French authors than any other American publication of the time. . . . Helping to pave the way for the host of little magazines that sprang up in New York a decade or so later, *M'lle New York* gave impetus to the undercurrent of revolt in America against the moralistic conception of literature, art and life. . . . Thompson and Huneker anticipated more powerful iconoclasts, the most famous of whom was H. L. Mencken."

In fact, Mencken was ultimately to use the underlying idea of the Thompson-Huneker fake feud as the foundation of his amusing book, *In Defense of Women,* and this was not plagiarism: by the time he adopted it it was in the public domain, if only because Vance Thompson had long since bowed out of serious literary circles. The end of Thompson — his end, that is, as a rebel — is a bizarre story, and starts off with his publica-

tion of a work on diet, one of the very first of the hundreds of
volumes that have since appeared on that vast subject — *Eat
and Grow Thin*. It became a best-seller, so much so that certain of his enemies, irritated by his success, declared that it had
really been written by Mrs. Thompson. Vance did not reply to
these allegations. The erstwhile essayist on Ibsen, Verlaine and
Knut Hamsun went abroad to live, settling down in Nice on the
French Riviera, and there he wrote another book, entitled *Woman*. Unlike the sly Mencken, this time the erstwhile
misogynist praised women without tongue in cheek. Perhaps
living in France and once more luxuriating in Old-World culture sweetened his character. Whatever the reason, he never
recanted. Vance Thompson died in such respectability that it
was difficult for his contemporaries to credit, when they thought
of the past, the rackety old days of *M'lle New York*.

He was not alone in incurring the disapproval of his boon
companions by making a hit. Bohemian philosophy as well as
necessity was exemplified when little magazine editors didn't
pay their contributors. To ignore profit, Bohemians believed,
was a touchstone of character, and one could not work for gain
without sacrificing one's professional purity. A painter who sold
his pictures was sure to be accused of compromise, of selling
himself down the river. The worst one could say of a book was
to call it a potboiler. Even so, it happened. Once in a while
someone struck the magic note and became a public favorite,
though he sacrificed the respect of his old friends in doing so.
Robert W. Chambers, for example, never lived down his success: as novel after novel soared high on best-seller lists, his old
companions were increasingly disgusted. Chambers had once
shown promise, they told each other, in the days when he still
wanted to be a painter. *Then* he studied in Paris on the Left
Bank: *then* he was a charming fellow. Now, with his fatal facil-
ity with plots, he wasn't worth the ink he spilled.

It must be admitted that Chambers was unregenerate and never gave any indication of regret for his wicked ways. Instead, he hit back at Bohemia in his novel *The Outsiders,* published in 1900. Oliver, a young painter of American nationality but European upbringing, comes to America and gets his first glimpse of New York. Like Saltus, Thompson and Huneker — in short, like a large number of aesthetes of the time — he is appalled by the crass ugliness of everything. "The flat skyline, the thin brick skin of the city under which its gigantic bones of iron protruded in ribs and ridges and rusty scars, attracted and distracted him. To him, as yet, it was merely strange, not hideous. He wondered how a nation could so completely overlook the vital necessity beauty, — he wondered *why* they had overlooked it. He . . . had passed his youth among the serene landmarks of an older civilization, where symmetry was born with life itself, where moderation was the first law of beauty, and where beauty, beginning as a necessity to embryonic intelligence, grew to the dignity of religion, — and left on mind and matter an impression ineffaceable."

But Oliver was not completely like Huneker and the others. Where *M'lle New York*'s writers pointed out a congenial way of life to those who, in Schwab's words, were "exponents of artistic (and sexual) freedom," the hero of *The Outsiders* shies away from sexual freedom like a skittish horse at sight of a blowing newspaper. He is so upset by the very existence of sex that, like the man at the analyst's, everything he sees reminds him of it. Above all, he is scandalized by the *mores* of the Bohemians he falls among — an odd reaction in a painter, but the conviction is borne in upon the reader, page by page, that Oliver is odd altogether.

Befriended by a young Englishman, Duncan Wayward, Oliver finds a room in the same house. Wayward lives in style, now and then drinking a cocktail or "a Schwepps and a pony," and keep-

ing in trim with his fencing. Yes, fencing. Our friends the foils
are back with us in sinister form: the reckless Wayward insists
on fencing without buttons. Even more disturbing than Wayward, thinks Oliver, is the group of girls who occupy other
rooms in the same house. They haven't got a chaperon, though
Dulcie, the youngest, ought not to be in the big city at all, considering her age. Oliver is not quite a milksop. He is only
slightly staggered when one of the maidens unblushingly offers
him a glass of wine, but to see Dulcie smoke a cigarette is too
much for his self-control.

"Why do you smoke?" he asks her, softly. "Nobody does it
now, you know, on the other side." From the way she flinches
at this snub and bites her lip and drops the cigarette, he knows
that he has had a good effect, but it is not enough; one tiny reform is only a drop in New York's bucket of wickedness. He
realizes this afresh when he attends a party of Wayward's. "Everybody smokes cigarettes when they see fit"; he marvels, horrified; "there are decanters, too." Even such depravity, however, becomes insignificant when Wayward exhibits his collection of slippers, each of which is a trophy of some woman's
shame. Oliver's shocked reaction abashes the young rake, who
adds apologetically, "There are not twenty in all."

"After a short silence, Oliver said; 'Isn't this whole thing
tinctured with decadence?' "

Harsh words, to which Wayward made no reply. "He's the
Earl of Firth's youngest son," another man explains to Oliver.
"But he's like the rest of us — one of the unclassed — a rank
outsider."

Poorer and poorer as time goes on, the starving Oliver faints
in the street, and is rescued by a friendly Bohemian who takes
him to the latter's residence, the Monastery, 260 Washington Square. The owners have to collect the rent with fixed

bayonets, Oliver's new friend tells him proudly, and the agent is afraid to come around very often.

"Do you see those parlour windows? Ramon Quesada, the Vice-Consul from Yucatan, lives there . . . Then, Mora Lessly, the wit, inhabits the next floor. I don't believe he does anything in the world but just inhabit places . . . Sidney Jaune, the novelist, who writes Volapük tinctured with a weak solution of Henry James and peppered with Cafe Americaine French, edits the American edition of *The Pink Rat* on the same floor. . . ."

Oliver takes up residence in this Bohemian beehive and slowly recovers his strength. But it is not long before he is freshly alarmed by signs of vice, when he discovers that the Monastery tenants occasionally give parties in one studio or another, there to entertain "the worldly of the gentler sex . . . They were young women who wrote for the daily papers, others who adorned the metropolitan stage and concert halls, some who painted, some who sang, some who composed fashionable garments and hats; others still who were about to do something for a living and had not yet decided what to do but were waiting for suggestions.

"An invitation to the Monastery was a thing to be desired; the very word 'Bohemian,' draws certain sorts of people as sugar draws cockroaches."

In spite of his misgivings Oliver is persuaded to attend one of these parties, and there he encounters Dulcie. It is terrible to think that they should meet here, surrounded by smokers and drinkers, but before he can leap to the natural conclusion she assures him that this is her first visit. Relieved, he loses no time in taking her home. Dulcie, who is living in a humble rooming-house, admits that she is working in a sort of sweatshop, and that the employer is kind to her. Of course Oliver knows immediately that this man has designs on her virtue. In despair, he says,

"Try to hold out, Dulcie; they're liars — every one! . . . And — the danger is everywhere — *everywhere* — at Wayward's, at the Monastery, on the street, here in your own house — by day, by night, — you know it, Dulcie? . . . Everywhere, from men — from the best of them particularly!"

Hard as life has been for Dulcie, it now, not surprisingly, appears worse. She gives up her job, and promptly becomes destitute, so Oliver brings her to the Monastery and conceals her in an inner room. It goes without saying that the relationship is Platonic. Yet, for just one moment, there is danger of the novel's becoming pornographic. Let us not go into details. It is surely enough to say that evil feelings overcome the young people, and they kiss! To be sure, it happens only once: even so, it is an awful shock for Oliver.

"He attempted to realize what they had done. Self contempt and humiliation staggered him, drove him into his own room, where he stood staring into space."

And worse is to come. The prurient world learns where Dulcie is, and a scandal ensues. The most innocent girl cannot go on forever ignoring innuendoes, and Dulcie's grief when the truth breaks on her is boundless. "To think of the horror of such a thing! Do other people believe that I — I — am that kind of a girl?"

Yes, they do. They are wicked Bohemians, they are outsiders who don't recognize decency when they see it. Finally Oliver and Dulcie know that they love each other — about time too, thinks the reader who has gone through some hundreds of pages and knew it long ago — but before they can marry and consummate their love, Dulcie dies.

*   *   *

It seems hardly fair to blame the American people for this nonsense, as if Chambers's characters were drawn from life. Of course they weren't — such people never existed. But it is significant that he was popular, that his high-flown, impossible sentiments did agree with the public ideal. Americans admired Oliver's battle for purity and shared his indignation with such dissolute people as he declared artists to be. It is more than a mere incongruity that one of American's outstanding artists, the dancer Isadora Duncan, was Chambers's contemporary, since it was his very existence — or, rather, the widespread attitude for which he was spokesman — that sent her out of the country and kept her away most of her adult life.

Perhaps this vivid, tempestuous, rebellious and exasperating woman should be blackballed from the Honorable Society of American Bohemians, for she rejected America, just as Whistler and Stuart Merrill did, but it is almost impossible to leave her out, her name was such a byword in America as well as Europe. Moreover, though Whistler and Merrill tried hard to remodel themselves and become Europeans, Isadora continued to consider herself American though she lived abroad, until her unhappy visit to the States comparatively late in her life, when she brought her Russian husband along on a tour and ran afoul of her compatriots' indignation with all things Russian.

Before that, Isadora had seldom railed against her native land — many a voluntary exile has said far worse than she did — because it was not in her nature to reject completely any part of herself, even her nationality. Whatever Isadora was, Isadora felt, was the right thing to be. Of course, after the débacle things were different and nothing was too bad to say against America. So she said things, whatever popped into her angry head. Whenever Isadora lost her temper she did it properly. Perhaps every nonconformist or Bohemian has a certain amount of venom to get rid of. Most of them turn their wrath on the symbols of authority they suffer under when young, but Isadora's childhood knew little authority; she had no cause to resent her mother in that way. It is possible, then, that when she flew out at last against the land of her birth, it was merely a delayed adolescent tantrum.

Certainly, from the very beginning, her home life was unusual. Her father had abandoned his wife and children because he was caught out in a financial swindle, and had left Mrs. Duncan just as she was on the point of giving birth to the child who was christened Dora — a name she herself later altered to Isadora. Mrs. Duncan divorced her husband, then set to work earning a livelihood for the rest of the family by teaching piano. They often went without enough to eat, and seem to have moved constantly from one lodging-house to another, but Mrs. Duncan had a stubbornly cheerful outlook and plenty of vitality: Isadora could look back on many pleasant hours when her mother discussed with the children music and art and philosophy.

Isadora began dancing as soon as she could walk. She claims that she was still a young girl helping her sister Elizabeth to run a dancing school when she formulated her own revolutionary concept of the art. All the family worked whenever they could to help out with money, and Isadora earned fees for appearing as an entertainer before society people at afternoon teas and charity benefits. Even in those early days her technique must have shown signs of distinction, but it is a question whether her modest success at San Francisco parties owed itself to her theories, which she expounded to reporters whenever she got a chance, or to her youth and prettiness and the well-advertised fact that she danced in flimsy draperies and would not use the tights or stockings other *danseuses* considered proper. It did not matter to the Duncans. They were glad of her earnings because the money could be put by for their dearest project, the promotion of Isadora. Always willing to take a chance, Mrs. Duncan went along with cheerful readiness when Isadora announced that she now had enough money to go to Chicago, where she would, presumably, have more scope. In Chicago Isadora arranged a series of recitals, during the first of which several ladies walked out in furious protest against her sketchy attire. Isadora was not intimidated. Hadn't she the authority of ancient Greece behind her? Dancing, like life itself, should be natural and free, without constriction. She had a mission to spread beauty through the world and liberate the human spirit from its chains, and no handful of dirty-minded dowagers was going to frighten her.

But professional work was slow in coming. She got a short engagement at a roof-garden, but the Chicago venture would have been voted a failure if she hadn't been introduced to Augustin Daly, the famous producer, after one of her performances. He said complimentary things about it and suggested that she look him up sometime in New York. Other people might have thought this invitation too vague to take seriously, but the Duncans were always optimistic, and immediately set about scraping up funds to buy their way east. Sure enough they got there, and Daly, hoist with his own petard, found Isadora a dancing turn at a theater. It was only a small part, however, and she felt out of place among so many others. More satisfactory were recitals in private houses, rather on the order of the performances she had given in San Francisco; there she could dance her own inventions, and, for that matter, the money was better too. While Isadora enjoyed her little vogue among the ladies of the Four Hundred, Elizabeth Duncan set up a teaching-studio at the hotel where the Duncans were living. One night the hotel burned down and all their possessions were lost. The Duncan children rejoiced. They were destitute! They were free! Now was the very moment to go abroad.

Typically, Mrs. Duncan fell in with these plans and was as enthusiastic as any of the others. Abroad? Why, of course — what a splendid idea! In Europe they would be able to see Greece, fountainhead of culture and beauty. She could scarcely wait to get started. Isadora attempted to raise the necessary money from well-heeled women who had in the past engaged her to perform for their parties. She was full of happy confidence that they would give it to her: after all, it was in the sacred cause of Art, wasn't it? But the general reaction to her blithe request shocked and disgusted her. Though they had all that money, most of the ladies refused to give any of it to Art's cause: one of the dowagers was so recalcitrant that Isadora had to faint gracefully on the drawing-room carpet before she would hand over fifty dollars.

Only slightly ruffled by the struggle, the Duncans sailed off to England in a cattle-boat without so much as a change of clothing to take with them. They were much distressed by the lowing of the cattle, and Raymond became a vegetarian then and there, and remained one until his death. They must have had names and addresses to refer to in London, but as Isadora recalled it they considered themselves absolutely on their own because they liked it that way. They spent days wandering blissfully about the city seeing the sights — "driving about in penny 'buses in a state of perfect ecstasy . . . and in the amazement and delight of everything around us, we absolutely forgot how very limited were our resources . . . It was not until some weeks had passed that we were awakened from our tourist dream by an irate landlady asking for her bill to be paid." The Duncans couldn't pay, so the landlady threw them out, keeping their few bits and pieces of luggage.

For four days the family walked around, spending the nights on park benches, and then one of them thought of a stratagem. They moved into a luxury hotel, explaining that their luggage was lost. Food was ordered from the room service, and everyone ate and slept to their hearts' content. When it looked as if a reckoning was imminent, the Duncans slipped out of a back door, much refreshed. It was dishonest, you or I might say, but the Bohemian Isadora never looked at matters in that bourgeois light. She held that it was the duty of rich people, and rich people's hotels, to support geniuses — and, as Isadora said, "I was never able to understand, then or later on, why, if one wanted to do a thing, one should not do it." Nevertheless, whether or not they felt justified in bilking the hotels, the Duncans had not enjoyed that four-day ordeal. After they had got hold of ten pounds and felt on a level with the world again, Raymond expressed the sentiments of them all: "We must never again subject ourselves to the insults of these low, common lodging-house women."

It was nice to have the ten pounds, but Isadora's art was not getting much further in London, so the Duncans went on to Paris. They adored Paris, and France in turn adored Isadora. Soon she was happily immersed in the study of Greece, and practicing, and teaching, and giving performances at parties. Sometimes she would round off a performance with a speech in which she held forth on her theories of "natural" dancing versus the popular style of ballet — it was a habit that grew on her in later years. Her audience was usually startled by her words and sometimes she had a brisk argument on her hands, but people respected Isadora. She even had great success with fellow artists. She toured Europe with the famous American dancer Loie Fuller and her troupe, and when she had the hang of it she organized tours for herself. At last Isadora Duncan was launched.

It was in Hungary that the twenty-three-year-old artiste

took her first lover. She had not been held off for reasons of prudery, but because her mother's Bohemianism did not extend so far as to include approval of sexual freedom: Mrs. Duncan kept a sharp watch on her daughters. On one occasion Isadora had escaped her vigilance, but the man elected to initiate her refused the responsibility. Now, in Budapest, she fell in love with a good-looking actor, and the affair was passionately consummated. Mrs. Duncan and Elizabeth expostulated in vain.

"The anxiety of them both was so unbearable," wrote Isadora in her memoir, "that at length I persuaded them to go for a little trip to the Tyrol."

This encounter was soon forgotten, but it was supplanted over and over, and the other female Duncans could never get used to the idea of Isadora's love affairs. The family group did not break up, but its unity was cracked; in an important respect Isadora was now on her own. However, she took all the other Duncans to Greece, where they wore the ancient dress and staggered the natives by going sandaled on pilgrimages and wandering through Athens in their draperies. The world watched. By this time everything Isadora did was news, and she lived the rest of her life as a personage — laughed at by some, revered by others, but still a personage. Her travels, her affairs, her ideas, and — in the end — her weaknesses, were reported and commented upon. For a while she ran a dancing school in Germany. She bore a daughter to Gordon Craig, the stage designer, and later, as the mistress of an American millionaire named Paris Singer, had a son. Both children were killed in a car accident in Paris, a shocking circumstance that changed Isadora's character but did not slow her down. The German school cost so much that it had to be given up: later, in despair of ever persuading the capitalistic governments of France and Greece to back her in a similar project, she offered her idea to the new Soviet Union. The Russians assented, so Isadora in 1921 bade goodbye, as she thought, to the Western world, and started a new life.

Moscow was a sad disappointment. The Russians neglected Isadora, and there was no realization of her vision of a school, a building equipped with studios and dormitories for a thousand children. Indeed, it was difficult to find lodgings at all. Moscow was underhoused, officials were jockeying for position, and food was in short supply. Nobody cared at all about dancing schools. But Isadora persisted until something had been accomplished — not on a grand scale, but still, something. Fifty children came to live with her, to dance every day. On a national holiday she produced some of these pupils onstage, where they did a few simple steps. The audience was enthusiastic, and when Isadora followed up the act with a dance of her own, an interpretation of the "Internationale," everyone went wild. It became her most popular number. And so life in Russia improved. She suffered from the discomfort and the bad food and drink — Isadora loved the fleshpots — but otherwise she had all an artist wants and needs: admiration, interest, and hope of achieving the ideal, the school that was to revolutionize mankind. Then she fell in love.

This was no novelty in Isadora's life: she adored men and was never shy in saying so. Unfortunately, as she grew older the men grew younger. She was now past forty, and fat, while the object of her latest passion was in his twenties — Serge Essenine, a curly-headed poet, a good-looking blond peasant who had won fame for his poems. They could not talk to each other, Isadora never having learned to speak more than a few words of Russian, but this difficulty does not seem to have hindered the relationship. It was disconcerting, however, to find that she could not simply live with him, as she had done with her lovers in the hidebound bourgeois West. The liberated Russians couldn't understand such an arrangement, and she was told that

Essenine would not be able to travel with her on her forthcoming world tour unless the pair were married; passport difficulties at the border were cited in explanation. What to do? Isadora held the greatest contempt for marriage as a bourgeois device, a ridiculous formality, a strait-jacket. On the other hand she needed money, and the tour was intended to raise some: they were so short of funds at the school that her pupils went hungry. She submitted to officialdom, married Essenine, and in 1922 the pair set off for Western Europe and the United States.

By land or sea, it was all a stormy voyage, and the element that contributed most to all the turbulence was alcohol. Essenine drank heavily, and so, to a lesser extent, did Isadora. But where her love of champagne, which had grown progressively stronger after she lost her children, was manageable, he was one of those people who should not take alcohol at all. Serge would collect a retinue of expatriate Russians, give them a banquet at Isadora's expense, and then, with their help, tear up the place, smashing windows, mirrors and ornaments. The celebration was sure to end with the entire personnel of the tour being kicked out of the hotel. Isadora had to move out of more than one luxury establishment in Paris, and was constantly dunned by enraged proprietors. She loved her darling boy nevertheless, daily taking him to shops where Essenine bought great heaps of clothes. Never a very well-balanced youth, this irruption into a world of luxury, where food and drink and general splendor were unlimited, toppled his reason.

He was actually locked up for a time in Austria, and the couple got away from France only one jump ahead of the police. In America, trouble of another sort met them at the docks when they were held at Ellis Island for some hours on suspicion of being undesirable visitors from the Soviet Union. Immigration officials accused Isadora in particular of planning to engage in political insubordination. Wasn't she notoriously immoral? Worse, she had voluntarily sacrificed her American citizenship. It was all very suspicious indeed, but Sol Hurok, the entrepreneur who had set up the American tour, soon got the pair sprung. Though Hurok was pleased rather than annoyed by the incident, because so much publicity attended it, Isadora worked herself up to a fine, towering rage with her native country. The customary speech she gave after the end of her first concert in Carnegie Hall was a fairly temperate one, considering the source, but as the tour progressed she became more and more denunciatory of the American attitude toward Russia. In the end she was delivering really fiery orations. Once, in Boston, at the climax she pulled out a red flag and waved it. When word of this shocking gesture got around, a lot of Isadora's engagements were canceled, and Hurok tore his hair. He tried to keep her quiet, but nobody in the world could do that — not when Isadora's blood was up. Even if she promised to be good and shut up, after five minutes there she was, half soused and talking away as hard as ever. Whenever the spirit moved him Essenine too would sound off, spouting away in Russian that few could understand. It certainly gave the audience a good money's worth, and people came to the recitals hoping for just such fireworks, but more stayed away. Cancellations ruined the prospect of a considerable profit.

On departure, Isadora published in the press a goodbye letter to America which contained a memorable passage: "I am not an anarchist or a Bolshevik. My husband and I are revolutionists. All geniuses worthy of the name are."

*   *   *

It is a moot point what effect all this had on America's Bohemia. The ranks had long been drawn up in battle array,

artists on one hand, Philistines on the other, all combatants
sneering at each other. That is the general picture as drawn by
Bohemians, but is it quite accurate? Not by 1923, at any rate,
the date of Isadora's indignant withdrawal from the scene.
There were many members of the middle class who went to
concerts and exhibitions and Isadora's dance recitals, and appreciated them. The bourgeoisie was beginning to tolerate
Bohemia, at last.

The Bohemian artists themselves naturally considered Isadora a heroine; she was their voice and their bravest pioneer.
An attack on her freedoms, especially freedom to love and live
wherever she liked, including Russia, was an attack on all of
them: what difference if she had herself repudiated the
American nation? The principle remained the same. Besides,
it was Russia she had chosen, and Russia was in high favor with
Bohemians. The Soviet was rebellious: the Soviet was therefore worthy of approval, and Isadora's espousal of Communism's
cause was just exactly what Bohemia would have expected of her
gallant soul. It did not matter that she had probably never read
Marx in her life; a large number of themselves didn't bother
to read him. As she said, all geniuses worthy of the name were
revolutionists. Viva Soviet Russia! Viva Isadora!

For all that, what remained of the lady's career is a tragic
story. Essenine in France, on the return journey, misbehaved
so violently that his wife had to send him back to Russia ahead
of her own return, if only to keep him out of prison in Paris.
Throughout the marriage she had been amazingly gentle and
forbearing, as if all she wanted now was to keep her boy at any
price, but Essenine was a pathological case, and her loving care
was not enough. After he had gone she found that he had pillaged her belongings and was smuggling large sums of money,
not to mention Isadora's wardrobe, back to his friends and

family. Isadora never complained about this. But she was not to see Essenine again: a year later he hanged himself. When the Soviet government told her that his not inconsiderable estate was now hers, she turned it back to his relatives.

After the death of Essenine, Isadora lost interest in the Soviet Union. For the following few years she lived in France, drinking too much, taking money wherever she could get it, and becoming little more than a nuisance to her friends. She died in a car accident, but more spectacularly than her children had: her shawl caught in the car's rear wheel and strangled her.

*   *   *

Some years later, the revolutionist writer Max Eastman wrote of her in an essay entitled "Heroism Plus Heroics: Difficulties in Worshipping Isadora Duncan." He viewed her dancing with strong enthusiasm, and gave her credit for having brought in comfortable fashions that gave beauty and release to a whole generation of young girls. On the other hand, he confesses, "I was repelled by her conversational and behavioral heroics, her confusion, all through life, of gesticulation with gesture." He mentions "the admirable force of character with which Isadora insisted on being half-baked," and in an amusing passage tells of one time, when he had written a poem to her dancing, she invited him to tea, then pulled him into the bedroom where she insisted that he work the ouija board with her. Eastman submitted with a bad grace: he thought ouija boards ridiculous. The finger spelled out the name "Ingrid," and he said something like, "Who the hell is Ingrid?" With her head coyly cocked to one side, Isadora replied that Ingrid would be their baby's name. Isadora's affairs were always front-page news, and that was Max Eastman's first thought. "As a progenitor of supermen, I am by instinct reticent," he writes in explanation of why he suddenly recalled a dinner engagement and hurried away.

Eastman, who was still a Marxist at the time of Isadora's Russian adventure, visited the country during her sojourn there. In some outlying town he encountered the dancer on tour: her prize Russian pupil later mentioned the meeting in a book, adding wonderingly that though Comrade Eastman had lunch with them that day, they never saw him again. This, says Eastman, is true; he didn't want to see Isadora, being unbearably irritated by her lack of comprehension of the Soviet's aims and meaning. As for her marriage to Essenine — "In the name of Art . . . she lured into her breast and bed this self-abandoned, dissolute, already suicidal genius-bum, a lyric-hearted playboy-singer turned into a sot by a city he could not love and a revolution he did not understand . . . this blind union was a disaster to them both, as well as to the hotel furniture."

CHAPTER 9

Four Ladies

EUROPEANS HAD long suspected that American women were awful. Explorers had said so, and now, with the twentieth century well into its stride, they were able to see the truth for themselves. More and more Americans crossed the Atlantic to visit Europe, their ladies descending on capital cities like the Valkyrie. Insouciantly they would take a place by storm, shopping, inspecting museums, sweeping splendidly into theater and opera house, putting their children out to grass on European culture, marrying off their daughters to impecunious aristocrats. European men were divided between admiration and terror of these Amazons. How pretty some of them were, but, alas, how bossy!

It was all the fault of the husbands, said the Europeans wisely. American men must believe that their women were goddesses: at least, they behaved as if they did. There was truth in the allegation. We have seen how grievously the mavericks, Huneker and Saltus, shocked the country with their cavalier treatment of their wives, but a more startling illustration, because it is positive, is the Harry K. Thaw story. Thaw, son and heir of a Pittsburgh millionaire, came to New York soon after the turn of the century and lost no time earning a name for dissipation and eccentricity. Falling in love with young Evelyn Nesbitt of the "Floradora" chorus, he took her, as the euphemism has it, under his protection. Then he proposed that they marry, but Evelyn sadly said that this could not be, and the reason she gave was in the true Robert W. Chambers tradition: she was not *worthy* of marriage, she said, because she hadn't been pure even when Thaw first came along. Harry agonized over this confession, and would not rest until he had extracted from her the name of her first seducer. She said it was Stanford White, the celebrated architect who had designed a number of good things in New York, including the Washington Square Arch.

White's name could not have come as a complete surprise to Thaw, since all Broadway had been aware of the liaison, but he behaved as if it were. He beat his beloved with a horsewhip until he had elicited a detailed account of the affair, which had begun, said Evelyn, when she was only sixteen. White invited her to dinner in his rooms and gave her a glass of champagne. Sipping it, she immediately fell unconscious and remained that way for some time. When she came to her senses, it was too late. She'd been ravished. Oh, the horror of it. Evelyn wept and Harry smote his brow.

Now that she was purged by confession, they were married, in April, 1905, but the bridegroom's mental turmoil continued. He was obsessed with the thought of White, often lying awake at night to dwell on the wronging of Evelyn. Sometimes he would burst into tears. Yet he did nothing about it for more than a year after the wedding. On an evening in June, 1906, he and Evelyn took a party to the new Madison Square Roof Garden, where an entertainment was being held to celebrate its opening. Stanford White, who had designed the Garden, was there, sitting alone at a table not far from the Thaws and their guests. All was quiet for a while. Then, in the middle of the second act, the Thaw party got up to leave. They were filing past

White's table when Harry suddenly pulled out a revolver and fired it three times, shooting White dead.

Thaw was tried twice for murder, both trials being long and wrangling. By dint of pleading insanity his lawyers got him halfway off, but he had to go to an asylum from which he didn't get out for nine years. One of the speeches made for the defense might well raise modern eyebrows. "He knew not, he reasoned not," roared Thaw's lawyer of his client, "but struck as the tigress strikes the invader who comes to rob her of her young. He struck for the purity of the home, for the purity of American womanhood, for the purity of American wives and daughters . . ."

In a country where such ideas floated around, it is not surprising that even Bohemia should have been invaded by the feminine principle. Not that *all* women in Bohemia took over the reins; this never happened. Only four were genuine female leaders, but they were powerful while they lasted. Yet it was no quadrumvirate — they didn't work together, except once in a while, and the only trait they possessed in common was an interest in nourishing genius. It is said that behind every man of genius stands a woman. This may be true, but the woman conjured up in the mind by these words is a helpmeet type, the ideal Hemingway wife, a soft creature who lives only for her man. Our four were not in the least like that. Poets and painters seeking a mother-figure would have done better to get out of the way of any one of them — Harriet Monroe, Margaret Anderson, Gertrude Stein or Mabel Dodge. That so many did not indicates great courage and even greater foolhardiness.

The eldest of them, Harriet Monroe, was least of all like an Egeria. Her life's crusade to help poets came of sad experience in a world that lacked appreciation of what she considered her own craft. She was born in Chicago in 1860, the daughter of a prospering lawyer. She was no Bohemian, but in spite of all her rigid respectability she asserted great influence on that rebellious crew. Neither was she a rebel, save against the public's attitude toward poetry.

As a girl Harriet had ambitions to be a poet and playwright. There seemed no reason to worry about livelihood — the family was comfortably off — but by the time she was grown up her father had lost his money, and she had to find work, no easy task in the 1880s for young ladies of refinement, at least in Chicage. Harriet became a free-lance journalist, reviewing books and plays and art exhibitions. Though she found time to write poems, disposing of them was quite another matter. Now and then she did succeed in selling one, usually to some magazine editor who needed a few lines as filler for a short page; such tiny triumphs only brought home all the more clearly and brutally that no poet in America could live on his earnings.

This fact was on her mind when she heard the news that there was to be a World's Fair in Chicago in 1893, the "Columbian Exposition." After smoldering thought, she approached the exposition's Committee on Ceremonies and told them that they should "recognize the neglected art of poetry" by commissioning her to write them an ode, to be read aloud on their Dedication Day. Those words were always Harriet's battle-cry — the neglected art of poetry. Over and over, whenever she got the opportunity, she pointed out the facts of this neglect. She said that other Americans who tried to live by the arts, painters and architects and novelists and musicians, might claim with justification that they had a hard time, but they did have a chance now and then to win some prize or award. There was no prize, anywhere in America, for poetry. It was the forgotten art. We applaud her stubbornness in never giving up the battle and at the same time marvel that she could have entertained the slightest hope of bettering conditions for poets. Who was to read their poetry, if and when it appeared? Puzzled publishers might well have asked the question at a time when Kipling was considered highbrow and housewives by the thousand, the mainstay of the publishing industry, were contented with *The Heavenly Twins.*

Harriet would have retorted, "Give the public the chance to find out."

Campaigning, speaking her mind, pushing her idea with tough insistence, she persuaded the Committee to accept her proposition. They bought her ode in advance, for the staggering sum of a thousand dollars, and she went home and wrote it. She had been brought up on Whittier and Wordsworth and Bryant, good meaty poets who took their time to say what they had to say, so there was no underwritten nonsense about that Columbian Ode: the Committee could not complain of being sold short weight. It included songs for a chorus of five thousand, but that was nothing compared to the historical scope of Miss Monroe's vision — "first, a salutation to Columbia followed by the procession of nations to the festival, led of course by Spain; second, back to the past — the coming of Columbus and the choral song of his sailors; third, the awakening of America — the wilderness, the pioneers battling with harsh nature and savage man, and conquering with a song of triumph; fourth, the procession of the great dead . . ."

On the day of days the poem was read aloud to the throng by an imported actress, and Harriet, sitting among Chicago's most important people, must have exulted in the thought that she had struck a blow for the cause. The exultation did not last. It was annoying, though not a tragedy, that the Ode itself, printed in pamphlet form and exhibited for sale in the fairgrounds at twenty-five cents, moved very slowly, but it was far

worse to discover that the New York *World* was running it in
their daily edition, along with a report on the dedication ceremonies, without having obtained permission from anyone —
and, of course, without having paid.

The matter of authors' rights, copyright and so on had not
yet been settled in America. It was anybody's guess if Harriet
had a case to take to law. In her father's opinion she had, and
on his advice she sued the *World*. The complaint was heard in
New York in December, 1894, and Harriet won, the jury declaring that the *World* had violated her rights. She was awarded
damages of five thousand dollars. Getting the money was wonderful, of course. Knowing that she had set a precedent for all
authors who came after her was even better. Yet, thought Harriet, it would have been best of all to have earned that money
directly with her own proper work as a poet.

Bitterly she lists in her book her earnings from all sources,
year by year. In 1900, $573; in 1902, $750; in 1910, $1636 —
and of these small sums only a tiny fraction came from published
works. The rest she earned with a bit of school teaching, and
an occasional reading, or lecture, on contemporary poets.
Truly, she observed, the people in her profession had a desper-
ate fight.

There were compensations, and she did not consider herself
unhappy. She won a little success once in a great while, on
which her heart could feed. And she loved Chicago. It did not
seem to her the intellectual desert that many others have called
it. There were lots of artists, she would have said indignantly to
such criticism: every Friday they gathered at Ralph Clarkson's
studio, which they named the Little Room. And Chicago had its
new Art Institute, its new symphony orchestra, and Anna Morgan's dramatic school. You couldn't call it a cultural desert by
any means, Harriet assured herself. Some of the rich men

subsidized whole dramatic seasons, importing artistes to perform, and the wife of one of them, Mary Aldis, turned a cottage on her Lake Forest estate into a little playhouse where she and her neighbors acted in plays they wrote or translated themselves. In 1912 Maurice Browne, an Englishman who had come to live in Chicago because he married a Chicago girl, established a genuine Little Theatre, the first of many in America. All this activity was enjoyable, but Harriet kept comparing the success of the other arts with the failure of her own to gain recognition. Why were poets supposed to be merely funny — "the butt of the paragraphers and cartoonists"?

She was fifty years old when she made a memorable journey around the world, and in London was introduced to the works of the American Ezra Pound. She had never heard of him and was not likely to meet him — the young man had chosen, it seemed, to make his home in Europe — but the poems impressed her, and she kept his name in mind. In Chicago once more, all Harriet's old resentments seemed to come back stronger than ever, no doubt because of the contrast between home and the great world outside. Suddenly she had a staggeringly exciting idea. She would start a magazine exclusively for poetry.

Hobart C. Chatfield-Taylor, to whom she went for counsel, was a rich man with sympathy for the Bohemian way of life because he had a talent for writing. In the 1880s, when he was young and wild, he was one of the founders of the Whitechapel Club, a rowdy collection of journalists, artists, writers, and gentlemen of leisure who, like himself, were discontented with their lot. The Club held its meetings in a rough-and-ready place where the center table was a huge coffin, and all the gas-lamps were shaded with human skulls. Murder weapons and macabre drawings decorated the walls. It was then that Chatfield-Taylor had the bright idea of running for election on the platform, "No gas, no water, no police." The Club backed him unanimously, but he didn't win.

Of course all this had been a long time ago. By 1912, Chatfield-Taylor was a little less self-assertive, for he had won himself a reputation as a biographer. He appreciated Harriet's ideas, and encouraged the idea of the magazine. He helped her draw up a list of likely prospects, and outlined the proposition she was to submit to them: if one hundred of these people, Chicago's art patrons, pledged to give Harriet Monroe fifty dollars a year for the next five years, she would be able to start *Poetry: A Magazine of Verse*. Five years should surely be enough to find out if the magazine was viable, said Chatfield-Taylor. Miss Monroe went to work on the lines he indicated, and got the money.

It remained to fill the pages. She read a lot of American and British publications, listed the names of those whose poems she thought good, and wrote to them all. One of the first, of course, was Ezra Pound, who answered immediately, and with great enthusiasm. "I may be myopic, but during my last tortured visit to America I found no writer and but one reviewer who had any worthy conception of poetry, The Art," he said. Would Miss Monroe be interested in other sources than American? If so, he could oblige, for, he assured her, he did see nearly everyone that mattered. In reply Harriet offered him the post of foreign correspondent, though, she implied, it was likely to remain unpaid for a long time to come. Pound was not put off: he got to work right away. Almost before Miss Monroe realized it he had extracted a promise from Yeats of "something," and come up with a number of suggestions, names she had never heard of, such as "the very great Bengali poet Rabindranath Tagore" who, Pound explained to the ignorant Chicagoan, was

HENRI MURGER
He began it all

EDGAR ALLAN POE
Bohemian before his time?

WALT WHITMAN
Most famous "Cave Dweller"

ADAH MENKEN
In spirit always one of them

JOAQUIN MILLER
"Byron of the Rockies"?

BRET HARTE
Adaptable Bohemian

JAMES HUNEKER

" 'Goodbye, dear Jim . . . God rest your splendid soul.' "

STEPHEN CRANE
Self-imposed exile

JACK LONDON
A passion for political rights

MABEL DODGE LUHAN
Determined experimentalist in her Indian period

ISADORA DUNCAN AND SERGE ESSENIN

*" 'My husband and I are revolutionists. All geniuses worthy
of the name are.' "*

EDNA ST. VINCENT MILLAY
"Miss Millay was *the Village."*

FLOYD DELL
Textbook case

MARY AUSTIN
Excellent witness

JOE GOULD
The outer fringe

ALLEN GINSBURG
"But then, everything in Bohemia changes, or ought to."

going to be the sensation of the winter, though no one except a few of the élite had heard of him as yet. The Yeats poems arrived soon, and also a selection by an American who signed herself H.D., very strange but beautiful. There was also something from Richard Aldington, another of the names Harriet had not heard of. His "Choricos" was the first sample she had seen of the new school of poetry that Ezra Pound seemed to be fostering, which he called Imagism.

So far so good. Through Pound, Harriet was receiving contributions more exciting than she had dared to hope for. In the home office she installed an associate editor named Alice Corbin, a young, pretty, talented poet married to the painter William Penhallow Henderson. Alice had taste and daring. Between them the women got ready their first number, with poems by Pound, Arthur Davison Ficke, and William Vaughan Moody among others. A Chicago artist, Ralph Fletcher Seymour, was responsible for the make-up and the cover. *Poetry* was on the stands before October, 1912.

The response was most encouraging: a first printing of a thousand had to be repeated within two weeks, and newspapers far and wide took notice. It amused editors that Chicago of all places should have produced anything so esoteric. "Poetry in Porkopolis," was one Philadelphia headline. Even Shanghai's American-owned *China Press* reported the event: "Chicago, anxious to overshadow its packing-house reputation by repute as an art center, will hereafter be the home of the subsidized muse." After a few more issues, however, this note of good-natured japing was, in many quarters, replaced by resentment. Miss Monroe and Miss Corbin printed such peculiar stuff! What was the big idea? Unconventional poetry does not arouse quite the incontinent rage that is so mysteriously evoked by extraordinary painting, but a lot of *Poetry* readers were startled

and frightened. One offering that worried them was Vachel
Lindsay's "General William Booth Enters into Heaven." Then
there were the Imagistes, or as they soon became known, in
more Anglo-Saxon fashion, the Imagists. Most non-poets remained unmoved by Imagist capers, but poets and poetry critics
went up in smoke when they read Pound's exposition, "A Few
Don'ts by an Imagiste," in the March, 1913, number. One
gathers that it wasn't so much the *vers libre* aspect of these
experiments that upset them; after all, the nation had survived
similar shocks administered by Walt Whitman, and now the
good gray poet himself was a classic. But the Imagists broke
more laws than those of rhyme and metrical rhythm. You had
to *work* to understand this stuff, if indeed it meant anything at
all, which most readers doubted. There were protests and
cries of outrage, some written direct to the office, some printed
in other periodicals. So much the better for *Poetry*. Miss Monroe and Alice Corbin were happy to reply at every opportunity,
and defended their poets with spirit. *The Dial*, bulwark of con-
servatism, kept them very busy at this; one of their editors regretted that *Poetry* was "being turned into a thing for
laughter," and singled out Ezra Pound for particular attention.
Later he extended his compliments to Vachel Lindsay (metrical
rubbish), Tagore (prosy), and Yeats, whose verse in the magazine, he declared, was much the least poetic of any he had yet
printed. Other letter-writers were on *The Dial*'s side, William Rose Benét for one, Conrad Aiken for another — though,
as Harriet points out, both these dissidents later accepted much
they fiercely rejected in the beginning.

The more one thinks about it, the more remarkable
her achievement appears. One determined spinster working
away in Chicago — of all unexpected places — had managed
against all odds to raise poetry's position in the public eye

and invigorate its followers. Harriet Monroe was the pioneer, and *Poetry* can justly claim to have made many discoveries. Before anyone had heard of T. S. Eliot the magazine printed him: Miss Monroe describes how she and Alice Corbin read the first lines of "The Love Song of J. Alfred Prufrock" when it arrived in the mail, and were breathless with excitement. *Poetry* published early efforts of James Joyce, Robert Frost, Edna Millay, and Amy Lowell.

In other ways too it brought the world to Chicago. Mrs. Alice Rossin, the daughter of Alice Corbin, has told me of the consternation caused in the office by the news that Rabindranath Tagore, whose "Gitanjali" *Poetry* had published, was to arrive in town very shortly with a son, a daughter-in-law, and also, it seems, an aunt. Of course they must be *Poetry*'s guests — the editors were eager to assume the responsibility — but where could they live? It was too large a party for the Henderson ménage or Miss Monroe's little flat, and a hotel was out of the question. This was not, as Miss Monroe has tactfully said in her memoirs, because *Poetry* didn't have enough money. The money could have been managed. No, it was because the Tagore party was dark-skinned. The staff had grave doubts if a good hotel in that community would consent to take Indians, even the Eastern kind.

Mrs. Rossin said, "Mother telephoned William Vaughan Moody's widow. She didn't ask, she just said, 'You're going to have guests. The Tagores are staying with you.' Harriet Moody had a big house, you see. She was a little surprised; she said, 'Oh, am I?' and Mother just said, very firmly, 'Yes. It's no use arguing.' That's how it happened, and Mrs. Moody decided that she liked having everybody meet there for highbrow conversation with her guests, so *Poetry* always sent their distinguished visitors to stay with her after that."

It was all fun, though Miss Monroe's career on *Poetry* was not one of undisturbed triumph. Ezra Pound quarreled with her, as he usually did with editors, and left the organization. And there was more unpleasantness when Alice Corbin, who developed a bad case of tuberculosis, went with her husband and daughter to live in the dry uplands of Santa Fe, doing work for *Poetry* at long distance. The disease was arrested, and Miss Corbin was to live on in New Mexico for years, but Miss Monroe was not pleased with the arrangement and tried to squeeze her associate editor's name off the masthead without going through the necessary preliminaries. A row ensued, but the matter was at last settled out of court. Then there was the *Little Review*, a rival magazine started by the cheeky young Margaret Anderson in 1914, practically on *Poetry*'s doorstep. Harriet always said that she was glad the *Little Review* existed, but she made some tart remarks about some of Miss Anderson's claims, which she felt infringed on her own. There were other little rifts in the lute, too. Poets are notoriously touchy. But on the whole, Harriet Monroe earned, over and over again, the right to be proud of her remarkable accomplishment.

She continued indefatigable until the end, and met her death in thoroughly characteristic fashion. In 1936, having attended a PEN Club congress in Buenos Aires, she thought that as long as she was in South America anyway she had better see the Inca ruins in Peru. The fact that she was seventy-six years old did not seem to constitute an obstacle, but the altitude was too much for her, and at Arequipa, 7500 feet up, she suffered a fatal cerebral hemorrhage.

*   *   *

One of *Poetry*'s many peripheral effects was that Amy Lowell, through its pages, heard of Imagism. Miss Lowell, a strapping girl from Brookline, Massachusetts, was an enthusiastic follower of the magazine from the start. In the year of its first appearance, 1912, she herself had published a volume of tight, conventional verse. Ezra Pound's work and ideas captured her admiration, and she determined to track down Imagism to the fountainhead. That is what she did, by crossing the Atlantic and bearding Pound in his den. It was a friendship that did not last long, as both poets were temperamentally set on having their own way. Miss Lowell reorganized her own work, to its considerable improvement, and that was all right with Pound. But when she took all Imagism under her wing, wrote a book about it, and gave the public the idea that Imagism was hers and not Pound's, he quarreled with her and left the movement altogether. Later he offered his services to Margaret Anderson on the *Little Review,* just as he had earlier done to Miss Monroe on *Poetry.* Miss Anderson was delighted to have his help. It is interesting that he should have continued to look toward Chicago rather than New York as a place with some hope for the future. Chicago too was American, it is true, but he must have had hopes for it in spite of that.

Margaret Anderson herself was very much a product of the Middle West. Born in 1891, she came to Chicago from Indiana at the age of twenty-one, the year *Poetry* first appeared. She came to the big city not because of any one specific ambition: she simply had an overriding desire to get away from home, where life was easy and her parents protective. "I was extravagantly pretty in those days," she writes, " — extremely and disgustingly pretty. I looked like a composite of all the most offensive magazine covers." The photograph frontispiece for her book, *My Thirty Years' War,* bears out this statement.

Combined with prettiness was an ornery nature that showed no signs of having changed when she wrote her book. "I have

never been able to accept the two great laws of humanity —
that you're always being suppressed if you're inspired and always being pushed into the corner if you're exceptional. I
won't be cornered and I won't stay suppressed . . . I am no
man's wife, no man's delightful mistress, and I will never, never,
never be a mother." Nor was she.

For a while at the beginning she worked in book reviewing
and then as a clerk in a bookshop, but she became restless with
that: she wanted to do something more exciting. According to
her own account, she woke up one night and decided to start
a magazine in order to have "an existence in which conversation was possible." That was why, in 1914, the *Little Review*
got its start. Not for Miss Anderson the steady, far-seeing, middle-aged preparations Harriet Monroe had made, for Miss Anderson was none of these things. Instead she grabbed whatever
money she could get from friends, then whistled off to New
York to sell advertising — a rackety beginning on rickety foun-
dations, one might say, but the *Little Review* did last for fifteen
years. In the words of Alson J. Smith, author of *Chicago's Left
Bank*, it served as "the bell-wether of the *avant-garde* in American letters." Of course, *Poetry* was already serving in the
same capacity, but Miss Anderson's periodical was at once less
and far more than that pioneering magazine. She never confined herself to poets. If she was a crusader at all in the sense
Harriet Monroe was, her cause was, basically, self-expression in
all fields, and her enthusiasms were catholic.

At the best of times she had little money; at the worst she was
heavily in debt. Fortunately, financial reverses didn't bother her
in the least. She really didn't want to make money except for
the sake of the magazine. All she wanted for herself was a piano
and a view, and she usually managed to get both without paying
out much coin of the realm. For some time she lived in a large

lakeside apartment, inherited in an empty state from relatives who had left town. Absence of furniture did not trouble her, and was actually an asset when Emma Goldman came, for Emma highly approved of this uncluttered, unbourgeois existence. Margaret wanted Emma to approve: with all her customary quick enthusiasm she had recently embraced the cause of anarchism.

Emma suggested giving a party, and they invited Ben Reitman, Emma's lover, Big Bill Hayward the labor leader, and a number of other friends of compatible views. More conventional tenants of the building were terrified of being bombed — the popular idea of Emma Goldman's crowd was that they carried bombs in their pockets and used them on every possible occasion — and they complained to the management, so Margaret had to take her piano and move out. Fortunately this happened in the summertime, and she found it easy and even pleasant to set up housekeeping in a tent by the lake, where she remained until late autumn. Floyd Dell and Ben Hecht and Max Bodenheim would call on her there, leaving their latest literary efforts pinned to the tent-flap if she happened to be out. The editor had only the clothes she stood up in, but it didn't matter at all. She says that as her blouse was made of georgette, she just washed it out every night in the lake, and wore it next day. Here we must entertain a doubt: surely the blouse wouldn't dry overnight in Chicago, especially near the lake? It wasn't even nylon — nylon was as yet unknown. Let us admit that she may have stretched the truth now and then, as many Chicagoans of that era seem to have done. Why not? She was a lovable legend anyway. And the *Little Review* in its crackpot fashion was also lovable, taking up in turn every wild idea that came along — Futurism, Dadaism and those that followed.

Margaret soon tired of things as they were and decided in 1917 to take the *Little Review* to New York. With her associate editor, the mannish-looking Jane Heap, she remained in Greenwich Village — where else? — for five years, until she got restless again and moved the ménage to Paris and the Left Bank. In 1929 the *Little Review* went out of business. Magazine post-mortems recalled its outstanding contribution to the cause of literature: the publication, for the first time anywhere, of part of James Joyce's *Ulysses* during the New York phase. They were stirring times, with the Postmaster General burning all the copies he could lay hands on and the editors being tried in court for having outraged morality. Miss Anderson was found guilty and fined one hundred dollars, and a marvelous time was had by all.

Margaret Anderson was a true Bohemian of the old breed, but our next subject in this monstrous regiment is Gertrude Stein, who, like Harriet Monroe, ought not — perhaps — to be in these annals at all. The objection is not that she wasn't a Bohemian. She was certainly a citizen of that nation without territory, but she was not, save by birth and passport, American: she lived in France, making only one visit to her native land from 1903 until her death in 1946. However, even though it was *in absentia,* her contribution to America's Bohemia and the movement toward new art was enormous. She cannot be ignored.

Witter Bynner once said that the life and career of Gertrude Stein, like that of her great friend Alice Toklas, was completely revolutionized by the California earthquake of 1906. "If it hadn't been for that, those women would have been ordinary well-off San Francisco matrons," he declared, but though this is an amusing theory it won't hold water — as Bynner no doubt was aware. Gertrude Stein was never closely tied to California, though she spent a part of her childhood in Oakland. The family had financial interests in other places as well. She was born in Pennsylvania, and taken as a small girl to Europe, where the Steins remained for a long time. After graduating from Radcliffe, she studied medicine at Johns Hopkins, spending the summers in Florence with her brother Leo. Leo was a collector and art critic, and Gertrude, making the rounds of the galleries with him, came to the decision that her tastes lay in that direction rather than in science's. When she had spent three years at Johns Hopkins, therefore, she went back to Europe. Leo had moved from Florence to Paris, and that is where his sister too bent her steps.

All three of the Stein children, Mike, Leo and Gertrude, had independent incomes: all three became interested in modern painting, and Gertrude would go with her brothers on their buying expeditions. With Leo she haunted the shop of Vollard, the only dealer in Paris who handled Cézanne's work. The Steins bought together, as partners, paintings by Daumier, Manet, Renoir and Gauguin — "They were rather awful but they finally liked them, and bought two Gauguins . . . It sounds like a great deal but in those days these things did not cost much," she writes in *The Autobiography of Alice B. Toklas*. Then they found Matisse. After the earthquake, when Mike and his wife went to San Francisco to see what had happened to the family property there, they took with them three small Matisse paintings, the first by this artist to cross the Atlantic. A young woman named Alice B. Toklas, who lived in San Francisco, was so impressed by the Steins and their paintings that soon after they returned to Paris she followed, in company with another young woman, to make a closer acquaintance with European culture. She had heard a good deal about Mike's clever sister, and was almost afraid to meet such a brilliant woman. Gertrude had taken a flat at 27 rue de Fleurus, with a large studio where painting covered the walls. Alice understood that Miss Stein was sitting for her portrait to a new Spanish painter named Pablo Picasso — all the Steins were interested in this man. But painting was not Gertrude's chief interest, it seemed: she was busily writing, and had finished a book, *Three Lives,* which she intended to have privately printed, because no trade publisher would accept it. Since then, Gertrude Stein's style of writing has become familiar, though not necessarily a pleasure, to everyone, but at that time it seemed most unlikely that any publisher *would* consider it. In spite of this, she was sure of what she wanted to do, and worked away. And, no matter what one may think of her writing, she was undoubtedly receptive to new impressions, as this passage from the *Autobiography* bears witness. She is speaking of her first sight of Matisse's work, his "Femme au Chapeau" at the autumn salon,

> . . . the first autumn salon that had ever existed in Paris . . . a step in official recognition of the outlaws of the independent salon. Their pictures were to be shown in the Petit Palais opposite the Great Palais where the great spring salon was held . . . There were a number of attractive pictures but there was one that was not attractive. It infuriated the public, they tried to scratch off the paint.
>
> Gertrude Stein liked that picture . . . They decided to go over to the salon and look at the picture again. They did. People were roaring with laughter at the picture and scratching at it. Gertrude Stein could not understand why, the picture seemed to her perfectly natural . . . It upset her to see them all mocking at it. It bothered her and angered her because she did not understand why because to her it was so alright, just as later she did not understand why since the writing was all so clear and natural they mocked at and were enraged by her work.

As the years passed on the rue de Fleurus, the studio and the writer in it became a pilgrim's goal. Americans especially wanted to meet her — all those who were eager for change in the arts. Gertrude's Saturday evenings became one of the things you had to attend if you aspired to belong to the latest, smartest movements. Alice Toklas lived with her; the two friends stayed together for the rest of Gertrude's life. Her so-called *Autobiography* was, of course, simply Gertrude Stein's device for writing about herself in the third person, but it is far easier to read than much of her other work. The *Portrait of Mabel Dodge*, for example, is — or seems to be — an essay on words rather than a portrait of anyone.

Mabel was one of our redoubtable four, living at that time at the Villa Curonia outside Florence, an old house which she and her architect husband Edwin Dodge had remodeled, and where Gertrude and Alice came to visit. Mabel herself liked her controversial *Portrait* very much, and had it privately printed. It was the only one of Gertrude's *Portraits* to be so honored, which is perhaps why it became the best-known and was so often cited in argument by Gertrude's champions as an example of her work. On one occasion it was read aloud by Oliver Gogarty in a Dublin pub — people were always comparing her technique to James Joyce's, so perhaps this is not as odd as it sounds. There seems little point in such a comparison; the only thing the two writers have in common is their courage in striking out along new paths as they did, but according to Hemingway's malicious *Moveable Feast,* Gertrude was always silent on the subject of Joyce.

Gertrude became more and more controversial and thus more important as a figure, but it does not follow that everyone began to accept her work. Many of her best friends couldn't understand it at all. " 'Alice, tell me, is it alright, are they really alright,' asked one of these friends, Mildred Aldrich. 'I know

Gertrude thinks so and Gertrude knows, but really is it not fumisterie, is it not all false.'" On another occasion, much later, when the name of Gertrude Stein was a household word, she and Miss Toklas visited Richmond, Virginia. "At dinner I sat next to James Branch Cabell," records Alice Toklas — really Alice this time, in *What Is Remembered,* her own book — "who asked me, Is Gertrude Stein serious? Desperately, I replied. That puts a different light on it, he said. For you, I said, not for me." Edwin Arlington Robinson wrote teasingly to Mabel Dodge, who had shown him the famous *Portrait,* "How do you know that it is a portrait of you, after all?"

When Mabel brought her lover Jack Reed to the rue de Fleurus he did not make a hit with the ladies, but her protégé, Robert Edmund Jones, did. It was through Mabel, too, that young Carl Van Vechten came to call. He was an enthusiast about Gertrude's work and actually persuaded friends in Paris to publish something of hers in their little magazine, *The Galerie Lafayette.* What probably helped her along much more, however, was Mabel's own article, the first she had ever tried to write, on the subject of Gertrude Stein. It came out in *Arts and Decoration* in New York, on the famous occasion of the International Art Show of Modern Art, held in the Lexington and Thirty-Fourth Street Armory in 1913. "In a large studio in Paris, hung with paintings by Renoir, Matisse and Picasso, Gertrude Stein is doing with words what Picasso is doing with paint," wrote Mabel. "She is impelling language to induce new states of consciousness, and in doing so language becomes with her a creative art rather than a mirror of history."

The appearance of this article was of considerable importance to both women: it gave Gertrude's reputation a fillip in New York, where it was needed, and it proved to Mabel that she was capable of producing something besides a beautifully furnished house. After the article's appearance, Gertrude, much gratified, wrote often to Mabel in New York, trying to get her help in publishing something in America, but the friendship soon cooled. Mabel's theory as to why this happened was that Alice Toklas, jealous of her, edged her out of Gertrude's friendship much as she had edged out Leo, for the brother and sister were estranged, having quarreled bitterly over Picasso. There might, however, have been an element of a quite different jealousy in Gertrude's coolness. When Mabel asked Leo why his sister had changed toward her, he laughed and said it was because there was a doubt in Gertrude's mind as to who was the bear and who was leading the bear.

After the Great War, which the ladies at rue de Fleurus weathered without leaving France, the American invasion of Paris began in earnest. Alfred Kreymborg and Harold Loeb, who planned to publish their new magazine *Broom* in Europe so that they could save expense through advantageous currency exchange, Sherwood Anderson, Robert Coates, Man Ray, Louis Bromfield, Muriel and Paul Draper, Scott Fitzgerald, Paul Robeson, and dozens more came to pay their respects to Miss Stein. Younger American writers and painters felt that they were not in the swim until they had familiarized themselves with her writing and, if possible, with her self. She was always willing to see their work and to comment on it. She appreciated Sherwood Anderson's writing none the less because he admitted that she had had a great effect on it. For a time there was a flourishing friendship with Ernest Hemingway and his first wife Hadley. Acid comments were made on both sides after these relations broke off, but Hemingway admits that she helped him with advice and criticism when he was a beginner.

She died in the American Hospital in Paris, in 1946. "I sat next to her," wrote Alice Toklas, "and she said to me early in the afternoon, What is the answer? I was silent. In that case, she said, what is the question?"

Since her death the Gertrude Stein controversy has faded out a good deal, but some of her work is still required reading in American Literature classes, and it strikes the ear oddly to read contemporary comments like Max Eastman's — "her silly book, *Tender Buttons* — equivalent in every respect except sheer passion to the ravings of a lunatic," and, again, "the subtly influential, and yet basically degrading, baby-talk cult of Gertrude Stein . . ."

*   *   *

Like Gertrude, Mabel Dodge was an experimentalist. Unlike Gertrude, she had no channelized drive to succeed in any one particular art. She knew she had no great talent and was quite correct in seeing herself as a receiver of ideas rather than a promulgator. In her prime, social questions were beginning to loom large on Bohemia's horizon: to some extent she was caught up in the struggle, but only because of her love affair with John Reed. Mabel was too rich, and too fond of being rich, to subscribe sincerely to Socialism. Besides, many others had been Socialists, and she liked to claim to be first in things. She was one of the first Americans, for example, to be psychoanalyzed, and also the first to use checked gingham for curtains: one feels that these boasts were of equal importance to her. She was a taster of experience, a nibbler. She would never have gone overboard like Margaret Anderson, who would rush straight into the fray and immerse herself. Mabel's method of rebelling was at once simpler and more complicated: she merely wanted her own way.

And she usually got it. Most of what she wanted she was able to buy — houses, space, influence in whatever circle she was frequenting. Born in Buffalo just before the 1880s, of a well-off family, she chafed all through her childhood at the constrictions of Buffalo life; the dullness, the meaningless and sometimes cruel conventions of behavior. Marriage — her second marriage; the first had ended very early when her husband died — brought an amount of freedom, but she was too restless to submit to the status quo, though Edwin Dodge was indulgent. In Florence, ever looking for something else, seeking the latest in art and philosophy, she got herself involved in an Italian high-life scandal, until even the good-natured Dodge grew angry and made her come to New York.

It was 1912. Mabel detested New York. For a while, fitting up an apartment at 23 Fifth Avenue (at the corner of Ninth Street, within the limits of Greenwich Village) kept her busy. She made it perfect, the colors mainly white, with here and there a glitter of crystal. Then Mabel was idle again. Mabel moped. Alone in ugly New York, bereft of friends, she resented Edwin more than ever, until she managed to become convincingly ill and stayed all day in bed. Edwin moved out and she recovered. Fortunately, however, before he left she met, through some of his architect friends, the young music critic Carl Van Vechten, who rallied round and took her out. And Edwin also brought home the sculptor Jo Davidson, who now became a constant visitor at 23 Fifth Avenue.

Soon New York did not seem ugly at all, and Mabel's days were full. She met the Hapgoods, Hutchins and his wife Neith: Hutch wrote a column three times a week for the *Globe,* and Neith wrote too, when she wasn't looking after their four children. Mabel in her memoirs describes Hutch as a great talker and says that she made an excellent listener for him, but there were frequent occasions when he was called upon to listen in his turn; she told him all her troubles, and the process must have taken hours and hours. And she made the acquaintance of Alfred Stieglitz, the artist in photography, who kept a private gallery over his studio for modern painters and sculptors. Probably it was through Stieglitz that she met James Gregg, who was doing public relations for the approaching International Show at the Armory in 1913, and through whom she came to write the Gertrude Stein article which launched her so well.

- That show was vastly important to American history, drawing together as it did artistic cliques on both sides of the Atlantic. It had a great impact inland as well. In spite of her birth pangs over *Poetry*, Harriet Monroe came from Chicago to cover it for the *Tribune*, and she tells how it all came about. Arthur B. Davies, president of the new Association of American Painters and Sculptors, directed the young hopefuls of the Association in preparing the show — Davies and Walt Kuhn had toured Europe to collect five hundred of the two thousand exhibits. Harriet listed some of the foreign entrants — Ingres, long dead but much respected now by radicals, who was being shown in America for the first time; Delacroix; Degas, Renoir, Manet; the three late founders of Post-Impressionism, Cézanne, Van Gogh and Gauguin; Matisse, Redon, Picasso, Picabia, Seurat, Signac, Toulouse-Lautrec, Maillol, Augustus John. In spite of the popular notion, she said, the "much-advertised extremists" did not overshadow the rest of the show, which she considered, on the whole, remarkably sane; but she admitted that at the preview the Cubist and Futurist gallery was the great attraction, filled with a gaping and laughing crowd. And no wonder, said Miss Monroe, for Marcel Duchamp's "Nude Descending a Staircase" looked like a pack of brown cards in a nightmare, or a dynamited suit of Japanese armor . . . Among Americans she noted the names of Robert W. Chandler (sic), Arthur Putnam, Glackens, Jerome Myers, John Martin and George

Bellows. "It is a live show," she concluded, with approval. She overheard the following comments in the Futurist and Cubist room:

"It makes me fear for the world; something must be wrong with an age which can put these things in a gallery, and call them art . . ." "It is modern psychology, it is scientific analysis, penetrating, destroying old standards, revitalizing art . . . concentration . . . power . . . color and form reduced to their simplest . . . fundamental rhythms of motion." "It's the grandest joke of the age . . . Look at that *Procession in Seville* will you. Puzzle, find the procession." "What is it, Mother? Is it playing with blocks?"

Whatever one thought of those paintings, one had to admit that art would never be the same again.

The exhibition over, Mabel Dodge settled in to a life that pleased and excited her. Hutch was a great one for writing in support of causes — prison reform, modern art, birth control, the eight-hour day. He took Mabel to meet Emma Goldman, and Mabel also met in that apartment Ben Reitman and the notorious Alexander Berkman, a former lover of la Goldman. She felt deliciously frightened of the anarchists at first but soon got used to them, and they came to see her in turn, on Fifth Avenue. She got very matey with Lincoln Steffens, the editor and political reformer, and Margaret Sanger, and bright young Walter Lippmann, and the painters Marsden Hartley and Andrew Dasburg, and many more. Soon she was presiding over a weekly Evening — she always spelled it with a capital — which became a feature of New York life; a mingling of socialists, trade-unionists, anarchists, suffragists, poets, lawyers, murderers, old friends, relations, psychoanalysts, IWWs, single taxers, newspapermen, artists, clubwomen, clergymen and a few out-and-out nuts, all of them "stammering in an unaccustomed free-

dom a kind of speech called Free." She thought she could de-
tect in all this an important development. "There was the beginning, in those days . . . of a new attitude toward the artist," she recalled in her memoirs. "His sacrosanct vocation was
being slowly questioned, his divine right to all forgiveness by
virtue of his calling was being disposed of, little by little."

As a matter of fact, it was a new Mabel who became aware
of this development, reacting with all a convert's zeal against
the Mabel who, only a year or so earlier in Italy, had been happily absorbed in sacrosanct art and divinely righteous artists.
That she was sharing in this dawning spirit, this realization of
art as a moralistic force, was due to her love affair with Reed,
radical young poet and journalist. Before meeting this youth
Mabel had been able to take Socialism or leave it alone, along
with all the other causes one heard about. Mostly, she let it
alone. Politics did not interest her. It was nice to have Big
Bill Hayward at her Evenings because she liked important people, people everyone was talking about, but without Reed she
would never have found herself enlisted in Big Bill's war against
capitalism. After all, as she could not have helped asking herself, if it weren't for capitalism where would Mabel Dodge have
been? It was impossible to say, but one could be sure she
wouldn't have been in that glittering white Fifth Avenue flat.
She does not seem to have discussed this awkward point with
Jack Reed or his left-wing friends: if she did, she has left no
mention of it. She found it satisfying enough that she was caught
up in the latest movement now sweeping Bohemia. Why indulge in misgivings? Why worry about logic? She was in love.

Reed, then in his middle twenties, was a Harvard graduate
and one of the protégés of Lincoln Steffens. He worked on the
American. He wrote poetry and had made a name for himself
with an amusing long collection of verses, "The Day in Bohe-

mia," dedicated to Steffens, which described how blissful it was
in that dawn to be alive at 42 Washington Square, where he
had shared a floor with three friends.

> Below's the barren, graceless, earthen ring
> Where Madame, with a faith unwavering
> Planted a wistful garden every spring. —
> Forever hoped-for, — never blossoming.
> Above, th' eternal washing droops in air,
> From wall to window hanging, everywhere!
> What poet would not yield to their allure
> "The short and simple flannels of the poor!"

At the time Mabel met him, Reed had just become an associate editor of the leftist magazine *The Masses*, whose chief
editor was Max Eastman. Jack was excited by his adventures
in Paterson, New Jersey, where the silk-mill workers were on
strike. When he went over to New Jersey to cover the situation
in a story, he was arrested on what he claimed was a grossly
trumped-up charge, and sentenced to twenty days in prison.
Bill Hayward was already in prison, and he introduced Reed to
the famous Carlo Tresca, another roommate. It bade fair to be
an interesting twenty days, but the New York newspapers got
onto the story and played it up until the New Jersey officials
threw Jack Reed out of prison again, though he had served only
four days of his sentence. He was now on fire to help the strikers, and insisted on taking a party — Mabel, young Robert Edmund Jones the stage designer and equally young Walter Lippmann — to see the goings-on for themselves. They were much
impressed, especially when Jack assured them that the strikers
could not hold out much longer. They were starving. They
needed money.

What to do? Carried away by a new indignation, Mabel
thought hard. Somebody suggested putting on a pageant about

the strike, at Madison Square Garden. In her memoirs, Mabel says that it was her idea. There have been others who contest this claim, but it doesn't matter — whoever thought of it, the group rapturously adopted the idea on the spot. Hayward approved, other leaders approved, and soon everybody they could interest in the project was hard at work. Bobby Jones did the scenery, Reed the outline, and a number of genuine strikers were brought over from Paterson for crowd work onstage. Artistically the pageant was a great success: unfortunately it was a flop financially. The producers' means had permitted only one performance because it cost so much to hire Madison Square Garden, and on this rock the ship was wrecked. By the time the cost was counted and the deficit announced, Reed had gone. With Bobby and Mabel and Carl Van Vechten he was on the high seas, bound for a nice long rest at the Villa Curonia, living the sweet life as Mabel's lover.

After a while he came back, but the tug of war continued, Mabel against the Cause. The affair has gone down in Party history as a morality play, with Jack Reed, the hero, a bone of contention between Mabel Vice and Communist Virtue. Without doubt there were times when Reed himself saw it in that light. More than once he tore himself from her arms. Whenever this happened, observers were heard to remark caustically that it wasn't necessarily a case of moral struggle, since Mabel must have been hell to live with. The play went on; the lovers, like boxers in a clinch, swayed back and forth. Now she had him, now she hadn't. The battle took them to the Mexican border, over which Jack got away in a burst of speed to report the Villa war. But he returned, and they went back East to Provincetown, or New York, or Croton.

A lot of Villagers were in the habit of spending the summer in Provincetown, living in quaint little fishermen's cottages and putting on plays. There were George Cram (Jig) Cook, and Susan Glaspell, and the Hapgoods, and Helen Westley: the Provincetown Players were just being organized, and when these people weren't putting on plays, they talked. How they talked! They talked about art, and life, and beauty; they talked about their psyches; most of all, at least at that time, they talked about Mabel and Jack. Mabel and Jack were perfectly willing to join in these discussions, especially Mabel. Whenever she was upset she called a convocation of friends to talk things over. When she was absent they wrote letters about her to her. It was like living in a pre-war Russian novel: the loyal chorus — Hutch Hapgood, Bobby Jones, Bobby Rogers, Lee Simonson and the rest — was so busy over Mabel that it is hard to see how they had the time to work with the Provincetown Players.

But Reed was not neglected either: he too had his adherents. Outstanding among them was F. Sumner Boyd, an English radical and, according to Reed's biographer, Granville Hicks, "perhaps the first thoroughly informed Marxist Reed had ever known." Certainly Boyd was the first "informed Marxist" to realize that Jack Reed could be an asset to the cause. The very qualities that had hitherto irritated other sincere revolutionaries and put them off — his weakness for the dramatic gesture, his vanity, his romanticism — would make him all the more persuasive and convincing to prospects in bourgeois circles, with their lamentable fondness for — if we may anticipate a phrase — the personality cult. Boyd cultivated Reed and cherished him like a delicate plant.

Mabel hated Boyd. "He seemed to me just a cad," she wrote, "but he flattered Reed and loved him, too."

The adoption of John Reed for serious work as a Marxist did not change his temperament all at once — Boyd would not have wished it to. In 1918, long after Reed had said a final goodbye to Mabel, he did something characteristic. The *Masses* had been killed off by the authorities, who forbade its passage through the mails: it rose like a phoenix from the ashes as the *Liberator* and carried on under much the same editorial board. Always in financial difficulties, it was supported at that time by a man named Burleson, whose politics did not please Reed. He had been working as hard as ever on two stories, one on the imprisonment of Eugene Debs, the other on the IWW trials, when he decided to resign, and sent in a letter with the finished work. "I've thought about it a long time," he wrote to Eastman, "and I make this decision not without emotion, remembering our long work together on the *Masses.*

"But I feel that I must take my name off the editorial page. The reason is, I cannot in these times bring myself to share editorial responsibility for a magazine which exists upon the sufferance of Mr. Burleson . . ."

Eastman replied with barely sheathed bitterness: ". . . Personally I envy you the power to cast loose when not only a good deal of the dramatic beauty, but also the glamor of moral principle, is gone out of the venture, and it remains for us merely the most effective and therefore the right thing to do."

The romance of Mabel Dodge and Jack Reed had come to the end so ardently desired by his political friends on the eve of the Great World War. As he became more involved in Socialism he withdrew from Bohemian ways, and bent all his attention on Russia. The Socialist Party of America split, and Reed went with the left wing. He married a girl named Louise Bryant — Mabel met her, and was acid in her description, but the marriage held until the end. After the Russian revolution he visited the country and wrote *Ten Days That Shook the World*, which was read widely, and made his reputation. When he next went to Russia it was in secret, as a delegate for the party: he found it much tougher going this time, for the balance of power had shifted and he was on what the authorities considered the wrong side. Making his long-overdue exit, he was caught and in Serbia thrown into prison. He got out at last, back into Russia. He was still there, planning to return to Chicago, when he sickened with typhus and died.

The Russians used his name until the Greenwich Village playboy became a heroic legend, in America as well as Russia. But Mabel Dodge was tired of politics, and dropped Socialism. She did up another house or two, fell in love with an artist, and continued those delightful long discussions of herself with faithful old Hutch. She wasn't changed, but Bohemia was. Jack Reed had done something irrevocable to it.

CHAPTER 10

A Kind of Freemasonry

I N THE earlier decades of the twentieth century Europeans often declared that the United States of America was not a real nation. It was too large, too unwieldy. How could people scattered all over that territory, with thousands of miles between them, possess a sense of unity or a common outlook? The doubts of the Europeans were justified to some extent. Distance did matter, separating community from community until a man in Colorado, for example, would become completely indifferent to happenings in Maine or West Virginia. Regionalism was rampant. Unconsciously, each segment of the country evolved its own styles of dress, food and accent.

There was one class in America, however, that transcended such invisible boundaries — the Bohemian. From seeds of culture planted here and there, from the Atlantic seaboard to the West Coast, colonies had grown up; groups that were alike in many ways — so-called nonconformists who actually did conform to a pattern from abroad. A young artist or would-be artist in a small, unsympathetic town in Mississippi or Missouri or South Dakota, who hadn't a hope in hell of getting to New York, let alone Paris, perforce sought out others like himself, if only in self-defense. They clung together in state universities, in local big cities, or wherever else they found kindred souls. They worked on newspapers or in church choirs. They put on amateur plays and arranged painting exhibitions. They formed a minority, and so, among them, there grew up the usual accompaniment of minorities, all over the world — a kind of freemasonry. Out of these small groups, now and then, a leader appeared, a person with stiffer backbone than the rest. Ultimately, such a one made his pilgrimage to Mecca. In the 1890s Mecca would have been London or Paris, but now New York, too, was a big city. Many Bohemians, feeling they need look no further for the Promised Land, stopped in Greenwich Village.

Few know as much about the eastward drift of the artist as the writer Floyd Dell, who went through it all and might well claim to be a textbook case. He was a thorough Midwesterner, born in Barry, Illinois, in 1887, the youngest son in a family living on the verge of destitution. His father was a butcher who owned his own shop for a while, but was thrown out of work in the financial depression of 1873 and never again reached a similar state of prosperity. The Dells drifted from one town to another, and Floyd's brothers went to work as laborers as soon as they were old enough. Floyd, however, was both delicate and intelligent, and his mother insisted that he be left in school as long as possible. The Dells were settled at last, in Iowa, by the time Floyd finished high school. At seventeen he had begun to make a name among the locals as a poet. It helped, no doubt, that in appearance he lived up to the common idea of a poet — good-looking in a frail, sensitive way, with dreamy eyes. Even his clothes were right for the part. Having discovered that the upkeep of white starched collars was prohibitively expensive, he wore a black silk scarf around his neck. Many a matron sighed fondly when she looked at him and thought of young Shelley, or Byron, or Keats.

His first paid work was in a candy factory, where two impor-

tant things happened to him: he fell in love with one of the girl
workers, and witnessed an industrial strike. The love affair
evaporated, but the strike had a lasting effect on a boy predis-
posed by the vicissitudes of his background to an interest in the
wrongs of the capitalistic system. He became a Socialist. He contributed his services as editor to a little Socialist monthly paper,
the *Tri-City Workers' Magazine*, and made speeches at political
meetings where even veteran workers listened respectfully to
the eighteen-year-old boy, because education, even at high-
school level, was rare among them. Then Floyd landed a job
as reporter on a Davenport paper. The dignity of such a position at his age staggered him: for a while it seemed that life
had little more to offer. As a reporter he met a number of men
who became lifelong friends. One was Harry Hansen, later
well known as a literary critic in Chicago and New York. Another was George Cram Cook, a prosperous businessman who
had once taught Greek in the West and still entertained dreams
of adopting the classic Greek way of life. For this and other reasons Cook considered himself ill-adjusted to Davenport society — which was nothing to what Davenport considered him
when he deserted Mrs. Cook and set up housekeeping with another girl. He abandoned his business interests and moved with
his mistress to a farm on the outskirts of town, declaring that
they were going to rediscover the simple verities. For a while
Floyd lived with the couple in their bucolic setting and watched
all the unconventional goings-on with fascination, but after a
while it was not enough to witness the lives of others. He began
to feel an itching foot, and looked longingly toward the nearest
metropolis, Chicago, until in 1909, the year he turned twenty-
one, he quit his job and went.

There his rise was rapid. Within a year he was editing the
Chicago *Evening Post*'s new weekly, the *Friday Literary Re-*

view. He married, and for a while the young couple came dangerously close to sinking into the bourgeois class — at least they had an apartment in Rogers Park full of paid-for furniture. But Margery Currey, Floyd's bride, was not the sort to drag a husband into a conventional existence. She agreed with most of his tenets, and was herself a working journalist. Floyd Dell became a critic of importance. People waited for his literary pronouncements and then obediently read the books he recommended. For a man barely in his majority he wielded a surprising influence. The Dells were the center of the city's artists and writers. It was at one of their parties that Margaret Anderson announced her plan for the *Little Review,* and when the magazine appeared, Floyd Dell was one of its chief supporters. His thin, rangy figure hurrying along Michigan Boulevard to some lecture or literary tea was a familiar sight to Chicagoans, who looked after him proudly. It was not long before he and Margery deserted Rogers Park and moved to more amusing quarters on Stony Island Avenue at Fifty-Seventh, in the south of the city. There stood a row of little houses, relics of the Columbian Exposition, which had been built as temporary stores along the avenue that had led to the Exposition's main gate. With their prim little ornamented fronts they looked like dolls' houses. Each had a large plate-glass window and one large room heated by a stove: there was no plumbing and no running water of any kind. Being cheap, they were taken over by impecunious artists and writers who dressed them up with bright paint, hung homespun curtains at the windows, erected flimsy partitions, and generally lived the good life. The Dells rented two of the dolls' houses that backed against each other, and announced that after consideration they had decided that theirs was to be a companionate marriage with one house for each. Though the ménage, like the rest of the neighborhood, was Bohemian to the

last degree, Dell says that he was not attracted to the usual romantic portrayal of the artist's life, an attitude easy to understand in a man who subscribed to Socialism.

"The Bohemian world of Murger did not please me; it was
too pathetic — people were always dying in those garrets, and
dying without an idea in their silly heads," he wrote in his autobiography, *Homecoming*, published in 1933. "The Bohemia I
approved of was the one seen for a moment in every history of
Parisian revolutionary uprisings, in which Bohemian students
fought and died behind barricades in each crisis of liberty . . .
I never cared for or could abide disorderly, pig-sty, lunatic Bohemianism. The Bohemia I learned to like was . . . a quiet
and seclusive place, not a show-off place . . ." There was always something solid and serious about Floyd Dell: he was no
roisterer.

But he looked the part, he looked very Murger. Some of his
friends decided that he ought to wear a high collar with a black
stock and carry a stick and gloves — "And I did it," he said to
me in 1964, laughing gently at himself. His portrait painted in
this get-up, which now hangs in the Newberry Library in Chicago, could pass anywhere as a picture of an eighteenth- or nineteenth-century dandy of the Left Bank. In *Homecoming* he
tells an anecdote about it: Sherwood Anderson and Floyd Dell
were friends in Chicago — in fact, when Dell went to New York
on his next migration he took with him Anderson's manuscript
of *Windy MacPherson's Son* and peddled it around until he
sold it to an English publisher, but that is another story. In
New York, in 1913, Floyd joined the staff of the *Masses* and
discarded his poetic stock and so on in favor of the blue flannel
shirt favored by the workingman. All his colleagues on the
magazine wore them. "They were expensive, those shirts," he
told me. "They cost ten dollars apiece, but as Socialists we
felt we had to have them." Months went by and he forgot he

had ever appeared in any other kind of clothing, until one day his old friend Sherwood Anderson dropped into the office to bring him the latest news from Chicago, wearing a black stock and high collar and carrying a cane and gloves. Dell thought it a quaint, Old World effect, like an eighteenth-century masquerade, but at the same time wondered what the idea might be. Then — "dimly, as in a dream" — he recalled his own trademark of earlier days, and realized who it was that Anderson was imitating.

Yet in its time the stock-and-cane ensemble served Floyd well, when as Chicago's chief professional poet and literary pundit he recited or read the works of modern writers to rapt gatherings. Sometimes these performances took place as purely social exercises among friends, but on other occasions Floyd picked up useful fees, giving lectures to groups of seekers after culture on the "Gold Coast," as the Lake Shore Drive is known in Chicago, or in stately homes out on the North Shore. It was at one such meeting, he says, that Vachel Lindsay, hearing him chant "Lepanto," got the idea for his "General William Booth Enters Heaven."

Occasionally the Dells would go with friends to spend a weekend at the Dunes, a natural playground at the lake's edge, across the state border in Indiana. Artists and poets and painters and intellectuals loved the Dunes. Some had shacks, others set up tents, and there they cooked meals over bonfires, and sat talking late into the night. One of the subjects most ardently discussed among Floyd's friends was love, love in all shapes but most especially the sort known as "free love." It was generally conceded by these thinkers that sex repression was one of the greatest sins of their world, and he dates the deterioration of his first marriage from the time he attempted to put these opinions into practice.

"We talked ourselves into trouble," he said recently. "My

closest friend at that time had a wife who was quite attractive, and this girl decided that she was in love with me. She told me so. Not only did she tell me; she talked it over with her husband. According to her version, that conversation ended with his agreeing that we should have an affair and get it over with. She said, 'It's all right with him, so let's.' At first I objected. I said that it might be all right for her and her husband, but I didn't have my wife's permission. All she said to that was, 'Well, why don't you go and ask her, then?' So that's what I did. That's how we all behaved in those days — we tried to be honest and free at the same time. My wife said, 'All right, if that's what you want, go ahead,' and this girl and I had the affair. The strangest thing about it was that her husband and I would talk it over occasionally, dissecting our feelings. These days it sounds incredible, but that's how it was then. He was remarkably detached — very much interested, as I remember, in contraception, the whole subject of contraception. During one of our talks, however, I learned that he hadn't been quite as complacent about me at the beginning as his wife had represented. He admitted that she'd been talking about me so much that he finally said he'd rather she went ahead and *had* the damned affair than hear any more about it. Well, we went on having these talks until he said he was getting jealous of me, so we called the whole thing off. The affair, I mean, not the talks.

"As for my wife, our marriage didn't last much beyond that time. I started drifting around, falling in love with other women, and the end was inevitable. There was a young actress in Maurice Browne's theatre, and then there was another girl, and — anyway, we separated. That's one of the reasons I went to New York." He thought about this in silence for a moment, then spoke with fresh animation. "But my friend and his wife, the one who started it all, they're still married to each other, still together. I found out after our adventure that it wasn't their first experience of that sort, nor the last, either. That girl was always falling in love. Why," he said, a certain amount of indignation strengthening his voice, "she busted up marriages right and left!"

He looked up at a portrait of the young Floyd Dell, hanging on a wall. "Bohemia," he said thoughtfully. "What is it exactly? I've thought about this time and time again. It changes, of course, it alters. But I think there are some things you've got to have in such a community. It must be in a big city, with a university nearby and a good library. You've got to have an old section of town falling into decay, where the rents are low. Paint is what makes Bohemia — bright colors to hide the dingy old brown and cover up the rusty old iron. We used a lot of bright orange-red paint we'd found to be good for that; it hid the blemishes and prevented more rust. It was used for utilitarian purposes rather than esthetic, but people forgot after a while why they'd chosen it to begin with, and it became a virtue rather than a necessity to slap brilliant hues all over the place."

In New York Dell fell in love again, and his girl moved into his rooms, where they lived together openly. Though it seems unbelievable to us, this behavior shocked the other Villagers. Personal freedom, yes, but this was nothing short of license, they said to each other. Nobody cut Floyd, but his friends showed their disapproval by not including his sweetheart in their invitations to him. Floyd would not accept this treatment. Arguing, fighting, holding out, he won the struggle at last and forced them to agree that any person had the right to live as he thought best, without incurring the censure of queasy Bohemians. But time passed, the original affair passed too, and after a number of other adventures he asked himself if this was really the life he wanted. He had two wishes, he decided — to

achieve "continuity and stability" in his work and his love life.
Like his alter ego Felix Fay, the hero of his novels, "He was
tired of writing short things . . . and tired of little love-af-
fairs, however beautiful . . . He wanted to finish the long
novel . . . and he wanted to stay in love with a girl and be
married to her for the rest of his life." Psychoanalysis was just
dawning on American intellectuals, and Dell resorted to it,
with satisfactory results. He found his girl — they are still married — and he finished the long novel.

"Oh yes, Bohemia changes," he said during our conversation
in 1964, "but the typical Bohemian still has a few unchange-
able attributes. He hates middle-class standards, and doesn't
mind hurting middle-class feelings, but it's a mistake to think
that he hates money. He has nothing against money itself, but
he's in revolt against some of the things that go with it — against
the genteel tradition altogether. Still, Bohemians have changed
very noticeably. Jerome Frank summed it up; he said, 'When
I was young we talked about sex and psychoanalysis: now it's
all politics.' "

Apparently forgetting his youthful admiration of the Parisian Bohemians who died on the barricades, the former editor
of the *Masses* shook his head sadly. Yet he was one of the Bohemians most firmly committed to the social struggle, and it was
Socialism that brought him into America's Latin Quarter. His
experiments with love on Stony Island Avenue and in Greenwich Village were interludes, and when we compare Floyd Dell
with his associates he seems to be less of a sentimentalist than
any of the others. Certainly he was a steadier type than his
friend Jig Cook, who went Bohemian in a quest for the true
Murgerland. He wanted to be a Murger artist, and he succeeded. When the farm palled and he fell in love with yet another woman, he deserted his first mistress and came to New

York with the new love, a quiet, serious, schoolteacher type named Susan Glaspell. In the Village he wrote plays, and he and Susan helped to create the Provincetown Players, but he would have made a rotten editor for the *Masses*.

* * *

But these people with origins in the Bible belt and the Far West should not lead us to conclude that every Bohemian in America was a frustrated outlander, fleeing from the cornfields. Rather more than fewer citizens of that country are city people. Many a Greenwich Villager had only a short trek to his land of heart's desire — from Brooklyn, perhaps, or the Bronx. There is no way to explain Alfred Kreymborg's decision to leave Yorkville, Manhattan, but to say simply that he must have been born with an instinct for the Village. It is certain that he did not rest until he got there.

Yorkville is still a strongly German district of Manhattan, one of those foreign enclaves so characteristic of New York, and in 1883, when Alfred was born, it was even more than now a town in itself. Alfred's German-born father owned a cigar store. The children grew up in an Old-World home, and music and chess were family pastimes. Alfred was one of those alarming infant chess prodigies, and might have gone on being a professional chess player all his life, but other interests got in the way. Growing up, he showed no aptitude for the occupations of everyone he saw going out to work. He had to earn money — his parents needed it — but he soon dropped out of the business school where they'd hopefully put him, and made out for a while as an errand-boy, office-boy, or with any other handy-man job he could pick up. Without knowing what he would rather have been doing, he hated these jobs.

"Getting on in the world . . . simply never occurred to

Ollie," he confessed in his autobiography, *Troubadour*.
". . . Business did not exist for him: he abhorred and despised
it. He knew that such an attitude in such a town was suicidal.
He tried to combat it, if only to help out at home. But his efforts were futile . . . something at the bottom of him — a
dream, a constitutional mania — seized and pulled him back."
Fortunately, he had a proficiency other than chess — he was
good at musical instruments. At last he found more congenial
work demonstrating player-pianos at the old Aeolian Hall on
Fifth Avenue, and the relief somehow brought him to terms
with himself. He knew that the time had come to move away
from the family house, because he was determined to be a poet.
He quit his job, with all the safety of time-clocks and pay day,
and took a room downtown on West Fourteenth. Certainly and
of course, we say to ourselves — where else would a moony boy
like that have gone but to lodgings so near to Greenwich Village?
But it was not quite like that. From 1904, when Kreymborg
made his move, until a certain day in 1913, he was unaware that
he lived at the edge of the Village. He didn't even know that
such a place existed. When a friend spoke of it he had to ask
where it was. The fact is, until about 1912 the name "Greenwich Village" possessed historical significance only. Its reputation as a center of Bohemia was only gradually won.

It was therefore independently that Kreymborg learned that
he himself was a Bohemian, a perfect type of one, who could
have gone straight onstage as the starving, struggling poet,
toiling through the night, collecting rejection-slips, and publishing a slim volume now and then. And his friends were in
keeping too — Marsden Hartley "the painter-poet," Ernest Roth
"the copper-scratcher," George Luks, Jo Davidson. He took his
art dead seriously. Once Joyce Kilmer brought him along to a
meeting of the Poetry Society, but Kreymborg hated it. He

couldn't bear the sight of all those complacent men making a profit out of their poems. He felt that the Club was full of "snobbish cliquery." Back at his rooms, he sat down and composed a satire on them called "Rhymesters de Luxe," which gravely offended Joyce Kilmer when it came out. Never mind Kilmer, thought Ollie. That business enterprise should have "stolen into spiritual America and contaminated nearly everyone concerned with creative expression — this was loathsome," he wrote indignantly.

His tastes, too, were defiant. He admired the modern painters whose works hung on Stieglitz's walls, upstairs over the photograph studio because they could not be shown in more conventional galleries. He liked Cézanne, Matisse, Brancusi, "and worst of all Picasso." It was all there in Kreymborg, everything needed to make him a Villager except for the fact that up until 1913 he didn't know that he was one.

Enlightenment came during his struggle to get backing for a magazine he wanted to create, which he had named in advance the *Glebe*. With the true little-magazine spirit he cherished a dream of publishing deserving poets, first conceiving the idea before Harriet Monroe had hers. Hearing of the project, the ever-watchful Ezra Pound sent Kreymborg a whole packet of work from friends — a lot of Imagist poems, and offerings from Joyce, Remy de Gourmont, and Ford Madox Ford. They all had to wait for a while. Kreymborg's first attempt failed before it got anywhere, but now in 1913 the climate of opinion was veering his way. Two things had set people talking about poetry and poets: Miss Monroe's magazine, with its accompanying rows over Imagism, and an anthology of poems, *The Lyric Year*, published in the East by one Ferdinand Pinney Earle. Earle had even advertised a cash prize of $500 for the best poem of the year, and bestowed it on Orrick Johns. Immediately he was swamped by protests from readers, who thought that the prize should have gone instead to young Edna St. Vincent Millay for her astonishing "Renascence." The controversy, while painful for Mr. Earle and Orrick Johns, was good for the cause. Suddenly the long-neglected Muse of Poetry became the leading topic of the day, and the time seemed ripe for Kreymborg to have another go at the *Glebe*.

He was spending the summer with two young artists, Samuel Halpert and Man Ray, in a New Jersey shack. The others got just as enthusiastic about the *Glebe* as its originator, drawing illustrations for it and planning the format. For a happy while they even thought they could publish it themselves in the shack, because some friend gave Man Ray an old printing press, but the press got smashed up on the way and Kreymborg had to look around for another method. Somebody suggested that he appeal to the Boni brothers who ran the Washington Square Bookshop in the Village, and probably drew a map for him in the bargain. Ollie visited the Village and found the Bonis, and recognized the terrain at once as his natural habitat. He was overjoyed with everything he saw and heard. Even if the Bonis had turned him down he would have thought the trip well worth it, but they didn't turn him down. They liked little magazines: they had already backed one or two, and, in time, they published the *Glebe*. True to tradition, it didn't last long, but before vanishing it printed some fine things. One of its firsts was William Carlos Williams. After it folded Kreymborg moved on to *Others*; years later he was to be one of the editors of *Broom* during its European phase. In the meantime he had found the Village, and that was the main thing.

Washington Square in 1913 was no longer the place we have known so well under various pseudonyms. Furbished up by the unfortunate Stanford White, who had designed the Arch and the Judson Hotel opposite on the "genius side," the park looked more respectable than it had in the old days. Nobody threw dead cats and dogs into the fountain any more, but rents were still cheap on the genius side, though on the north, the Mabel Dodge side, only richer people could afford the rents. The bookshop of Charles and Albert Boni took its name from the Square, but actually it stood on MacDougal Street, serving in a second capacity as an informal gathering-place for ebullient Villagers who used the walls for a bulletin board. The delighted Kreymborg examined all the signs, garish and gay in their bright colors — advertisements, he recollects, of the Liberal Club, Guido Bruno and his garret, the *Masses*, the *New Republic*, the Washington Square Players, Polly's Restaurant. None of them meant anything to him then, but in due course he was to investigate them all.

His memory is faulty to some degree. Guido Bruno, for example, was not to make his appearance for two more years, after which he poured out publications at a fantastic rate, and put himself on show to sightseers as a quaint Bohemian. Nor could Ollie have seen anything at that early date pertaining to the Washington Square Players. Their time, too, was yet to come. For the rest, however, his list is accurate. The Liberal Club and Polly's were almost one and the same: at least, they occupied the same building and attracted the same people, though as Liberal Clubmen they talked, while at Polly's they ate *and* talked.

Polly, Paula Holladay, was an Evanston girl who effectively conquered her bourgeois background by becoming an anarchist and taking for paramour — and cook — Hippolyte Havel, an ex-lover of Emma Goldman. Mabel Dodge describes Hippolyte as a Russian Nihilist with a "broad, low, intelligent brow, and long, black hair; he was very small, and very obscene in his talk."

According to all accounts he was abusive as well. The public would hurry to Polly's to receive the accolade: in certain circles, nobody was anybody until Hippolyte Havel had cursed him for a bourgeois pig.

Polly's was in the basement. Upstairs the Liberal Club held its meetings. It had started out as a splinter group from the original Liberal Club, founded by Lincoln Steffens and a group of friends uptown on Eighteenth Street: it owed its separate existence to a schoolteacher named Henrietta Rodman. The question that precipitated the split was Henrietta's marriage. According to New York law of the time, no female teacher could be married and yet hold her job in the public schools, and Henrietta considered this unfair. To test it, she married and dared the civic government to do its worst. It did: it fired her. Henrietta proposed that the Club make a campaign of this issue, attacking the rule as an example of outworn tyranny. The others would not agree, so Miss Rodman broke with them and set up her own Club in the Village, where a number of members followed her. It is pleasant to record that her struggle against the city won the day, and that after a year's enforced idleness she was reinstated and permitted to go back to work, but marriage for female teachers was only one of Henrietta's many causes. She protested unceasingly, always urging one idea or another upon the world — the abolition of corsets for women's attire, sandals instead of shoes, bobbed hair — an almost terrifying innovation for the times — free love, birth control, women's suffrage, nudism. No historian has claimed that she was perfectly balanced mentally, but she attracted much admiration and loyalty nevertheless. Her taste for causes fitted in perfectly with the spirit of the Village. The sex angle (as advertising men would call it) of her protests attracted some to the Club downtown, but all was not sexy, as even Floyd Dell would be forced to admit: the Liberal Club was, in the main, political in its interests and sponsored countless debates, formal and informal, on social matters. For a while, in fact, no Village protest was worth a damn unless it was worked up and worded at the Club.

The staff of the *Masses* used its headquarters nearly as much as they did the proper magazine office — more, if we count the time spent consuming Polly's meals. The *Masses* could probably put up a better claim than magazines like the *Glebe* to being a mirror of Village opinion just before and during the First World War; its editors and readers were interested in more than art. It was started in 1911 and edited by a man named Piet Vlag, but didn't hit its stride until the next year when the editorship was taken over by Max Eastman and his associate, Floyd Dell, just arrived from Chicago. Eastman, another small-town boy, came from upstate New York and had graduated from Williams College. A good talker and a noticeably good-looking man, tall, with prematurely white hair, he was a serious Socialist and a serious thinker, a type we don't today associate with Greenwich Village, though at that time it was not at all incongruous. But Eastman wasn't a conventional political agitator, either. In time he incurred the wrath of the Left Wing, and when the moment of decision arrived he was to denounce Communism. The Left Wingers then retorted that he was merely a playboy who had trifled with the sacred cause — an unfair allegation. Yet, in the words of Hoffman's book *The Little Magazine*, the *Masses* editors and their contributors formed an "interesting and curious" group that was not purely Socialistic either. "For them revolt was essentially a personal matter; and, though Marxism and other forms of socialism did form a background for much of their thinking, they looked upon the constraints of bourgeois society for the most part as personal inconveniences or as objects of ridicule and satire . . . Socialism of this early period — that is, before the revolution in Russia had given Marxism a bargaining power with intellectuals and artists — was a mixture of social realism and poetic romanticism."

The editors of the *Masses* printed poetry as well as protest-reports, and Floyd Dell contributed a lot of articles on sexual mores, a subject that would not have interested Marx or Engels. When, during the war hysteria of 1917, the magazine spoke out in favor of pacifism and was suppressed, the manifesto of its first number in 1911 was recollected by very few. "Socialism has more to gain from a free, artistic literature reflecting life as it actually is, than from an attempt to stretch points in order to make facts fit the Socialist theory," it had proudly declared. By the end of the war, that statement was hopelessly out of date.

*   *   *

It was in 1913 that the *Masses*, to raise money, sponsored the first of the famous Village balls. It was so successful that the Liberal Club promptly followed suit with a "Pagan Rout," the first of many. "In Costume $1, Without Costume $2," read one of their advertisements; the idea being to encourage the Village gentry to use ingenuity and artistic talent inexpensively. The Routs were held for years, until, when they got too pagan even for the Village, they were abandoned. As for the theater movement, it started slowly, in the wake of several performances of the regular little theater type. Albert Parry chronicles its history. The Village's theater began in 1912, he says, when Everett Shinn of the Tile Club put on burlesques in his studio for the amusement of friends: "More Sinned Against Than Usual" and "The Prune Hater's Daughter" were two of his titles. A year later, when Jack Reed's "Moondown" was printed in the *Masses*, somebody at the Liberal Club had the idea of producing it there. The venture, proving successful, was followed by a lot more offerings. Floyd Dell wrote a play solely for the purpose of Club production, and so did other members. The footlights' glare caught the imagination of Villagers, and those who spent the summers in Provincetown began putting on plays in an old building on the pier there. Leading spirits of this summer movement were Jig Cook and his friend Susan Glaspell, who wrote together the very first of the Provincetown Players' productions, "Suppressed Desires." More followed. Several seasons elapsed before the Provincetown group decided to present their work to New York City. In the meantime the Washington Square Players had already gone professional; they opened in 1915, the Provincetown Players a year later.

All in all the little colony was growing fast. For a long time the Liberal Club, Polly's and the bookshop remained the inner core of the Village, but other clubs and restaurants kept springing up like mushrooms, and young people poured in from north, south and west. Young people had been coming to New York for years, but now they had a particular goal in the Village, and there they concentrated. Commercialism showed its ugly face — Guido Bruno brought into the district an attitude of opportunism that most of his neighbors deprecated, by setting himself up as a professional freak. Soon there was more of the same. All over the district, especially in the crooked little streets behind the Square, appeared lighthearted signs advertising restaurants with eccentric names, studios whose occupants specialized in lightning portrait-painting, and weird nightclubs. Not all the old Villagers, as first settlers, condemned these developments out of hand: that would not have been in the Bohemian spirit. They agreed that Bruno lowered the tone of the place, but most other arrivals were welcomed.

Everybody liked Bobby Edwards, in spite of his freakishness.

A long, lanky, spectacled man, Bobby started his Village career in 1910 as a maker of ukeleles out of cigar boxes, but he had other talents and soon moved into the entertainment field with an act he did in a restaurant, singing songs he had composed and accompanying himself on a ukelele. As he became popular, he organized his followers into the Crazy Cat Club, which many of the town's notabilities joined. When Arthur B. Moss began to publish the Village's own weekly, the *Quill*, Bobby agreed to write a regular column for it, and he continued to work for the paper, writing witty comments and news items, until Moss, leaving New York, turned over the whole thing to him. Often the new editor burst into poetry, and occasionally printed one of his songs complete with music. I recall one that started out:

> Oh, waiter, do not put those chairs upon the table.
> Oh, waiter, leave those chairs upon the floor.
> For we would all go home if we were able —
> Oh, waiter, don't disturb us any more.

CHAPTER 11

Something About Bodenheim

T HE First World War's explosion had so great and diverse an effect generally on the United States that its particular impact on American Bohemians went unnoticed. Later the editors of the *Masses* were to make themselves heard, so vociferously proclaiming their disapproval of the hostilities that they were considered a nuisance: later still the Philistines decided that the journal was a threat to law and order, and dealt with it accordingly. But the first impact in 1914 concerned many more Bohemians than were represented on the staff of the *Masses*. It hastened the weaning process of Bohemia, forcing the Murgerites to throw off the influence of Paris and London, which cities were now practically incommunicado. More than that, the war stiffened the backbone of other colonies within the States. If Greenwich Villagers ceased to yearn for the Continent, so did hinterland Bohemians give up, temporarily, their dream of going to New York. It was no use going away: New York was ruined — the war had spoiled the fun if it, and one might as well make the best of things at home. Thus, until the day of decision in 1918, light-hearted vagabondage all but faded out, and of course after that date all of Bohemia was — for a while — swamped.

During the non-participating years, Chicago did not quite

ignore the war, but paid only lip service to it, as the city's newspaper files attest. Admittedly, some attention was bestowed by
Bohemians on their lost critic Floyd Dell and his goings-on in
the East, but his Chicago friends obviously still felt a bit sore
at Dell for abandoning them just as if, in spite of all evidences
of culture, the Art Institute and *Poetry Magazine* and so on,
he considered them unworthy. (America's Bohemians were
beginning to show strong chauvinistic feelings.) But, if apa-
thetic toward the international struggle, Chicago was sharply interested in national affairs, and the city's intellectuals felt themselves deeply committed to the battle of the Wobblies against
capitalism. Margaret Anderson wrote one of her most fiery
editorials for the *Little Review* of December, 1915, about the
death of the IWW leader Joe Hillstrom — the legendary Joe
Hill who had organized the workers from San Francisco up to
Maine, in every mine and mill, by teaching them to sing. Joe
Hill had recently been martyred, shot in a Utah jail. "For God's
sake, why doesn't *someone* start the revolution?" wrote Margaret.

The South Side colony still existed, of course, but artists and
writers were congregating in larger numbers in the vicinity of
the old Water Tower north of the Loop, on Chicago Avenue.
Towertown offered low rents in run-down houses near Lake
Michigan and Lincoln Park. A little to the west of the area
lived Italians, Greeks, Germans and Hungarians, a circumstance
that meant foreign restaurants where Bohemians could afford
savory meals in romantic atmosphere. The lunatic fringe dis-
ported in Bughouse Square, as the public named Newberry
Park across from the Newberry Library on Walton. When the
philanthropist Newberry made over this property to the city,
he had stipulated that the right of free speech must prevail on
that plot of ground, and every orating crackpot in town had
the freedom to propound his message within those limits no
matter what his subject — dress reform, pure food, pacifism or

outright sedition. No policeman could lay a finger on him for expressing his opinions in Bughouse Square. Nearby was the Radical Book Shop. The Near North Side was, in short, a happy little neighborhood for any eccentric. It is no wonder that Jack Jones started up his Dill Pickle Club nearby.

Jones had lost one eye and his faith in the IWW, of which he had formerly been a member, but though he forswore the radical labor movement he could not bring himself to desert the climate of ideas. Hence the Dill Pickle, a combination forum and playhouse. Other clubs proliferated in Towertown — the Hoboes College, Reitman's New Church — but they didn't have the Dill Pickle's *panache*. Its premises were a renovated old barn, never closed. Jack offered shelter to destitute friends, visiting radicals and artists with nowhere else to go. He opened his doors to all lecturers, even those whose ideas were opposed to his own. One-act plays were produced there — Ben Hecht wrote one that scandalized Chicago and brought extra publicity to the Club — and on Sunday night the program always provided a speaker to hold forth and then stand ready to defend his thesis against all comers. The club's house organ, a little magazine edited by Jones, was called the *Dill Pickler*. In later years, during Prohibition and the era of gangsters, the Dill Pickle slipped into the role of tourist trap and became a regular Chicago nightclub with the customary, occasional flurry between thugs and police, but at the beginning, as a genuine center for the meeting of minds, it must have been great fun. In a letter to Albert Parry published in *Garrets and Pretenders*, Mrs. Edna Fine Dexter, a one-time habitué, talked lovingly of the old days when bobbed-haired girls and deeply thoughtful boys spent hours of the night on the barn's flat roof under the stars, discussing such subjects as "Nietzsche and Prudhomme and Havelock Ellis."

All old-time recollections of Chicago's Bohemia include the

gentlemen of the press. This is as it should be; a newspaperman becomes a fifty percent Bohemian almost as automatically
as he gets his job. Reporters are seldom more than fifty percent Bohemian. The weekly paycheck keeps them from total
immersion, but Hecht dipped into the dangerous waters more
deeply than most of his confreres; in the end he became an out-
and-out artist, deserting journalism altogether. Some years
after the heyday of the Dill Pickle he published his first novel,
Erik Dorn, and set tongues buzzing with shock all over
the country. I myself have good cause to remember Erik.
When I was a high-school student in Chicago I once took along
a copy of the novel to the dentist's, reading it with rapt attention while waiting for my turn in the torture chamber. Sum-
moned, in my apprehension I left the book on the table in the
waiting room. Another patient, a middle-aged matron, picked
it up and read a bit. Scandalized by the contents, she raised
hell with the dentist — an unfortunate, mystified man, who had
never read a novel in his life — and then took her name off his
engagement book, refusing to have her teeth fixed by anyone
who supplied such filth to his clients.

I doubt if *Erik Dorn* would whiten many hairs nowadays,
but it was a daring book for the times, and this side of his character was uppermost when Ben Hecht befriended Max Bodenheim. Their association, marked by humorous quarrels in public, has been compared by Albert Parry to that of Potash
and Perlmutter, but it was more than an act: for Hecht it was
hard work. You had to be determined and vastly tolerant to
stay friends with Bodenheim. He was a good-looking youth in
his early days, though Villagers who knew him at the end would
find this hard to believe, after he had sampled too many Pierian
springs. Born in the early 1890s in Illinois, Missouri or Mississippi — nobody seems quite sure — he decided at the age of

seventeen to be a poet. His father, an industrious shopkeeper, was not sympathetic to this idea, and Max ran away and went on the bum. After wandering and consorting with hoboes for some time, he joined the army. His term of service was lengthened by a stay in the penitentiary for hitting an officer over the head with a musket. In *Letters from Bohemia,* Hecht says the lieutenant involved "had been ridiculing Private Bodenheim as a Jew." When Max got out of jail he came to Chicago to pursue his career as poet, carrying the bulging briefcase that became part of his public image. In it, says Hecht, were all his unpublished poems, a change of underwear and socks, rejection slips, and a bottle of Tabasco sauce.

The general portrait of Bodenheim, proudly hateful, was painted by himself. Hecht says that he had "a mystic sense of himself as an unwanted one. No one asked him for lunch or dinner . . . It wasn't true. Bogie was often a guest in my home" — even though his table manners were calculated to spoil the host's appetite. But it is true, Hecht admits, that Bodenheim was more disliked, derided, denounced, beaten up and kicked down more flights of stairs than any other poet the writer had ever known or heard of. Hecht says indignantly that Bogie's seven books of poetry attracted little attention in spite of their merit, but the neglect probably owed itself to the fact that Bodenheim's poetry was not in the mode. Besides, though it wasn't bad, it seemed rather pallid compared with the pungent flavor of Bogie himself. His novels, too, would not be remembered if it weren't that one of them, *Replenishing Jessica,* having had the good luck to be condemned as obscene by John S. Sumner, naturally became a best seller. As a high-school girl I considered myself an expert on obscenity, but I didn't see much of that quality in *Replenishing Jessica,* though I looked for it earnestly. What did strike me as remarkable was a passage in which Jessica, the heroine and a very rich girl, daringly decided to go out and mingle with the common people on a bus. In preparation for this venture she donned a red velvet suit trimmed with ermine. No, Bodenheim's novels were not immortal. It is for his life and death he is remembered. These were lurid in exactly the fashion Philistines felt they had a right to expect of Bohemians.

With a mocking grin he would say to Hecht, "Nobody seems to like me. Do you think it is because I am too aware of people's tiny hearts and massive stupidities?"

Hecht: "They are too aware of your big mouth. Why don't you try ignoring their imperfections, after sundown?"

Bogie: "I was born without your talent for boot-licking."

"He crowed with delight and whacked his thigh . . . it is this strut I remember as Bogie's signature. Ignored, slapped around, reduced to beggary, Bodenheim's mocking grin remained flying in his private global war like a tattered flag. God knows what he was mocking. Possibly, mankind."

Bogie was comparatively gentle with Hecht: usually he snubbed those who wished to be nice to him. When, in 1917, America entered the war and even Chicago had to take cognizance of the situation, he played a trick on a group of people who had pacifist sympathies. He declared that he was a conscientious objector but would undoubtedly be drafted, whereupon they hid him away in an apartment and kept him in luxury for weeks before discovering that he had volunteered for the army and been turned down, on the grounds that he had already served and been dishonorably discharged. Nevertheless Bodenheim had friends, men tough enough to stand for his peculiarities and women who fell in love with him. One of the men was a sculptor acclaimed by Bogie and Hecht as the greatest artist living — Stanislaus Szukalski, son of a Polish-born blacksmith in Chicago. Stan once smashed his own work with a cane when he saw it in the Art Institute, placed in a spot he didn't like. He was good-looking in a skinny way and wore his hair long, with a beret. He married a young Chicago heiress, much against her family's wishes, and moved into a luxury apartment high up in one of the skyscrapers on the Gold Coast.

The same winter I got the dentist into trouble over *Erik Dorn* I went out carol-singing on Christmas Eve with a small party led by my new brother in law, Mitchell Dawson. Mitchell, who wrote poetry in his law office, knew Towertown well. Sometimes when he was courting my sister Rose the pair had visited the Dill Pickle, and often they took me to the poetry readings across from the Tower itself. It must have been his idea that night that we serenade the Szukalskis in their eyrie — the rest of us didn't know them. Rose demurred, but we overrode her and took the elevator up all those stories to the apartment. Outside the door, in a luxuriously carpeted little passage, we lifted up our voices in "God Rest Ye Merry, Gentlemen," swinging our lanterns in time to the beat. The door opened and there stood Szukalski, his bride peering out curiously behind him. They invited us in for a drink, and showed us around. It was a rather somberly splendid place, I remember, except for his studio, all white and spacious and neat. Rose said to Mrs. Szukalski, "Really, this is an imposition. We're so sorry — we just felt crazy, you know, and did it on an impulse," and Mrs. Szukalski said not at all, they were delighted. On the way down in the elevator Mitchell said accusingly to his wife, "You apologized! . . . Yes you did, you were apologizing, I heard you." But recriminations were dropped in favor of a long, solemn discussion as to whether Stan could possibly be *happy* up there with all that money.

Szukalski and Bodenheim were founder members, in days be-

fore Stan's marriage, of the Vagabonds, a club whose meetings
were held in the Szukalski studio. There they entertained literary lights and pretty girls, who scuffled for the privilege of
filling the bowl of Bogie's pipe, a four-foot carved bamboo im-
plement from the South Seas, the bowl of which rested on the
smoker's foot. Bogie used to ornament the stem with ribbon
bows. During this period he and Hecht were getting together
in the evening at regular intervals, at Hecht's house, where
they wrote plays, and all went along smoothly enough except
that Hecht grew tired of hearing Bodenheim's constant vituper-
ation of practically everybody. He therefore made a rule that
the poet should not utter one word of complaint in his house,
at least on working evenings, and Bogie agreed. One night
Bogie arrived late and disheveled, gripping in his teeth all that
remained of the famous pipe, a fragment of stem. It was a bitterly cold night, icy underfoot. He said he had slipped and
fallen as he got off the streetcar, shattering the pipe. Hecht com-
miserated with suitable lightness on the little tragedy, and the
friends got to work. It was not until the next day that the host
heard that Bodenheim had broken his shoulder as well as his
pipe in the fall. He hadn't said a word about it. That would
have been complaining.

The last person in the world to feel chauvinistic, Bodenheim
decided in 1910 to have a look at New York. He knew Alfred
Kreymborg through correspondence — Kreymborg had published some of his poems in the magazine *Others* — so he wrote
to the editor asking for help. Kreymborg got him a room in
Bank Street where he himself lived with his wife, and waited
with interest to see what the poet looked like. He proved to
be, said Kreymborg, "the queerest of the queer," with one arm
in a sling and the famous briefcase gripped under the other.
Though very young, he "spoke with the weariness of an aged

man." Ollie introduced him to some of his colleagues, who also contributed to *Others,* and listened in delight as Bogie and Marianne Moore spun "long subtle thoughts in colloquy," always addressing each other with elaborate courtesy as Mr. Bodenheim and Miss Moore. Max's poetry Kreymborg considered "mature to the last degree," and Kreymborg's wife mothered Max. All in all, Bogie was probably as happy as he could be — for a while. As if in exchange for this loan from the Middle West, Kreymborg went to Chicago for a long stay. He loved it. "The crude braggadocio of the natives had forthright power, irresistible charm. Here was no dependence on New York, and *via* New York an abject prostration to Europe; but egoism, naïveté, joy."

However, egoism, naïveté and joy were not enough to bring Max Bodenheim back to Chicago for good, once he'd seen New York. He returned, but went back to the Village again and again, until in 1920 he became an out-and-out New Yorker, and new generations, visiting the Village, would have been surprised to hear that he had not always been one of the local characters there.

CHAPTER 12

Back at the Ranch

MABEL DODGE was not having a good war. It had been vexatious from the very beginning, when the opening of hostilities caught her with a house-party in the Villa Curonia and her guests all hurried away with what she considered unbecoming haste to secure passages for themselves to America. She herself refused to budge, upon which her favorite in the party, Carl Van Vechten, basely went off on his own. This was outright desertion, and she didn't speak to Carl for years afterwards — a decision she had cause to regret when she herself got home, at her own majestic pace and with dignity unimpaired, because it meant she had nobody to play with. Everyone else was scurrying around on errands that did not interest her. The love affair with Jack Reed was over, and she could find nothing to do but mope around the old stands — New York, Croton, Provincetown.

One day in New York she dropped in on the exhibition of a painter people were talking about, the Russian-born Maurice Sterne, just back from Bali with a lot of new pictures. The paintings did not please Mabel, who reflected that though the man could draw his colors were muddy. The more she viewed, the more sure she grew that this Sterne had missed his calling — anyone with such a woeful lack of color-sense and such a good grasp of form ought to be a sculptor rather than a painter. Nevertheless she bought one of the paintings, and not long afterward the artist came to call. He proved attractive. Mabel imparted her theory about his proper field of activity: he did not agree, so they met again and again for further argument. Sterne was strangely stubborn. In spite of her repeated admonitions, he went right on painting, and would not even try his hand at sculpture, but Mabel too could be stubborn. She argued and argued. All at once, somehow, they married.

In Mabel's reminiscences she gives a dreary account of this, her third marriage, but the dreariness is undoubtedly hindsight. After all, she stayed with Sterne for a while, and that is something she would not have done if she hadn't wanted to. Then in 1916 he went out to New Mexico to visit a painter friend of his, Paul Burlin — a trip that was to have important consequences.

Van Doren Coke traces the growth of New Mexico's artist colonies — in *Taos and Santa Fe, the Artist's Environment* — from as far back as 1882, when Frederic Remington, seeking Indian subjects, first visited the state. Remington came back several times and in 1902 spent quite some time in Taos, about which he was enthusiastic for its beauty and remoteness from the ugly ways of civilization. By this time Joseph Sharp of Ohio had also discovered the untouched West, and he too lived for a time in Taos. Later, in Paris, Sharp got friendly with two compatriot painters studying in the same atelier — Ernest Blumenschein and Bert Phillips — and told them of his private cache in a wonderful unknown country. Blumenschein and Phillips pricked up their ears. "We were ennuied with the hackneyed subject matter of thousands of painters, windmills in a Dutch landscape; Brittany peasants with sabots," wrote Blumenschein years later. In 1898, after a preliminary reconnaissance, he went to Colorado with Phillips and the two friends spent the summer sketching, then, as autumn drew on, bought a wagon and started out for Mexico. They were two days' ride from Taos when the wagon broke a wheel, and Blumenschein had to ride into town to get help. He was so entranced with the surroundings and the fall color of the trees that he made up his mind to forget Mexico and stay right there, and Phillips, when he followed, agreed to do the same. Blumenschein for a time continued to spend at least half his year in the East or in Europe: in Paris with Phillips he met Irving Couse and told him about New Mexico, and soon Couse too moved in. Herbert Dunton, who studied under Blumenschein in New York, came out to get material: *he* stayed. Faced with the difficulty of selling paintings in a remote town far from customers, the friends organized the Taos Society of Artists, and through this agency sent out traveling exhibitions of their work. The colony became better and better known. From Chicago came Walter Ufer and Victor Higgins, in 1914.

In the meantime Santa Fe, sixty miles to the south but equally clear-aired and altitudinous, was collecting artists of its own. The seeds of rivalry were there from the beginning; today, though highways have rendered insignificant the journey between the towns, Taos residents shake their heads pityingly if the unaware tourist praises Santa Fe, while at mention of Taos the people of Santa Fe pull down the corners of their mouths as if they were eating something bitter. Coke names the Californian Carlos Vierra as Santa Fe's first artist, who came in 1904. Five years later he was joined by Kenneth Chapman, an anthropologist who also painted. There followed, first on exploratory visits and then as residents, Gerald Cassidy, Paul Burlin, Olive Rush, Sheldon Parsons, Walter Rollins and many others. By 1916, when Maurice Sterne listened to the blandishments of his friend Burlin and came to see the place, Burlin had built a house for himself in Santa Fe. It was the same year William Penhallow Henderson brought his wife Alice Corbin of *Poetry* to the sanatorium on Monte Sol, where she speedily improved until she was able to live at home with her husband and child, occasionally going to the doctor for a check-up. There were many such half-invalids in the city.

Enchanted with Santa Fe, Sterne wrote to his wife telling her that she simply must come and see what it was like. Mabel hated to be shown things, and though she did come, she was reluctant to do so, determined not to like Santa Fe. And she didn't like it. She thought Paul Burlin's wife, an ethnologist named Natalie Curtis, a tedious woman. Natalie talked a good deal of her work collecting Indian chants, but Mabel was positive that the woman couldn't possibly understand the true nuances of the red man's music: nobody but Mabel could understand things like that. She observed specimens of America's aborigines as they moved about the streets of Santa Fe in their buckskin boots or moccasins, and knew immediately that they had a special quality, a rare life-force that the other Anglos were too obtuse to appreciate. How imperceptive were those other Anglos! How she disliked them! As a matter of fact, all artists were tiresome, and those of Santa Fe, huddling together as they did, playing house in their adobe dwellings, happy and complacent with their brightly colored sticks of furniture, were the most tiresome of all. They should have been trying to *know* the red man, instead of merely painting him. When Alice Corbin invited her to tea, Mabel's rage was overwhelming, and she took it out on Maurice. She said she had to get out of this stifling Santa Fe: she wouldn't stay even one more day in a place where people actually made dates with each other as if they were in New York, and expected you to drink afternoon tea. Mabel had not come all the way to New Mexico just to drink tea with other Anglos, and he need not expect her to do so. No, no. She would go to Taos.

As if trying to make up for her disappointment in not being first in Santa Fe, Mabel in writing this chapter of her life persisted in describing Taos as her own, own discovery, a place that Anglo-Americans were too unimaginative and timid to visit until she had blazed the trail. Very likely it was only by this method that she could continue to feel it worthy of her love. She tells how she horrified everyone in Santa Fe when she grabbed the name "Taos" out of the air and announced her intention of going, and how Maurice dragged his feet and called her crazy for thinking of it. But she insisted, she found transport for them: *Something* was calling her. The journey she describes sounds perilous: the reader begins to think of Taos as Burton thought of the source of the Nile, with this difference — Mabel, according to her version, discovered Taos. At this point in the narrative she does not mention the artists already living there, as artists had done for more than half a century.

In a way we can understand why she grew to look upon the town as her own private property. It was never that, but she did have an effect on it: she made it a different place. Where Santa Fe's colony of settlers had always been diverse, including writers, anthropologists, and tubercular patients as well as painters, Taos was a simpler community. It had a splendid pueblo, a handful of non-Indian locals, and a happy few painters who lived in the rather stodgy manner of their kind, putting color on canvas or talking about color on canvas. There were no TB people, no writers, and no anthropologists. It was Mabel who introduced diversity to Taos. A highly gregarious woman and an enthusiastic lion-hunter, she invited guests to come and visit as soon as she had found lodgings with enough space to accommodate them. One of the first of these was Gertrude Stein's brother Leo, but as a celebrity Leo could not hold a candle to some of those she planned to capture later on. The rented rooms were only a makeshift: soon she had bought land and was building a large house, with guest-houses nearby. Maurice was bored without his Santa Fe friends and kicked his heels for some time before he capitulated to his wife's original notion and took up sculpture. Mabel was gratified, but not very: she was now thoroughly bored with Maurice and had her eye on a Taos Indian named Tony Luhan. In 1918, when Maurice announced his intention of leaving, there was little discussion — if any. Exit Maurice, enter Tony.

Mabel's affair with Tony probably set more tongues wagging, for a longer period, than any scandal Taos had heretofore known. The noise grew to such large proportions that government agents a few years later threatened to make trouble for her on the grounds that Luhan was their ward. Furthermore, there was some question of her title to a part of the land she had bought. Was it not Indian property in fact? Certainly it abutted on pueblo territory, and some of the other Indians, disliking Mabel, were more than willing to press a complaint. She acted swiftly to frustrate her opponents by marrying Tony, and the official rumbles died away; of the unofficial ones, the chatter of Taos residents, she scorned to take any notice. But Tony, whether as lover or husband, did not constitute enough of an interest to fill her days. In 1921, before the fourth marriage took place, she began to correspond with the English writer D. H. Lawrence, urging him to come and live in New Mexico. Lawrence took months to think it over, but in the end he and his wife arrived. All his life he had carried around with him the idea, or dream, of setting up a Utopia somewhere in a distant land, where he and a few devoted followers would lead what he considered the proper kind of life, and for a time he and Frieda, his wife, thought that the New Mexico mountains were exactly what he had always sought. On a visit to England he attempted to round up the followers he needed, but succeeded in persuading only one, a painter, the Honorable Dorothy Brett, who accompanied the Lawrences back to Taos.

Mabel gave Frieda a ranch that she — or, rather, her son John Evans — owned higher up on the mountainside, and Frieda gave her in return one of Lawrence's original manuscripts. The Lawrences and Brett worked earnestly putting in order the tumbledown houses they found on the property, and they continued to love New Mexico, but Utopia never materialized, and Lawrence quarreled bitterly with Mabel. This was nothing new in him — he quarreled with everybody — but he remained angry with her for the rest of his life. After he died in Italy, Frieda brought back his ashes and buried them in a cairn on the ranch. She stayed in Taos until her death. Mabel stayed there, too; she died in 1962. Brett is still there.

One man with ample reason to remember the Lawrence incursion is Witter Bynner, who, though he was born in Brooklyn in 1881, has lived in Santa Fe long enough to be the dean of Anglo residents there. Recently he told me how, when looking around one of the local churches with a friend, he overheard the speech of a young priest who was showing the place to a party of tourists.

"If you're interested in the history of New Mexico's churches," said the priest, "you'll want to read 'Death Comes for the Archbishop,' the life story of our Father Lamy. It's by Willa Cather."

He pronounced the name "Cayther," setting Hal Bynner's teeth on edge, so as soon as the poet got the chance to speak privately to the priest he said: "Excuse me, but you aren't pronouncing that name properly. It's Willa Cather; rhymes with rather. I knew the lady well. I assure you that's the way she herself said it."

The priest thanked him, but a moment later Bynner heard him saying the name wrong to a new party. Afterward he came over to apologize: "I did it again; it just slipped out. Sorry. Excuse me, but do you live in Santa Fe yourself?"

"I've been here for years," said Hal.

"And what do you do?"

"I'm a poet."

"Oh," said the priest in patent disappointment. "Not even a painter?"

Bynner was a Harvard man. After graduation he worked in publishing houses. His own first publication was a book of poetry, *Young Harvard,* which appeared in 1907. As a lecturer on literature he traveled the States and learned to know the Middle West, naturally becoming familiar with the *Poetry* office in Chicago. Arthur Davison Ficke of Davenport, that home of many literary figures, was his close friend. Often when Bynner and Ficke met they talked irritably of the many modern schools of poetry, Imagism, Vorticism and so on, the proponents of which, they felt, were given to far too many pompous explanations. Toward the end of 1916 a book called *Spectra* appeared rather mysteriously, without fanfare. The poems it contained were written, it seemed, by two Pittsburgh people nobody had ever heard of — Emanuel Morgan and Anne Knish. Miss Knish had written the preface, in which she said that these poems were the result of recent experiments by which the Spectric group aimed at pushing the possibilities of poetic expression into a new region, "to attain a fresh brilliance of impression by a method not so wholly different from the methods of Futurist Painting." Anne Knish, too, had written the first poem in the book. It began:

The piano lives in a dusk
Where rich amber lights
Quiver obscurely

Emanuel Morgan followed with,

Spectres came dancing up the wind,
Trailing down the long grass
Shooting high, undisciplined,
To join the sun and see you pass . . .
The colors of the pointed glass.

It was nearly two years before the world learned Emanuel
Morgan was the nom de plume of Witter Bynner, and Ann
Knish was really Arthur Ficke. Before the discovery was made,
these two managed to fool almost everyone in the literary
world. Bynner later told William Jay Smith, who wrote the full
story of the hoax in 1961, that the idea and the name flashed
across his mind one afternoon when, en route to Davenport to
visit the Fickes, he went with two friends in Chicago to see the
ballet "Le Spectre de la Rose." Afterwards the conversation got
around to new schools in poetry, as it often did when Bynner
was there. Suddenly, glancing down at the ballet program on
his knees, he declared that for his taste the Spectric group of
Pittsburgh were the most interesting ones to watch. His friends
admitted that they had not yet heard of the Spectric school, but
said they would make a point of looking it up. After that, says
Hal, there was nothing for it to create the school, poets and all,
and the minute he reached Davenport he proposed the project
to Ficke, who threw himself into it with enthusiasm. That very
night they wrote a lot of the poems. As one of the book's first re-
viewers, the talented poet Witter Bynner, in the *New Republic*,
declared that the Spectrists had rendered the Vorticists, the
Imagists, the Futurists and the Chorists passé.

"I was correcting proof on the book when the editor of the *New Republic* happened to drop in and catch me at it," he remembers. "I had to say something fast, so I told him that the publisher had sent me the proofs for reviewing, and the editor immediately asked me to send him my article when I'd finished it." But the *New Republic* review was only the first of a great number of comments that appeared in print: everyone in the literary world of America, and some abroad, had something to say about *Spectra*. There were attacks in plenty, and parodies as well, but the poets got a lot of praise. Bynner as lecturer often mentioned them: he was against them at first, but slowly he came round. The school was enlarged by one more member, Elijah Hay, in reality Marjorie Allen Seiffert. There was even a special *Spectra* edition of *Others*. Not until April 26, 1918, was the hoax exposed, when a young man in the audience of a Detroit hall where Witter Bynner was lecturing stood up and asked the speaker the fatal question: wasn't it true that Bynner himself was Emanuel Morgan, and that Arthur Ficke was Anne Knish?

Bynner recalls that he replied, quite simply, " 'Yes.' . . . After all, what else was there to say?"

*   *   *

In 1922 there appeared at the University of California the first number of a little magazine, *Laughing Horse*. It was unusually clever, with a high-spirited sort of zaniness. The three editors, Willard, or Spud, Johnson, Roy E. Chanslor and James T. Van Renssalaer Jr., adopted bogus names for the masthead and wrote spoof biographies of themselves in the manner of the Spectrists, perhaps naturally, as they knew Hal Bynner well: he was an English instructor on the campus for a year before he went to live in Santa Fe. Bynner allowed them to quote from his works, and contributed several original things as well.

Horse was still a very young periodical when Spud went to Santa Fe to visit Bynner and there made the acquaintance of D. H. Lawrence when the English novelist and his wife, Frieda, passing through Santa Fe on the way to their first sojourn in Taos, spent the night at Bynner's house. It is notorious that Lawrence's friendship was always a chancy thing; after the couple, with Bynner and Spud, had visited Old Mexico together, he drew malicious portraits of both the Americans in his book *The Plumed Serpent*. But a writer is seldom at a loss in such warfare. Hal bided his time, until in his book *Journey With a Genius,* published in 1954, he was able to hit back. By that time the Lawrence-in-New Mexico legend had reached enormous proportions. Lorenzo had long been dead, but people in the neighborhood spoke, and still speak today, in hushed tones of his fits of temper. It is said that when a little bitch belonging to the Lawrences went into season and ran away for a few days with other dogs, her master whipped her almost to death. It is only fair to add that the story has been hotly contested. But there are other grudges: Lawrence paid the penalty of fame in that everything he wrote was seized upon by people he knew who claimed that it was about themselves, and they almost invariably resented it.

"I'll never forgive him for that story, 'The Woman Who Rode Away,' " a Taos woman told me. "I was there when he went to Blue Lake — we all rode up together in a party. It was the most beautiful pack-trip I've ever been on, and I kept it in my memory as a shining jewel until I read that story and recognized it for the same occasion. It was a *horrible* story. How could he have taken a thing as beautiful as that and ruined it?"

Opinions on that will, of course, differ.

Before the Mexico trip, Lawrence had written a letter for Spud's magazine. In spite of what he said in *The Plumed Serpent* he was fond of the youth, whom he called "the Spoodle," and it was at Johnson's request that he wrote this letter, which amounted to a review of Ben Hecht's *Fantazius Mallaire*. Irritated by Hecht's use of so many socially forbidden words, which Lawrence felt was pointless as compared with his own, he quoted many passages to prove how offensive Hecht's attitude proved to be. The *Horse* editors were well aware that they could not possibly print the letter as it stood, and Chanslor — Spud Johnson at this time being in Mexico — hit on the amusing expedient of substituting for every dubious verb or noun the word "blank." What emerged in print was extremely shocking, though not, one would have said, provably so. In the same issue was an article by Upton Sinclair, "Goose Step," in which the writer attacked the university authorities for knuckling under to the local business tycoons, and it was probably Sinclair's article even more than Lawrence's letter that stirred up the wrath of the powers. However, they used the Lawrence letter as their excuse for action. Chanslor was put into jail on the charge of printing obscene material; he was tried and acquitted, but he went east after that, and *Laughing Horse* too had to leave the campus. Spud Johnson took it over and published it first in Guadalajara, then in Santa Fe or Taos, whichever city he was living in at the time. For years it continued to flourish. Lawrence wrote other pieces for *Horse*: in 1926 there was a special Lawrence number. Sometimes Arthur Ficke, Mary Austin and Mabel contributed. In 1939, after a long life, *Horse* was discontinued.

Spud, still a Taos resident, said recently: "I finally stopped it because I was bored and it was boring. But people still give me horses — I suppose they can't think of any other kind of present." He looked rather glumly around the room, where horses of porcelain, glass, brass, felt and wood vied for attention with a paper mobile of Pegasuses in plenty. "I've never been crazy about horses, as a matter of fact," said Spud.

CHAPTER 13

Boat Without Oars

T O A good deal of Bohemia's fermenting growth, particularly in the California of the early years of the century, we have an excellent witness in Mary Austin. Her photographs seem nearly all to have been taken in her middle age or later, and agree with my memory of our one meeting, showing her as a sturdy, no-nonsense figure who, for some reason known only to herself, usually wore a hat of impeccable respectability if little aesthetic interest. Yet she was a witness of Bohemia, as I have said — a companion of Bohemians, a dweller by the roadside that leads to Bohemia. She was not herself a Bohemian. It is difficult to say why one is so sure of this, but one *is* sure. True, much of her nature was compatible with the state — she had intellect and nonconformist sympathies: she was a fierce champion of women's rights. But she had a certain cast of temperament that simply doesn't fit in. She was rather heavy and solemn in spirit: stately, with no glint of humor.

Until Mary took her degree in teaching, she was a Middlewesterner who had never been out of the Mississippi valley. Born in Carlinsville, Illinois, in 1868, trained in Indiana, Mary would probably have remained in those environs for a long time if not forever, but her brother felt the wanderlust, and he persuaded his womenfolk — Mary and her newly widowed

mother — to come out west with him and go homesteading.
None of them knew anything about the problems they faced on
arriving to take up life on the allotment, situated in the most
hopeless, miserably arid part of California, but they struggled
on for years before giving up. When Mary was not trying to
cope with violent extremes in temperature that killed the crops
before they had done more than sprout, she taught at a little
school in the district. There were Indians in the country. It
was a long time since these aborigines had been a threat to settlers in America: the memory of redskin sieges, guerrilla warfare
and wholesale scalpings had faded, and all Mary's white neighbors felt toward Indians were a few stirrings of dislike and dis-
trust. They said that Indians were dirty and shirtless, and would
steal if you didn't look sharp. But Mary took a different viewpoint. She found them fascinating, and went out of her way
to make friends with them, encouraging the storytellers, especially, to talk. Mary Austin was the founder of American anthro-
pology.

She married a man whose family was Californian; he too was
a teacher. Though this step took her away for good from the
tough existence of the homesteader, it soon became evident
that she now had other problems to handle, which might be
worse than the farm's. Austin was a shiftless soul, and there was
no way to change him: he was impermeable. Mary was well
along in pregnancy when he disappeared early one morning
from their small-town lodging-house, without giving her
warning or explanation. In fact they were due to be dispos-
sessed that day, for non-payment of rent, but Mary didn't know
it, and it was a shock when she found herself out of the house,
sitting on one of the trunks without the slightest idea of what
to do next. A boardinghouse keeper, passing by, took pity on
her and offered her shelter in return for cooking, a proposi-

tion Mary was very glad to accept. That night the missing husband returned, after dark but ready for his supper, which the
landlady grudgingly let him have. He rebuked Mary for having
gone without letting him know where she was.

She might have left him then, but women did not lightly
walk out on their husbands in the early years of the 1900s, even
when shiftlessness reached such extremes as it did in Austin.
The most vivid memories Mary retained from her youth in Illinois had to do with drunken husbands and their wives. She
knew all about men who beat their wives brutally and husbands
who foisted one child after another on women too weak to bear
them. Yet most of these women, though they might join the
Temperance League, did not walk out of their homes.
What drove Mary away from Austin at last was something she
considered far worse than shiftlessness: their child proved to be
a hopeless mental deficient. Worse, her husband had known that
there was a more than fifty percent chance that any infant he
fathered would be like this — the taint ran in his family. He
had never told Mary, and now, when she asked him why he
hadn't, he replied loftily, "In our family we don't talk about
such things." That did it. Mary put the little girl into an institution and left her husband. At this time the Austins were living near San Francisco, having changed their jobs on several
occasions. Mary knew and loved the city, so she took up her solitary residence there and finished a book she had been writing
about her homesteading experience and the Indians, *The Land
of Little Rain.* Published in 1903, it was instantly successful,
and Mary Austin became an established member of San Francisco's group of writers and artists.

It may be remembered that these Westerners had always
been more out-of-door in their tastes than had their eastern
colleagues. Now Mary, with a few other pioneers, went south

along the coast to Carmel and built a house on one of the hills.
"There was no town at Carmel then; nothing but a farm or two,
one or two graceless buildings, and the wild beach and the
sunny dunes," wrote Mary, some years later, in *Earth Horizon*.
"George [Sterling — Mary was very fond of him] and I were
very much alone that first year. It was the simplest occupations
that gave us the most pleasure and yielded the richest harvest
of impressions, observations, and feeling responses . . . [Ster-
ling] delighted to go striding, axe on shoulder, over Monterey
hills looking for pitch pine or bee trees or whatever arduous and
practical simplicities restored him to the human touch . . . or
the lot of us would pound abalone for chowder around the
open-air grill at Sterling's cabin, and talk, ambrosial, unquota-
ble talk." Possibly it was at this time that Sterling wrote the song
Witter Bynner transplanted to Santa Fe, where he used to play
the piano as he sang —

> "Oh, some say that
> Our Lord is fat,
>   And some that he is bony,
> But as for me,
> I know that he
>   Is like the abalone."

The San Francisco earthquake of 1906 sent more and more
artistic refugees to live at Monterey and Carmel, forming what
Albert Parry calls "the first rural colony of American men and
women of art and freedom." But it would be a mistake to put
down to the earthquake's account this tendency to return to
nature: California herself, with her mild climate and splendid
beaches, is enough of an explanation. Before the quake ever
happened, San Francisco's artists were seeking out the country
for relaxation and, finally, total escape from urban life. Wan-

dering was and is natural to the California Bohemian, who more
than any other of the brotherhood lives up to the secondary
meaning of his name as a gypsy or hobo. Indeed, he is so far
from settled that it is not accurate to refer merely to San Francisco's Bohemia, or to Carmel's, or — today — that of Venice
West: we can talk about Chicago's colony or New York's, but
when we approach the Pacific the only qualification that covers
it is "Californian."

Deliberately and with set purpose the pioneers of Carmel
kept life simple. Sterling, Mary, Jack London, Henry Laffler,
Jimmy Hopper, Harry Leon Wilson, Charles Warren Stoddard,
Ambrose Bierce, and, after the fire, Ray Stannard Baker, Jesse
Lynch Williams, Lincoln Steffens — all were agreed that Carmel
must not be spoiled. Sternly they resisted the efforts made by
outsiders to develop their haven into a popular resort. In 1912,
when Mary left, the place was still small, beautiful, and not
over-populated. In 1914 Robinson Jeffers brought his family
and settled in. For a few years more there was peace and beauty,
but in the Twenties a serious fight flared up between the towns-
people and some newly arrived estate agents, when the new
arrivals made a concerted attack on the local amenities. Albert
Parry has told of the struggle. The realtors, after some success
in buying land around Carmel and Monterey, moved on to the
next step, proposing to "improve" on their property before selling it off. At this the artists, who had kept a sharp, jealous eye
on developments, rallied their forces for the attack. They had
learned that exhortation did not suffice: hadn't a few outsiders
betrayed them by selling? Artists and writers therefore girded
up their loins and plunged into battle — or, rather, went into
local politics. It was a sacrifice to give up their leisure and their
private work in order to run for political office, but they did
it, and they had enough success at the elections to preserve control. The day was saved — for a time.

"The mile of beautiful beach remained untainted by business enterprises," wrote Parry. "The sidewalks and streets remained rustic, the Monterey-Carmel highway still zig-zagged . . . But business was creeping into this oasis of Far Western intelligentsia just the same." And the cost of living went up. Visiting Carmel at the end of the Twenties, Parry found rents were as high as those of New York, and the food was both bad and expensive. Besides, the spirit had somehow curdled. There was "too much adoration of such distinguished citizens . . . as Lincoln Steffens with his left-pink editorials in the *Carmelite,* or Robinson Jeffers with his idealized dark-haired twin sons; too much attention (for an intellectual settlement) to the first nudist group in Carmel; too conscious an attempt to have colored pavements." It was the same cutesy atmosphere that in the end spoiled Greenwich Village, against which even the great out-of-doors is not immune.

* * *

But Mary Austin's feelings, at least, were not harrowed; by that time she was safe on her way, moving, incongruous but impressing, among the artists and writers of her time. We catch glimpses of her stocky figure in Florence, Paris, London, New York. In Florence, she followed Isadora Duncan, without knowing who she was, for the pleasure of watching her graceful walk, and inadvertently tracked the dancer to the apartment of Gordon Craig, with whom Isadora was carrying on a torrid affair. Mary backed out quickly, but the women met again, more than once. Pavlova used to ask Mary about Indian dancing, an attention that pleased the ex-schoolteacher. "But it was not so with Isadora Duncan. There were times when Isadora highhatted me; when she forgot who I was and what occasions she had of meeting me before. There were times when she had been drinking, and other times when she was simply silly." Isadora had grown heavier, Mary noticed in New York, and slightly clumsy. Irvin Cobb said that she went galumphing around the stage like Grant's tomb in love.

Mary's chosen place, when at last she made up her mind to settle down, was Santa Fe. Apart from its other delights, she was near Mabel and Tony in Taos — for a friendship had grown up between the women that survived where most of Mabel's other friendships did not. It was Mary, says Mary, who urged Mabel to put an end to the growing "cabal" in Taos by marrying Tony. Mabel must set her own house in order by divorcing Sterne, and she must also make an allowance to Tony's Indian wife. All went as Mary had advised. "I went there often," she wrote, "for while there is practically no likeness between Mabel and me, very little consenting approval, there is the groundwork of an intelligent approach to problems of reality, and a genuine affection. There is about Tony a warm stability of temperament which makes him an acceptable third to all our intercourse . . ." No, definitely not a Bohemian, but at least a person to whom Bohemians talked. She left directions about her body after her death: it was to be buried on a certain mountainside, overlooking the New Mexican landscape she had loved. Her wishes were honored; her tomb was arranged as she had decreed. Then years passed, until one day a party of people who had admired Mrs. Austin went riding into the mountains to visit her grave. Among them was Hal Bynner.

"Nobody could remember exactly where it was," he said, "and there were no directions in town that we could find. We looked and looked, on several mountains before we gave up, but it was no good. I'm afraid we've lost Mary."

Hers was a remarkable career, but to my mind the most remarkable thing she ever said was in reply to a producer she met in New York. He had just produced a play that for one reason and another has not yet been forgotten — "Abie's Irish Rose." The critical pasting the piece received had hurt this gentleman's feelings, and it must have been with trepidation that he asked the great Mrs. Austin her opinion of it, but she answered, with full sincerity, that she liked it very much. "It is a true folk drama," she declared.

*　　*　　*

The South, reluctant as always to follow in northern footsteps, remained until after the First World War ignorant of her artistic — or, at any rate, Bohemian — potentialities. It had always been like that; southern intellectuals and artists found their private worlds sufficient for their needs, without forming colonies of boon companions. Unmoved, New Orleans had watched young Louis Gottschalk go out into the world to win renown: only the Gottschalks themselves made much fuss about that. And though Louisianians took a comfortable, quiet pride in George Cable and their few other literati, it is doubtful if many New Orleans gentry were aware of Lafcadio Hearn's presence until long after he had gone to other countries. The Southerners' attitude toward the arts was not inimical; they were not instinctively resistant, like the aggressive Yankee and Chicago merchants who distrusted music, painting and poetry. Southerners thought it right and proper that their talented young should show the benefits of a select background. They were like a kind old uncle watching his nephew painting masterpieces, as he strokes his beard and says indulgently, "Very nice indeed. He gets that from *my* side of the family."

Then, all at once, and early in the Twenties, Bohemianism hit New Orleans full force. Nobody has ever really explained the onset. Whether the city's bright new magazine *The Double Dealer* was the cause of this burst of creative energy or was merely one of its effects is a moot point; at any rate they must have been closely associated. Around *The Double Dealer* — started in January, 1921 — gathered a notable array of editors and contributors. The moving spirits of the publication were four: two New Orleans men who had been together during the war, Julius Friend and Albert Goldstein, with Basil Thompson and the poet John McClure. They had two hundred dollars with which to pay the printer, a man whose financial mainstay was the regular publicaton of a seed catalogue. Two hundred wasn't enough: they could never get the printer's estimate down below three hundred. There was not one moment during the paper's life, of five and a half years, when they were not running in the red.

But *The Double Dealer* kept going. Their offices were on the third floor of an old walk-up studio building. Once the staff gave a fancy-dress party to drum up funds, much in the old *Masses* tradition, but this was Louisiana and the proceedings were accordingly more demure. One of the ladies who had been present described them when she took me to see the Lower Pontalba Building where the town's big costume parties have always been held. An old red brick building, facing a similar one across Jackson Square, it is one of New Orleans's most prized historic possessions. She outlined the line of march for me, through the park and under the arches.

"They started off like always, with a torchlight procession through the square," she said. "You never saw more beautiful costumes in your life, and they looked even more beautiful by torchlight. One of the artists, Ronald Hargrave, had designed most of the dresses, so everything hung together; it wasn't the ordinary mixture you get at most costume balls. He'd done the decorations too. There was never anything so lovely." Her face still lit up at the memory.

"That period — well, it gave everybody a taste of what they thought Paris must be like," said Albert Goldstein reminiscently. "Some of us had actually seen France, of course, but a lot of the others hadn't, and for them, as Hamilton Basso said, it was like having Paris in our backyard. We had painters and writers and pretty girls and all that — nice girls, you understand." In an article he wrote in 1959 for the magazine *Dixie* — "The French Quarter's Golden Era" — he lists the writers who happened, by pure accident, to be living in New Orleans at that one time: William Faulkner, whose first article it is said, was printed in the *Dealer,* Sherwood Anderson, Oliver LaFarge, Roark Bradford, Edmund Wilson, and Lyle Saxon. Another of the group was the artist William Spratling, who later left to live in Mexico and revive the native arts there. Others came to pay shorter visits: Carl Sandburg, John Dos Passos, and Eugene Jolas of *Transition,* the little magazine published in Paris. Proudly Mr. Goldstein listed the countries in which his magazine circulated: the United States, Canada, France, Great Britain, India, Tasmania, and the African Gold Coast. He also listed the contributors — Ernest Hemingway (his first article), Mark Van Doren, Thornton Wilder, Ben Hecht, Louis Untermeyer, Howard Mumford Jones, Robert Penn Warren, Sherwood Anderson, John Crowe Ransom, Edmund Wilson, Ezra Pound, Robert Graves, Lord Dunsany, Allen Tate and Maxwell Bodenheim. "We even rejected Dreiser and Gabriele d'Annunzio," he ended triumphantly.

*   *   *

Then came a strange development in American history, when for once all were in the same boat together, Bohemians and Philistines alike — a boat without oars. Prohibition had arrived.

How did it happen? Ask the women of the households Mary Austin remembered, the wives of men who spent their weekly paycheck in saloons, the females whose only comfort lay in Temperance Leagues and services in Methodist or Baptist churches. They were the backbone of the movement, but they found help in plenty from reformers of all sorts. The war, which took away the men and sent public attention chasing other problems, gave them their chance. Most of them really believed that alcohol could be legislated out of existence. The Volstead Act was slipped through in 1919, and in the following year the noble experiment began its long, troubled and troublesome career. Prohibition affected every branch of American life, but its greatest impact may well have been on the Chicago and New York Bohemian colonies. Chicago had always been a tough town: Prohibition made it tougher. Chicago bootleggers, rightly sensing the softest spot in their society, made straight for the Near North Side, where they moved in to keep company with established rebels already mobilized against older laws. We have seen how the Dill Pickle was chosen by these merchants as their favorite hangout. The bourgeoisie quickly learned where to go, and took to shopping for their contraband in Bohemia. Being an outpost of liberty, a fort that defends every man's right to alcohol, may be a fine proud thing, but in Chicago the honor brought trouble in its wake, especially when competing gangsters took enthusiastically to shooting each other.

Nevertheless the life of the spirit continued in its peculiarly Chicagoan way, and recently I realized this vividly, going through Mitchell Dawson's papers. Letters from Bodenheim in New York indicated how the Chicago and eastern colonies were becoming interknit: Bogie seems to have served unwittingly as a kind of catalytic agent precipitating this association. The earliest one I found is dated 1916, and the return address is Alfred Kreymborg's in the Village on Bank Street. It is not what one thinks of as a characteristic Bogie letter; it is cheerful, even courteous. Success had worked the miracle, if only for a short time.

"I have written to almost nobody, since my arrival here. The adventures in fitting my outer-self into new situations, new people, and a new life, have completely absorbed at least part of me." He is publishing a book of poetry; he is actually selling poems for cash down to a new magazine in Boston; he is getting over a nice party the night before "at Skip Connel's apartment, attended by Williams [that would be William Carlos Williams], Bob Sanborn, Mary Caroline Davies, Dorothy Merrill, Horace Hobley and wife, Frances Gregg, and Kreymborg. There was no shop talk, everyone wanted to get away from that tiresome subject — poetry. And I forgot — Marcel Duchamps of Cubist fame was also there . . . I am now associate editor of Others, and my name will appear on the front page of all numbers, together with that of Kreymborg."

Then, back to normal. In 1919 Bogie writes with bitter scorn about a series of lectures in Chicago to which, it seems, Mitchell has refused to invite him. Instead of the usual friendly "Dear Mitch," the salutation is, "Dear Dawson." It is a long letter and I shall quote only a part of it: "To quote from your letter: 'We didn't know whether you'd get here, and if you got here whether you'd ever get back, and if you stayed what the hell we'd do with you . . . If this sounds thin to you, make the most of it.' Yes, I'll make what little there is to make of it." He did.

Bogie was not the only problem child Chicago artists had to cope with. Heaviest on their collective conscience, perhaps, was the Italian-born Emmanuele Carnavale, a lost soul of a poet. He wrote poems, but also spent frequent spells of time in mental homes. Between these incarcerations he drifted about, asking with increasing urgency for help.

"Oh Mitchie dear," he wrote from a hospital in Duluth, "Didn't you receive a letter in which I asked you for 15 dollars? To pay my next week in the hospital? Mitchie dear, brotherchen, whom should I ask, tell me? I need it . . ." Another, postmarked Italy — Em went back to Italy for a while, though he didn't stay there — "Dear Mitchell: Wasn't I the good boy not to have asked you for money all this time. Don't alarm yourself. I am not out to ask you for money yet, tho I am in dire need of it. I come at the request of a different kind I need a suit of clothes; I go around with a suit that shows my bare ass, and it is quite an indecent affair I haven't a jacket that fits me well and the last suit I wore until it could no longer be worn was given me by Bob McAlmon.

"Any old thing will do, as long as it doesn't show the light across in the posterior portion . . ."

In a letter dated July, 1922, Mitchell wrote to a friend who enquired after the poet:

Em went to the Psychopathic hospital in the winter of 1919-20. At that time he was God or at least he believed it was possible to become God — although we both decided that it was undesirable to become God without also remaining human. And then he had a new scheme of metaphysics — which was very old. Everything was everything. Then every thing was yes and every thing was no. Everything was nothing and nothing was everything. He almost believed himself a new Messiah. But he could also separate himself from these ideas and seemed to be perfectly aware of their psychopathic import. In fact, he told me circumstantially everything that had gone on in his brain from the time when Sherwood Anderson had driven him out of his house because he (Sherwood Anderson) was afraid he himself would go insane from having Em around. — I did not know what happened until Harriet Monroe told me he was quarantined in the Psychopathic Hospital . . .

He took a job in Lincoln Park. He couldn't stand it; begged to be sent to the Dunes. We sent him. He lived there all summer — naked and black — praying and shouting — lived on beans and cherries — scandalizing resorters — begging scraps of food — swimming far into the lake and crying for help. "The insane man sees more clearly," he said.

The first cold day drove him back to town. People gave him clothes and money. He developed a mendicant routine. We knew to a day when he would appear for dinner, cigarettes and a few dollars . . . I suddenly received a letter saying that he was again in the Psychopathic Hospital. This time he barely escaped commitment to an insane asylum. The doctors tried to scare him into being "good!"

Since that time Em has tried to work, but he really can't. It isn't a question of bracing-up — he is burnt-out. His right hand has a continual tremor. He is rational but cannot fix his attention on anything steadily for any length of time. He is restless as a child. He has none of his old pride and will suffer insults without any come-back.

Em has written a few fine poems and one or two reviews for "Poetry" within the last year and he may continue to produce good things from time to time. He associates now almost entirely with "incomplete personalities." You know the kind — Dill Pickle and little theater crowds. Chicago has a "Bohemia" which is several degrees worse than Greenwich Village. It fawns on anyone who shows the slightest degree of brilliance. Em flatters that bunch by associating with them and in return they make him feel a little of his old confidence and superiority . . .

I do not know what you mean by "psychic negligence."
Negligence on whose part? — A man like Em must outwit
society in some way or he will smash . . .

This was written after Dawson had settled for a life of middle-class discipline rather than the Bohemian way. In his
father's law firm, however, he continued to write poetry and
work for the general cause of literature.

"I feel, Mitch," wrote William Carlos Williams from his
New Jersey office, in an undated letter, "that by education, by
tradition, by inclination and training as well as by our present
accidental positions in the world we have a chance to work together with a better chance of success than any two others
in the whole movement. It is up to us. Not that I want to rush
ahead blindly just to do something. That is not my feeling at
all but I have already begun to think with you and that must
lead to a definite plan." Significantly, the movement to which
Williams here refers is not political but artistic, the cause of
modern poetry. The New Jersey doctor and the Chicago lawyer supported it with fervency, in just the same way that people
worked later for or against Marxism.

Modern poetry, modern art of all kinds, was *the* cause of
the day. Not that Williams lived in an ivory tower. In the same
letter he mentions a scare then current, of war with Japan:
". . . if war happens this time I'll enlist (at the first crack of a
gun, I was going to say), But I hate the mere thought of war
now so heartily that I don't know what I'd do . . . I can think
of nothing but Debs in the Levenworth [sic] prison, fool
though he may be, and I feel ashamed of myself. Not that I want
to be a Debs for I have little sympathy with him. I am not a
Bolshevist no matter how I may sympathize with the mob. I
am not like the mob. I am different and only feel for their fight
from a higher plane. That is the puzzle."

CHAPTER 14

Mostly About Vincent

I N NEW YORK the pace was, if possible, even more fervid. There too the law against liquor was broken from the time it went into effect; Greenwich Village, like the Near North Side, was a hunting-ground for those in search of bathtub gin and phony whiskey, and their name was legion, for a lot of erstwhile law-abiding citizens, hurt and bewildered by this official attack on their private habits, turned instinctively to the Village. Belatedly, they felt a sympathy with nonconformism . . . and anyway it was easier to get the stuff down there. Ranks of homecoming soldiers joined them, swelling the throng that trooped downtown every night, past Fourteenth Street to where the fun was.

Even uptowners knew exactly where to go — Barney Gallant's. Barney, a Latvian emigrant who bore the distinction of having shared quarters for a spell with Eugene O'Neill, had become a Bohemian by osmosis. As long as the Liberal Club lived he attended its meetings, but he became a businessman as well, co-owner of a restaurant, the Greenwich Village Inn on Sheridan Square. The Volstead Act seemed to Barney such rank foolishness that he ignored it. Quite openly after the fatal date he continued to serve liquor at his Inn, until — much to his aggrieved surprise — he was arrested and sentenced to thirty days in jail. Barney was popular, and the case aroused a lot of feeling in New York. In the eyes of his many friends, he was the great martyr of the season. After doing his time he went back to being a restaurateur, but, having learned discretion in the Tombs, he now supplied the public with liquor under the counter, like any ordinary bootlegger. Inevitably there were further run-ins with the law, but Barney bit the bullet, took his medicine when he had to, and prospered. In time Barney Gallant with his white tie and tails brought class to the Village, but nobody held it against him. It was felt that he had won his spurs.

Malcolm Cowley, in *Exile's Return*, tells of what it was like for him and the other youths who returned to the Village after the war. He had gone over with the ambulance corps in 1917, and his absence served as a punctuation for a process of change in Bohemia that would not otherwise have been so sharply defined. Before the war, he says, there had been two mingled currents, "two types of revolt, the individual and the social — or the aesthetic and the political, or the revolt against puritanism and the revolt against capitalism — we might tag the two of them briefly as *bohemianism* and *radicalism*." But in pre-war days it had been hard to tell the difference between these two schools of thought: Bohemians read Marx and all radicals had a touch of the Bohemian. They were all fighting for the same cause. "Socialism, free love, anarchism, syndicalism, free verse — all these creeds were lumped together by the public, and all were physically dangerous to practice," says Cowley. He recalls the Evenings at Mabel Dodge's, when Big Bill Haywood talked to poets and Cubist painters, how during the bread riots of 1915 the Wobblies made their headquarters in Mary Vorse's studio on Tenth Street. The Draft Law during the war changed all that, Cowley thinks, because rebels had to divide their ranks. Those who rebelled against puritanism were safe, but the political rebels were endangered. Some yielded and struck their colors by helping the war effort. Some fled to Mexico to get out of being drafted. Some went to Leavenworth. The radical current in the Village almost disappeared: "The Bohemian tendency triumphed in the Village, and talk about revolution gave way to talk about psychoanalysis" — later, as Floyd Dell has pointed out, to give way in its turn to the old talk once more, about revolution. "The *Masses,* after being suppressed, and after temporarily reappearing as the *Liberator,* gave way to magazines like the *Playboy,* the *Pagan* . . . and the *Little Review.*" (That *Playboy,* incidentally, was not at all like today's magazine of the same name.)

Just after the armistice, Cowley recalls, the Village was empty of young men, but soon it filled and overfilled. The Liberal Club, depleted of funds, drew its last breath and died, but two other social centers flourished in its place: the Hell Hole on Sixth Avenue and West Fourth, and the Working Girls' Home at Greenwich Avenue and Christopher Street. "The Hell Hole was tough and dirty; the proprietor kept a pig in the cellar and fed it scraps from the free-lunch counter. The boys in the back room were small-time gamblers and petty thieves, but the saloon was also patronized by actors and writers from the Provincetown Players, which was just around the corner. Sometimes the two groups mingled. The gangsters admired Dorothy Day because she could drink them under the table; but they felt more at home with Eugene O'Neill, who listened to their troubles and never criticized. They pitied him, too, because he was thin and shabbily dressed." But it was in the Working Girls' Home that Cowley was most conscious of the difference between the pre-war Villagers and his own group. "They," the oldsters, wore odd clothes, especially the women, who went in for Dutch bobs, embroidered smocks of vaguely Russian appearance, very short skirts, gray cotton stockings and sandals. Like loyal successors to Henrietta Rodman they didn't wear corsets, and so tended to show signs of pot-belly. "They had a look of unexampled solidity," says Cowley — it was terrifying to see a group of them advancing upon you. However, this costume was not worn by absolutely *every* female Villager. Some went in for tailored suits, and one girl always wore riding boots and brandished a crop. "We," on the other hand, wore ordinary clothes. Cowley's crowd, he says, had never been rebels, never broken with their parents or stalked out of church. His generation were not idealists. "The truth is," he concludes, "that 'we,' the newcomers to the Village, were not bohemians." For that period, at least, they were merely soldiers home from the war, looking for fun; and the Village was full to bursting with them.

*   *   *

If, as Cowley says, the radical element of the Village disappeared during the war, it was not long in making a reappearance when the war was over. No doubt a number of individual radicals were frightened away for good, but the spirit was born again, gathering new adherents. Of course the causes had changed, but there was no dearth of them. Labor still had grievances, the strike weapon was used again, and then, in 1920, there took place an incident that seemed so glaringly unjust as to put all smaller cases in the shade. In April of that year the Massachusetts police arrested two Italian immigrants, Nicola Sacco and Bartolomeo Vanzetti, on suspicion of being implicated in the murder of two guards, during the armed robbery of a factory payroll. The evidence against them was not strong, but they were indeed armed, and they had been in the vicinity when the crime was committed. Another fact the police considered highly suspicious was that the prisoners admitted to being anarchists. Though the two men denied that they were murderers as well, their captors were not inclined to give any anarchist — an Italian anarchist, at that — the benefit of a doubt, and the jury seems to have agreed. Sacco and Vanzetti were tried, found guilty, and sentenced to death.

Some enlightened members of the public took up the cause and agitated for retrial, or, at the very least, repeal of the death sentence, and the prisoners' defending lawyers managed to postpone the execution for seven years, during which time there were countless meetings, lectures and debates held on the subject. In New York, Villagers organized a protest march; Edna St. Vincent Millay was one of the marchers. In spite of all this, Sacco and Vanzetti were executed in 1927. There has never been a conclusive answer to the question of their guilt or innocence, but on one point there can be no doubt: the proceedings were shamelessly biased. As an English journalist, Rupert Furneaux, puts it, "Quite apart from the questions of doubt and delay, the Sacco-Vanzetti case presents many strange features to English eyes: the violent partisanship expressed by racial and political interests; the attempts by the District Attorneys to cajole and coerce witnesses, and the Motions for fresh trial, and the appeals from court to court."

Strange as it may seem, throughout America it was the Bohemian element that showed up best in the sorry business of Sacco and Vanzetti: they combined in protest. It was nothing new that Bohemians should sympathize with revolutionaries, but the widespread sentiment evinced on this occasion was something more than that customary easygoing sympathy. Had Bohemia a social conscience, after all? The Sacco-Vanzetti case would have sorely perplexed Henri Murger.

*   *   *

It was in that spring of 1920 that Edmund Wilson, four years out of Princeton, came home from an extended tour abroad.

Like any other young man with his intellectual leanings, he took an apartment in the Village, and in a novel, *I Thought of Daisy,* and a collection of essays, *The Shores of Light,* he has written a good deal about those youthful days when he was in and out of love with Edna St. Vincent Millay and bought his liquor at the corner drugstore in defiance of Prohibition, this being a Village custom. Of course he was in love with Miss Millay. In his mind, as in the minds of many other young people, Miss Millay *was* the Village. She had already been there for some time and had made her mark. It will be recalled that Edna Millay's poem "Renascence" was in 1912 the cause of sharp controversy over the "Lyric Year" prize. For the ensuing five years the public's wonder did not die down, that a poem so beautiful should have been written by a schoolgirl. Moreover, the situation was appealingly romantic. Edna was one of three sisters who lived with their mother, in very straitened cirumstances, in a small town in Maine: it sounded like the beginning of a fairy tale.

A group of women had organized themselves and obtained a scholarship at Vassar for Edna, but it took them two years to do it, and she did not graduate until 1917, when she was twenty-five. Already she felt old: there was so much she wanted to do in life! She went straight to Greenwich Village from Vassar. Her sponsors, who naturally expected her to embark immediately on a career as a poet, were startled to learn that she wanted to be an actress instead. But so it was: Edna applied at the Provincetown Players for a part in a forthcoming production.

Small, with dark red hair, a lovely voice, and a beauty that seems to have depended much upon her intensity and vivacity, the little Maine girl showed at the first try-out reading that she was at home on the stage. She was immediately accepted for the part. Just as immediately, she and Floyd

Dell fell in love. It was undoubtedly one of the serious passions of Dell's life, and he has never forgotten her: very likely his final irritation and disappointment with Edna Millay constituted one of his reasons — the unsatisfactory quality of temporary love affairs — for abandoning Bohemian ways. Even today, the men of Edna's era think of her with a mixture of fondness and exasperation. For a long time after her departure from the Village, her life of gallantry was hinted at and obliquely referred to. Since her death in 1950 it has been discussed outright, with enough anger and lip-smacking in accompaniment to puzzle modern youngsters. What, they wonder, was all this about?

Surely, even in 1917, few women were wholly faithful to one lover forever and a day — dozens of records testify that they were not, especially in Bohemia. What made the difference with Edna was that she was so frank about herself, at a time when other women were not — frank, that is, in her poetry. (She soon dropped her ambitions for a stage career and returned to writing.) It was the saucy, defiant spirit of the poems that shocked people, though they often memorized the lines for application to their own situations. There was

> I loved you Thursday, yes, but what
> Is that to me?

and the even more memorable one about the candle burning at both ends. It titillated and shocked readers, this spectacle of a girl kissing and telling, and it outraged her lovers, who had until then taken it for granted that it was a man's prerogative to love and leave. Yet they all forgave her: they couldn't help themselves. In *The Shores of Light,* Wilson, who was ardently in love with her, explains why: ". . . her relations with us and her other admirers had . . . a disarming impartiality . . .

when she came to write about her lovers, she gave them so little
individuality that it was usually, in any given case, impossible
to tell which man she was writing about." (Here he gives a
gentler portrait than that of the woman who in *Daisy* is called
Rita Cavanagh, but even his fictional Rita is forgiven by his fictional self when he reflects that she was pestered so unbearably
by suitors that she had to flee to France.)

Max Eastman enters the conversation with an essay of his
own, entitled "My Friendship with Edna Millay." He quotes a
passage of Wilson's in which the other man says that to fall in
love with Edna was an almost inevitable consequence of knowing her. Eastman goes on, "I shall have to confess that I tried to
fall in love with Edna Millay, believing it for a time to be my
romantic destiny, but regretfully failed." It seemed to Eastman that it wasn't so much an intoxicating effect, as Wilson
describes it, that Edna had on people: she seemed rather to
make people tense and self-conscious, as though life "which
had been flowing along naturally enough, had become an
enacted drama." Nor was she voluptuously beautiful — "she
had the legs and, at times, the expression of a maiden aunt."
But her eyes were of an incredible wild gray-green, her torso
was shapely, her voice thrilling. What put off Eastman, he thinks
in retrospect, was her "determination to be a poet, and not
some man's woman or even some child's mother." He adds,
later, "Strength of character is always a trifle alarming." With
this said and out of the way, he thinks that his judgment of
Millay's poetry may be all the more valid, since he saw it plainly,
undistorted by personal passion, and he admires most of it more
than the poems of any of her contemporaries.

Like Rita in Wilson's novel, Edna went to Europe in the autumn of 1920. All in all, she was not a Village resident very long,
at that period or later. Abroad, she was evidently happy for a

time — at least a friend thought so when he saw her briefly in France — but Floyd Dell has told me that she had miserable experiences generally, and had to undergo an abortion. She looked ill and unhappy when she came back in 1923. "That might be the answer," Rita said once when the narrator of Wilson's novel proposed marriage to her, but she didn't accept him, nor any of the others who offered for her hand. So it was with Miss Millay for some time, until, beset with family responsibilities, disenchanted, worrying unduly about her age, it must have been with great relief that she submitted at last, and married. Her choice was Eugen Boissevain, a businessman but no Philistine. Eugen had long been associated with the Village. He liked the atmosphere, and his late wife was very much of the Village: she was Inez Milholland, a strapping, brilliant lawyer who had championed labor and women's rights. But now he took Edna away from the Village, for her health's sake, and they settled on a farm, "Steepletop," in Austerlitz, New York.

When Eastman returned after a long time away from America — two years in Russia and another year on the Riviera — he was delighted to hear of the marriage: he and Boissevain had lived together, and he considered Gene his dearest friend. Max himself had married a Russian girl, Eliana, and the four people saw a lot of each other, most often at "Steepletop." In the early years of the Boissevain marriage, it appeared that Gene was giving Edna just what she needed, security and quiet and happiness. The fairy tale ought to end here, like all proper fairy tales, with the princess living happily ever after, but it did not: there was a long sequel, not quite so roseate. Edna changed, and Eastman describes it: "She seemed to be mysteriously sick a great deal of the time . . . She cultivated for all that it was worth the privilege of being sick." She took to spending most of the day in her bedroom, or if she was downstairs, she would fly up to that room whenever someone arrived unexpectedly, or a guest was noisy. She was, in short, a self-spoiled child who had decided in youth that she was a poet, that she was made of more delicate fiber than other people. "She babied herself and Eugen babied her . . ." Eugen was good, he was devoted, he stood guard over his "child" like a dragon. No poet ever had a more sheltered life, but was that what a poet really needed? Eastman doubts it. Certainly her poetry, after the first collection printed during her early married years, was not as good as it had been. It was not good even before she wrote the worst of the lot, the propaganda she published during the Second World War. And there was another factor contributing to her deterioration, he admits sorrowfully. Edna drank.

So, for that matter, did her husband. Eastman concludes that the pair had gone in too thoroughly for romantic solitude when they bought "Steepletop" and moved away from the world. Up there the quiet evenings, at first so enchanting, inevitably became longer and longer, and reached the stage where "the romance becomes a discipline." The Boissevains, stimulated by liquor, resorted to it more and more. The Boissevain-Eastman combination faded out. As far as Max Eastman is concerned that is the whole story, but Floyd Dell has an additional theory, that during one period when Edna was reputed to be seriously ill she was undergoing treatment for drug-addiction: he thinks it possible that the disintoxication she underwent at that time did not endure.

Edmund Wilson has a bit more of the story to tell. He had paid his duty-call on "Steepletop" soon after the Boissevain marriage, but a long time went by before he saw the pair again. It was 1948, and nineteen years had elapsed, when he went up to the farm a second time. He felt some hesitation about going at all, knowing that he could not honestly

praise Edna's latest poetry. Gene greeted him. When Edna
came into the room Wilson did not recognize her, she was so
changed — "somewhat heavy and dumpy, and her cheeks were
a little florid . . . She was terribly nervous; her hands shook;
there was a look of fright in her green eyes." He saw that Boissevain watched her closely and managed her as if she were a
baby, soothing her when she came near to bursting into tears
over some trifle. Though she quieted down in time, and became more like the girl Wilson had once loved so much, it was a
painful experience, and when he had the news of Edna's death
in 1950, he found himself deliberately thinking not of that last
meeting, but of a description he'd heard from a woman who
remembered seeing her years earlier, running around the corner of MacDougal Street flushed and laughing, hair swinging,
with a laughing Floyd Dell in pursuit — "a glimpse of Edna
as the fleeing and challenging Daphne of her *Figs from Thistles*
poem . . ."

"It was impossible to understand her," said Floyd Dell. "I've
often thought she may have been fonder of women than men."
He sounded wistful, as if that might be the most comforting answer.

CHAPTER 15

The Last Years

" AMERICAN literary men were flocking to Europe like crows in a cornfield during those years of debased currency," said Max Eastman of the days that followed the end of the war. He ought to know: he was there. Malcolm Cowley speaks with even more scorn of the American tourists who "followed the dollar." But the crows and the dollar-followers were not necessarily actuated by pure greed; for years it had been impossible to visit Europe — except of course, as a member of the armed forces — and in America the natives were restless.

Young people naturally longed for the forbidden land where things must be better than they were at home. There was a heightened consciousness of other lands, which owed itself to the returned soldiers whose noses had been rubbed in foreign earth and who could no longer believe that their home towns were the be-all and end-all of life. When Sinclair Lewis's *Main Street* burst on America in 1920, much of its popularity was due to such disenchanted veterans and a number of others who were infected by their discontent. If the great hinterland of the States was really as flat, smug, arid and immovable as Lewis described it — and thousands of Middlewesterners were sure, ashamedly, that they recognized the picture — then the sooner they got out of it the better. The result of all this ferment was a kind of double exodus eastward: those who could went to Europe, and those who couldn't were satisfied to come to Greenwich Village.

Not all of the latter sort were artists. Why, then, the Village? Because Greenwich Village had come to mean more than a mere artist colony. It stood for a fresh start, for cheap living, for liberty. It stood for fun. The little winding streets, the small houses, the quaintly named restaurants and shops, became a symbol of everything a youth might dream of out in Illinois or South Dakota or Oklahoma — gaiety, romance, dissipation — and they came in their hundreds from Illinois and South Dakota and Oklahoma, many without so much as a thought of literature, art, or merely saving the world. Nearly, but not quite, they swamped the serious artists who had not gone to Europe. A large group of painters and sculptors did not emigrate — Art Young, Jo Davidson, William Glackens, Reginald Marsh, George Luks, Al Frueh, Hans Stengel, and John Sloan: though John and his wife Dolly did move ultimately, it was in the opposite direction, to New Mexico. As for writers, they flocked in, more and more and more. What if some of the stars, Kreymborg and Cowley and Edna Millay and many more, did go away? Others took their places, so many of them that today the American writer who has not lived in the Village, even for a short spell, is an exception. As E. B. White wrote,

> In the days of my youth, in the days of my youth,
> I lay in West Tenth Street, writhing with truth.

Only one force pushed these hopefuls out of the magic vicinity — success. Greenwich Village was basically a jousting-ground for beginners and runners-up, not a place in which a man planned to stay forever. Here and there, every so often, a

Villager, after an energetic space of life battling and scrambling and playing and working, discovered that his labor had borne fruit — that he had won recognition and money. This discovery led to a. yearning for space and quiet, which are commodities not easily found below Fourteenth Street. Or the newly success-ful young man might want status, or a garden for his family, or merely a change: for whatever reason, he moved uptown, and though afterwards he might visit the Village to see his friends and favorite bartender, he never again felt quite the same about them. Without admitting it, he suspected that he was superior to the old crowd. Allen Churchill, in *The Im-proper Bohemians,* says that an aroma of failure hung over the Village, and explains it thus: "The solid middle class of America had always looked down on Village life as exclusively for the young, a phase to be lived through quickly and out-grown. Most Village Bohemians had sprung from the solid mid-dle class . . ." The population turnover, especially in the boom years, was rapid. Those who stayed on and on were usu-ally people who would have felt chilly and displaced anywhere else. By the Thirties, a textbook example of such a fixture was Joe Gould.

Bearded, dirty, well-spoken and impish, Joe Gould was a born misfit. The son of a doctor in a small Massachusetts town, he could never find a niche anywhere until he drifted to the Village, where he immediately felt at home. He spent the rest of his life there. With Bogie he frequented the Raven Poetry Circle and other groups, and at first he seemed much like any other Village eccentric, but years passed and Gould became a plain and simple bum. (See Joseph Mitchell's *Joe Gould's Secret* for a detailed account.) In his cleaner days — a term used in a rigidly comparative sense — people invited him to parties where he could eat and drink and hold forth, but as he grew older and dirtier and lousier, free refreshments were hard to find, even though he was a great man for parlor tricks almost to the end: he could dance a special Indian "stomp" or imitate a seagull.

He was believed to be engaged in a monumental work — everybody in the Village heard about Joe Gould's "Oral History of Our Times," which he said he was preserving in thousands of notebooks, jotting down the conversations he overheard in the street and putting them together in a cross-section of society to end all cross-sections of society. It was an arresting idea, which people naturally kept in mind. Mitchell writes that after his death in 1957, persons who had known Gould well spent a long time trying to find these notebooks, but Mitchell himself had a particular reason for doubting that they would ever be found. During Gould's lifetime he tried hard and vainly to trace even a few of those books, until at last he came to the conclusion that there weren't any. Gould practically admitted this. The truth is, though he may have started out genuinely intending to write the Oral History, his energy flagged. He was disorganized by nature. What little he did put down he repeated again and again. We might call it the longest mental block in the annals of literature, except that Gould can't be said to have joined the literary ranks at all. He left no cache of records, no small portion of the Oral History. His life's only accomplishment was that he lived it.

Flawed characters such as Gould's belong to Bohemia even though they are only at the outer fringe. They orbit the center at such long distance that they are barely within sight and sound of the true, working artists. Yet they go on, held by some magnetism, some dimly felt sense on both sides of kinship. Gould, even when his mental lesions overwhelmed him, still chose in his dream-world to be a writer, not a big-business millionaire, not Napoleon, and the Village recognized his right to be there. The Village accepted him. Even Villagers couldn't like him at the end. He was a pest, a nuisance and a dead-beat. Still, he was one of theirs: he was a nonconformist. They realized instinctively that those who believe in making life a kind of *Salon des Refusées* cannot pick and choose their outcasts.

Another example of Village tolerance is the Baroness Elsa von Freytag von Loringhoven. A refugee from Germany, she was a model for a while, and then began writing poetry, when she became the special charge of Margaret Anderson and Jane Heap in the *Little Review* office above the Washington Square Bookshop, before 1933 when they moved to Paris. In any society but the Village's the Baroness would have been certified. Among other eccentricities she loved to wear weirdly outlandish clothes. Sometimes she shaved and lacquered her head, and at least once wore a coal-scuttle upside down as a hat. Whenever the magazine staff found themselves unexpectedly out of stamps, they knew that the Baroness had stolen them to paste on her face for beauty-patches. In later years she returned to her native Germany, and there she actually *was* certified. The poor creature ended her life by suicide.

*   *   *

The Bohemian who tires of life, who gives up by retirement into insanity or suicide, is not necessarily one who has failed in what he wanted to express. There are people who refuse to conform to convention but are never happy in a state of defiance either. Even when such a man has won an amount of independence the weight of opposition seems to him too strong to bear, and he yields at the very moment when he might be considered victorious. This may explain Hart Crane, but we can't be sure, for the emotions and motivations of an alcoholic are impossible to follow.

He was never widely known, but he was getting to that point when he ended it all. Harold Hart Crane was his name as a boy, before he lopped it. He was born in 1899, in Garretsville, Ohio. His parents were on bad terms, and Harold sided with his mother. He was a sensitive child, not at all the kind of son his father wanted. Crane the elder was a prosperous candy manufacturer with a forceful personality, and Harold hated and feared him. Mrs. Crane left her husband while the boy was still a minor, so that though the home was dissolved, Harold still had to depend on his father for support. On two occasions he tried to work in Crane's firm, as his father thought he should, but the attempts were not successful. His ambition to be a poet was not calculated to make father-son relations any easier. "Why can't you do an honest job of work and write poetry in your spare time?" demanded Mr. Crane.

Hart broke loose from the candy factory and went on to many jobs. He was a mechanic bench-hand, a shipyard worker, a book clerk, an advertising writer, a newspaper reporter — and, just as his father had suggested, he wrote poetry in his spare time. This he placed in various magazines, the *Seven Arts* among them. Pound included him in his "Imagists" anthology. When Crane moved to Greenwich Village, as he did just before the outbreak of the war, he found it a tremendous experience. He was thrilled and delighted to live among the magazine offices and publishing houses that had always made up his inner life, and the disruption of all this by the war seemed to him a personal outrage. He was not drafted in time to go abroad: he was sent to Ohio instead, to do clerical work for the Army. Then the war ended and he came back to the Village, looking for a job, and Margaret Anderson put him in charge of the *Little Review*'s advertising — a kindly deed, but one with no common sense to recommend it. Hart had rooms upstairs over the office, but he sometimes encountered the Baroness on the stairs, and she so frightened him that he ran away. Imperceptibly, the *Review* job faded out.

Hart's private life, too, was unsatisfactory. He was a homosexual, which is an uneasy thing to be in any place, even the Village. He embarked on one love affair after another, always hoping it would be a permanent relationship and always disappointed, until ultimately he became cynical, and took his sex pleasures wherever he could, usually down at the waterfront among sailors. Sometimes he seems to have had sentimental afterthoughts even then, as the incident of Claire Spencer hints. In his young days, when he and his mother first left home, Mrs. Crane had made friends with Claire's mother, and their two children often went out walking and talking together. Claire, who became a successful novelist, married Harrison Smith, the publisher. Years had passed since those walks with Hart Crane, and it can be imagined how astonished she was when he suddenly upbraided her for deserting him, marrying another man, and ruining his life. Poor Miss Spencer could not account for these unreasonable accusations, but Crane was often unreasonable, especially after his mother died. It was then that he started to drink heavily.

Hart began to wander. In the late Twenties, the boom years, a writer could pick up enough to live on, even when he was not making a fortune, and Crane was no longer beset by poverty. He moved about, not staying in Paris like the self-styled exiles, but remaining there long enough to be a part of the group of poets and artists who contributed to *transition,* described by Cowley as the magazine of the exiles, and as "angry, sophisticated, high-spirited, tired, primitive, expressionist, objective, subjective, incoherent, flat . . ." anything, in fact, that the editors felt like being for that issue, at that moment. (Crane was particularly friendly there with Harry and Caresse Crosby, the glamorous pair who, though splashily picturesque and indubitably American, do not rate a position in America's Bohemia, strictly speaking, because they stayed away most of the time.) In America, Hart lived like most of his circle, spending much of the time outside of New York, roughing it in the country. Cowley remembers that he often passed Sunday afternoon in a place in New York State just across the Connecticut border with eight or ten friends — the Allen Tates, the Matthew Josephsons, the Cowleys, Robert Coates and others — in an unpainted, unremodeled farmhouse that his friend Bill Brown and Bill's wife were doing up, with Hart as carpenter's helper. Usually the party played croquet or just sat around drinking hard cider. Hart "would laugh twice as hard as the rest of us and drink at least twice as much hard cider, while contributing more that his share of the crazy metaphors and overblown epithets," but after a while he would grow quiet and slip away to his room. Soon the others would hear his phonograph playing a Cuban rumba, while the typewriter clacked. An hour later he would come out with a few sheets of manuscript, his eyes burning, his hair on end, too excited to listen to comment on the work, though he asked everyone to read it. Cowley adds that this pretty picture was not by any means the whole story of each poem: he had probably worked for weeks on it before he took to the cider, and he went on working afterwards — "painfully, persistently — and dead sober." Those were the days when he wrote most of the poems for his second book, *The Bridge.*

After the poems had been sent off for publication, Hart Crane needed more alcohol — so much, says Cowley, that he wasn't able to write down his ideas. "He drank in Village speakeasies and Brooklyn waterfront dives; he insulted everyone within hearing or shouted that he was Christopher Marlowe; waking after a night spent with a drunken sailor, he drank again to forget his sense of guilt." He was a hard man to handle, though between bouts he remained the person his friends loved. "Scenes, shouts, obscenities, broken furniture were the commonplaces of an evening with Hart, and for a long time nobody did anything about it . . . The 1920s had their moral principles, one of which was not to pass moral judgments on other people, especially if they were creative artists." Then, at the end of 1929, early in December, the Crosbys arrived in New York to pay one of their infrequent visits to their native land. Hart Crane gave them a welcome-home party in his room in Brooklyn Heights — he was very fond of the couple, who had encouraged him and published much of his work. About a week later Harry Crosby, who had borrowed an apartment from a friend, was found dead in bed there with the body of a young woman he had always called the Fire Princess. He had evidently shot her through the head and then turned the gun on himself. He left no letter, no word of explanation, and had not given any sign of special mental depression, but then Harry Crosby had never been an obvious man.

The Bridge was well received when it appeared, in 1930. Hart Crane was now accepted as one of the country's outstanding poets, but those who knew him realized that he was not working as he had done before. For the most part he stopped seeing his old friends, out of his sense of guilt. In 1934 he went to Mexico; on the way back he jumped from the ship's deck into the sea and drowned.

A volume of his letters, edited by Brom Weber, appeared in 1953. The public's reaction, such as it was, indicated that to many Crane was still a mystery they had no interest in probing. To quote one review: "Crane all too well fulfilled the popular picture of the Greenwich Village Bohemian. He drank to excess, was chronically in debt, dissipated in every direction, quarreled with his friends and relatives, and openly exploited his sexual aberrations . . . The recipients of some of Crane's letters have their courage with them in permitting the publication of the letters unretouched . . . Fortunately Crane was not simply erratic. He had genius."

*   *   *

The early Twenties in the Village had still been a time of innocence. In spite of Barney Gallant's frequent arrests, in spite of the drugstore gin and the Pagan Routs and the carefully unmarried ménages, there was to be found in those days an atmosphere genuinely that of a village, the sort of informality that can exist only where people know one another and respect each other's foibles. But things changed fast. As a bootlegging center Greenwich Village was the scene of parties that grew wilder and wilder through the years. Early settlers argued that the offenders were merely visitors from uptown, but the statement soon ceased to hold water. Residents misbehaved as badly as visitors. Nightclubs with determinedly quaint names sprang up everywhere. Tarts moved into the neighborhood, having found it a good hunting-ground for moneyed men who came slumming. University boys rushed to the Village to sow their oats. It got so that a man who came into his office with a hangover had only to say, in explanation, "I was down at the Village last night," to get sympathetic grins and nudges from his colleagues. The Village was no longer the colony of simple living and high thinking it had once been. Yet it was still the Village, a lodestar for the young, which is why Robert Clairmont chose it for his residence.

Clairmont was a good-looking young man from Pittsburgh, an aspiring poet who had an astounding stroke of luck. At the age of fifteen, working outside his school hours as a lifeguard

at a local swimming pool, he taught an elderly gentleman to
swim. The elderly gentleman died a few years later, when Clairmont was working his way through college, leaving the youth
half a million dollars. Clairmont resigned from his classes but
did not immediately plunge into an orgy of spending. Instead,
he studied the ways of money and learned to play the stock
market to such good effect that by the time he tackled Greenwich Village he had parlayed his inheritance to double the
original amount. For once the newspapers did not exaggerate
when they hailed him as the Millionaire Playboy; Robert *was* a
millionaire, and certainly a playboy as well. It was 1926 when
he appeared, moving into an apartment near Washington
Square that had formerly been occupied by President Wilson's
daughter Margaret. Very soon word got round the Village that
a miracle had taken place, that the handsome, genial young
newcomer was as openhanded and hospitable as he was charming. Vast numbers of free-loaders hurried to make his acquaintance and drink his liquor. Clairmont, never averse to a carouse,
outdid almost everyone around him in drinking and wench-
ing, but sometimes the noise was too much even for him and he
would go away for a while, leaving the party uninterrupted.
Occasionally he wandered up to Harlem, listening to the Negroes' music, which fascinated him. At other times he behaved
like an uptown playboy and hit the high spots on Broadway.
Girls rushed to his arms in droves. His friends numbered themselves in the hundreds, but out of all these he was probably
genuinely friendly with only a few — Maxwell Bodenheim, a
wild Irishman named John Rose Gildea, the poet Eli Siegel,
and another poet, Tom Boggs. Siegel was a leading spirit at
forums where poets would read their works aloud and argue
them out; Bodenheim often attended these meetings. Without
much difficulty they prevailed together upon Clairmont to fi-

nance a kind of little magazine, the first issue to appear on April
Fool's Day. *New Cow of Greenwich Village*, as the periodical
was called, was a great success. Somehow amid all this activity
Clairmont found time to write his own poems. The opening
one in his *Quintillions*, published by Dial in 1928, is titled
"Sadness Couplet":

> They tell who walk in love and all alone
> A mechanical piano has a sadness all its own.

Clairmont had been living in the Village only a little more
than a year when an eerie incident took place in his apartment.
The painter Hans Stengel had borrowed the rooms in the customary informal fashion of Clairmont's friends, in order to give
a party. Clairmont himself was away, probably having departed
on purpose to avoid the racket. What followed was told to me
by a girl who was Stengel's particular friend at the time.

"He'd been perfectly normal as I remember, and there was
nothing different about him that night. It was a regular Village party — we used to go to a lot of them, wherever we heard
one was being held; you know how it is. I was in the corner with
somebody or other, drinking and having a good time, not paying any attention to Hans, and then somebody yelled that he
couldn't get the bathroom door open, and we all helped pull
it. There was Hans hanging dead. He'd certainly done it deliberately. He'd rigged up the thing like a kind of booby-trap,
on purpose to make it hard for anybody to get in, and he'd
drawn a picture of himself hanging — a *funny* picture, my God,
with his tongue out — oh, it was awful. And we had to get him
down. Then the police came and asked questions all night. I
can tell you, it sobered me up for days."

Clairmont had to move. Otherwise life went on as before,
with a bow in the direction of Hans Stengel's ghost. In an obitu-

ary notice, Edmund Wilson — who had been a friend of the suicide's — surmised that the artist had lost heart because he
could never earn money doing serious work, at which he was
really good, but had to support himself with piddling little illustrations. I asked Stengel's former girl friend her opinion of
this theory and she said it simply wasn't true. Stengel had been
perfectly all right, she insisted. "If you ask me," she said, "he
killed himself to see what it was like to be dead."

*   *   *

Because Clairmont was attractive, rich, and a poet, girls threw
themselves in his path. They did the same with Bodenheim
because he was attractive and a poet, though not rich. It is implied in a gay little inscription written by Clairmont in a pres-
entation copy of *Quintillions* — "To Maxwell Bodenheim,
roué of the first order, a dangerous rival in affairs of the heart"
— that more than once they stalked the same quarry, but the
records don't bear out the implication. We hear little or nothing specific about Clairmont's girls except that there were lots
of them. Some of Bodenheim's, however, are named, described,
almost dissected for posterity. Many a reporter is still living
who can look back to Bogie's banner year, 1928, when it seemed
for a while as if no week could pass without some distracted female trying to kill herself for love of him.

For instance, there was Gladys Loeb, an eighteen-year-old
fugitive from the Bronx. She loved Bodenheim and lived with
him for a little while, then he discarded her. Gladys went back
to her room, turned on the gas, and passed out with his picture
held to her breast, but the landlady got there in time to open
the windows and save her lodger's life. Dr. Loeb, Gladys's
father, came downtown to fetch her home and had to fight his
way through the crowd of reporters who were writing down

everything his daughter had to say about her tragic, hopeless passion. The story had only a couple of months to subside before another girl, Virginia Drew, twenty-two years old, was making news through *her* love for Bogie. She too had been thrown out by him, and had talked to various people about it. Then she disappeared. Her relatives were still looking for her when Bodenheim went out of town in search of coolness and rest, without leaving an address behind. There would have been nothing particularly sinister about this omission in the ordinary way, but the police pricked up their ears when Virginia's body was found in the East River, for her death had apparently taken place soon after she was last seen in Bodenheim's hotel lobby. As the poet later explained, they had talked at length that night, and when she left he felt assured that she would not, after all, make away with herself as she had threatened to do. Further investigation proved that Virginia had left the hotel alone and that Bogie could not possibly have done away with her, but in the meantime his hideaway had been discovered — it was a cottage in Provincetown — and the gentlemen of the press set out immediately to corner him. So did Gladys Loeb; at least her father leaped to this conclusion when he found her room empty the morning after the news of Bogie's whereabouts was published. Dr. Loeb went straight off to Provincetown himself, arriving more or less at the same time the reporters did, and, as it happened, a good half-hour before Gladys got there. Bodenheim, who hadn't yet heard of Virginia's death, was annoyed by all the excitement, especially when Dr. Loeb demanded that he unhand Gladys. Bogie didn't have Gladys. As a matter of strange fact, he had no girl at all in the shack. He had just demonstrated this, throwing open his door to one and all, when Gladys arrived.

After a lot of talk, everybody adjourned to New York, where

a chastened Gladys was dragged back to the Bronx, and Bogie returned to his hotel room. Again he was the topic of the day: his name was in headlines everywhere. Then came yet one more addition to the saga. One of the Village "characters" was a girl named Aimee Cortez, whose habit at parties, whenever things got going with a swing, was to pull off her clothes and dance. As we know, Villagers were traditionally indulgent to the mentally unbalanced. Their attitude toward Aimee Cortez was not only kind but admiring; a lot of people called her the Mayoress of Greenwich Village. Now, Aimee had no particular connection with Bodenheim. She was not one of his retinue. Nevertheless she seems to have been fired by all the newspaper hoo-ha with a spirit of emulation. She chose Gladys Loeb as her model, and used gas. She too was found in a gas-filled room, holding to her heart a photograph of Bogie, but unlike Gladys, Aimee was dead when the landlady got there.

*   *   *

During his visits to Harlem, Clairmont made friends with many of the musicians, and conceived a warm admiration for the work of William Christopher Handy. In Handy's autobiography, *Father of the Blues*, he tells of his friendship with Clairmont. In the earlier days of their acquaintance, when they met casually and talked now and then, Handy had no idea that Clairmont — always hatless, usually wearing a brown shirt with no tie — had money. He put him down in his mind as a penniless artist or poet like many others who strolled in to listen to music. One day, when Handy was speaking idly to Clairmont of general conditions, he mentioned that he was in very low water and wasn't sure what his next step would be. In reply, Clairmont made a suggestion so unusual that the musician thought for a minute that he must be joking: Why didn't Handy give a concert at Carnegie Hall? Handy stared at Clairmont. In the Twenties,

jazz was never heard or even mentioned in Carnegie Hall, which
was dedicated to classical music. Not that Handy didn't feel for
himself much as this young poet seemed to feel — that his music was good, certainly good enough for the Carnegie. But there
was a bigger obstacle than prejudice against jazz: how could he
possibly finance such an undertaking even if it were permitted?
He said this.

"Well, let's see," said Clairmont. "How much do you think
it would cost?"

Handy said it couldn't possibly be less than five thousand dollars, and then, to his amazement, the young man in the brown
shirt said *he* would provide the money. He did, too. The concert took place and made musical history in New York. "I had
entertained an angel unawares and the five thousand dollars
was a gift from him," said Handy.

The famous date of "blue" Monday — October 29, 1929 —
began that disastrous week for the New York stock market, the
week that ultimately plunged the Western world into a long-
time depression. Up in Harlem the denizens read the first news
of the crash with varying sentiments but not much personal interest. What was Wall Street to them? What if a lot of white
stockbrokers *were* ruined? But Handy grew alarmed as the
days went on and the reporters, looking for human-interest
stories, found the fate of Robert Clairmont good for columns of
copy. It was said that the millionaire playboy had lost a fortune
estimated at $986,000 within the week. It was said that he was
standing in the breadline, along with many other once rich men.
Handy set out for the Village welfare center to find his former
benefactor, and after a long search ran him to earth — but not
in the breadline: Robert Clairmont had found a job with the
city authorities, and was giving out food vouchers. He was glad
to see Handy anyway. That night and several nights following
he slept at the musician's house, returning to his Village job

every morning. He didn't fade out of the scene immediately: at the end of a month's waiting, when it became evident that the market was not going to revive for a long, long time, he took his last thousand dollars and blew it on a big binge with his cronies, a ball at Webster Hall. Whatever reactions may have been evinced by other big losers, Clairmont remained unruffled — "the same smiling, modest man as before," said Handy admiringly.

Robert Clairmont never went back to the Village to live, though he kept in touch, writing poetry and for a while editing the magazine *Pegasus*. Today he lives quietly and comfortably on the West Side.

*   *   *

Though the depression era seemed endless to those living through it, in fact it lasted only ten years, or less than a sixth of Bodenheim's life, and we might well wonder why it should have had such a lasting effect on him. In the Twenties, before the crash, he was at the top of his career, occupying a fair if not top position among American poets. The notoriety of his affairs was not responsible for this — it was his work that earned him some amount, at least, of dignity. Other poets have scaled higher summits, but Bogie did pretty well. In 1926 and 1927, Edmund Wilson reviewed Bodenheim's writing; though he didn't like it very much he gave it a fair amount of respect — "though his books are rather disappointing when we set out to read them through, he appears to excellent advantage in the selection made by Mr. Conrad Aiken . . ." The lean years, however, brought an end to this quasi-respectability. Bogie emerged from the distressed decade a bum and seems not to have made any effort to become anything else for the rest of his life. He panhandled in the Village, haunting any restaurant that would permit his presence, offering to sell poems which he pretended to dash off then and there, or leaflets on which earlier compositions were printed.

"They weren't really his own poems, not toward the end," said one old Villager, discussing the case. "I happen to know the guy who wrote them for him. Bodenheim would buy about a hundred at a time, and peddle them . . . He was a pest. If you saw him coming you crossed the street."

Between forays he spent much time in the alcoholics ward at Bellevue. A grotesque figure who had long since lost his good looks, with cheeks fallen above toothless gums, unshaven face and unspeakable clothes, he yet, at the age of sixty, found a woman to marry him. This was his third wife, twenty-nine-year-old Ruth Fagin, who was not bad looking and who had taken a university degree, but whose career of teaching and newspaper work had often been interrupted by mental break-downs. After their marriage, Bodenheim and Ruth lived in the manner to which he had become accustomed, cadging money or drinks. Occasionally Ruth picked up men to sleep with, or Bogie found them for her. The two stuck together. They fought each other, cursed each other, but helped each other too, sharing whatever dingy shelter they could find at night. Into this squalid Eden came the serpent Weinberg, a dishwasher of twenty-five or so whose record of mental institutions was even longer than Ruth's. He was attracted to her, and hung around the couple until Bodenheim grew jealous. Jealousy seems ir-rational in a ponce; perhaps Bogie simply didn't like Weinberg. The night of February 6, 1954, was cold and wet, and the Bo-denheims were facing the unpleasant prospect of spending it out of doors when Weinberg happened along to suggest that they come home with him to his room. Against Bodenheim's inclination they accepted the invitation. In the room, Boden-heim settled down to read. Perhaps his wife and Weinberg thought him sunk in a stupor, or perhaps they were so befuddled themselves that they forgot he was there at all. They began to make love. Bodenheim ran at them furiously, and Weinberg shot him dead. Ruth then attacked Weinberg: he stabbed her to death. The police caught up with him very quckly, and he told the whole story, which the newspapers ran with huge headlines. Most people were surprised to learn from these reports that Bogie was only sixty-four. They had thought him much older: younger readers, indeed, had taken it for granted that he was as old as the Village itself.

When you think about it, this was a poor reward for Bodenheim's toughness. It *was* toughness of a sort, to have weathered, however badly, the storm in New York that followed Black Monday. At that time most of his contemporaries bowed to fate and went away from the Village, usually away from New York altogether, and probably saved themselves from the corrosive experience of poverty that pushed him off balance altogether. So many of the transplanted had departed that it was possible once more to look at the genuine, indigenous Villagers, the Italians and Greeks who had found it for themselves as a run-down, low-rent district they could afford to live in. The natives too felt the pinch — everybody did — but even times as bad as those couldn't last forever, and five or six years after the Crash the Village showed signs of life, as if blood were running in veins long frozen. The streets stirred. A few tourists came in, poking inquisitive noses into restaurant doors. Those Bohemians who had seen out the Depression woke up and stretched, like lizards after a particularly cold winter. The Village regained some of its luster, but was never again to be quite like its old self. Noises sounded like echoes, and even in the merriment there was an acrid tinge of imitation. It was now all too evident that somewhere along the way springs had broken.

CHAPTER 16

The Real Thing?

I T WAS spring in 1964 when I looked for today's Bohemia in San Francisco.

"Bohemians. Well now, let me see," said the first man I asked. "I'll tell you what we can do. My grandmother used to know a lot of artists. I'll call her up and — "

"Thanks, but let's do that later," I said. "Just now it's modern Bohemia I'm interested in."

"Oh. Well, I'm afraid I couldn't — "

My next friend suggested that I go to the library. But I'd read most of the pertinent books, I said: I wanted to know about contemporary Bohemian life. I was not surprised that he couldn't help either, because I'd already learned that people everywhere tend to connect Bohemia with the past, not the present. The reason is probably that Murger's book is more than a century old, and Americans don't like old words. Even for old ideas they want new terms, or misapplied ones such as "momentarily" instead of "in a moment." I should have said beatniks, or beats, instead of Bohemians, as a newspaperman finally told me.

"They're what you want," he assured me, for I was hesitating, thinking that the beats were probably merely a sub-group. "Mind you, if you're looking for old-time Bohemianism you can find that too — California's got everything. Try Sausalito."

Just to make sure, I did try Sausalito. I called on the leading painter of the colony, an elderly Hungarian who used to be well known as a modern in Paris and London. That was before the war. Now he lives on a derelict houseboat, one of a fleet of similar craft occupied by friends and colleagues. We sat in the saloon-studio among scattered paints and canvases. "Don't they call you the Mayor of Sausalito?" I asked, and he laughed.

"If they do, it's because I organized this crowd of us who live on the boats. We had to defend ourselves against some members of the city council, businessmen you know, who don't like artists. It makes them angry that we aren't occupying any land and so don't have to pay taxes, so they tried to get us out by condemning the boats, calling the region a health hazard, all those dirty tricks. But we organized. We fought them back, and finally convinced the majority that if they got rid of us they'd destroy one of the main tourist attractions of the town." Like Carmel, I said to myself, where the artists had to come down out of their ivory tower and mix into local politics. "You've seen the Marina, I suppose? The Bay Road?" asked my host.

Yes, I had; it was impossible to miss it. What must once have been a charming little road along the waterfront was now one of those overcrowded, buzzing thoroughfares that are a feature of all pleasure-resorts. A curved line of liquor stores, supermarkets and quaintish gift shops was all one could see from the vantage point of the ceaseless procession of cars. But those giftshops are what saved the houseboat brigade of Sausalito, because Americans on holiday, who used to buy only antique lamps and bits of petrified wood, have now started buying paintings as well. The boom began when they read about fortunes being made overnight in the world of art. Sausalito needs her painters.

I took my leave, walking down the narrow planking that connected the studio to land. On other boats I saw signs of life; women in slacks, bringing home paper bags of food, and men in paint-smeared clothes taking the air on deck. It looked familiar, but clearly it wasn't the whole story of Bohemia in California. I must go on searching.

That night the newspaperman took me on a tour of the city's night life, or an important part of it — one place after another of the kind described as "gay bars," where homosexuals meet and relax. There were a lot of them, these bars, all decorously run: no activity apart from desultory drinking, save for quiet picking-up, or cruising. Only one that we visited had as much as a show for the clients, which consisted of a series of numbers much alike, men dressed as women who sang and danced. None of the performers pretended to be pretty; there was nothing like the costumes and make-up that characterized a drag show. All of them were possessed of a spirit of savage mockery; I had the impression that they had gone out of their way to look as ugly as Dames in English Christmas pantomimes. But then it was no use trying to be pretty, since a city ordinance evidently insisted that such transvestite entertainers wear weird undergarments like black BVDs, with long sleeves and pants. The effect of this black knitted material behind spangled dresses was indescribable.

Yet I felt that the BVDs didn't fully account for the men's attitude of mincing anger. They were chronically angry, and afraid as well. They were there because San Francisco, for them and during that year, happened to be the right place; for the time being, the police were not bothering them as much as their colleagues would have done elsewhere. A lot of homosexuals keep themselves advised as to the situation in various states and travel accordingly, the law forever yapping in their tracks.

There are many pitfalls. In San Francisco it would not have done, for example, for two of them to dance together — that was forbidden; that would bring the law down on the place in no time. In New York, dancing together was not forbidden, but there were other oppressive rules in Now York, and for the moment San Francisco was better. Thousands of lives are governed and hectored by these legal oddities.

It grew late. Sitting in the fifth or sixth bar, eyes and lungs smarting from smoky air, stomach rebelling against too much Scotch, depressed by man's cruelty to man, I thought deep thoughts. Like any other minority, faggots have their place in Bohemia, because Bohemia is a refuge for people who can't get along in conventional society. Just the same, faggots were not all there was to see of San Francisco's Bohemia. I would certainly turn my attention to the beatniks, but first I wanted a good night's sleep, for gay bars are far from gay, and I was tired. I had just reached this conclusion when one of the boys, a nice-looking nineteen-year-old, sat down next to me and said, with a wise smile,

"Are you really studying Bohemia, Miss Hahn, or are you just having a ball?"

Having a ball? Before I disgraced myself by bursting into tears, I said goodnight.

*   *   *

"Big Daddy's the man to see," said my adviser. "Eric Nord's his real name. He used to be all mixed up with the beats of Grand Avenue at North Beach — that is, when the beats were there. You don't find anything like the crowd there used to be around, though. Sooner or later you'll want to see the City Lights Bookstore, but find Nord first and ask him how come his followers were all run out of town. I believe they've got together

at Venice now, near Los Angeles, but Eric came back. He's tending bar at Mike's Place on Broadway, east of Columbus."

Mike's Place was one of those big restaurant-cum-bars characteristic of San Francisco, where they used to build as if space
would never be a problem in the whole wide world. I got there
early in the afternoon when it was nearly empty. The bartender shook his head.

"He doesn't work here any more, but if you stick around he'll
probably be in for coffee."

After twenty minutes or so, when the place was filling up,
he nodded to me and indicated a group that had taken a table
near the front window. A tall, broad man with a fair beard,
wearing a beret on his balding head, stood up when I asked for
Big Daddy, and acknowledged that he was it. He had a soft
voice and gentle manners, and asked me to join the others, a
dark, fierce-eyed man whose voice was not fierce, who said he
was a poet at one of the universities, and a young Negro in a soft
hat.

"Yes, most of the crowd left town a long time ago," said Nord.
"A lot of them are in Venice, and some in Big Sur. I'm getting
out again myself pretty soon."

The poet soon took his leave, but the Negro stayed with us for
a couple of hours more. We wandered to another big bar where
a few people played coin-in-the-slot machines far back in the
shadowy rear. Up at the front there was a milk bar where sandwiches were for sale. Two high-school girls in short skirts, carrying books, came in and bought sandwiches, staring round-eyed
at Eric Nord, giggling to attract his attention, giggling even
more hysterically when he invited them to join us. They sat
down, ate their sandwiches, gasped a few remarks, and hurried
away. An adventure had been achieved. Then the Negro, too,
went away.

"It was the papers that named me Big Daddy," said Eric. "You may have read about my pad where the kids used to gather." I had, though not in the papers. Before going to look him up I read *The Real Bohemia* by Francis J. Rigney and L. Douglas Smith, which told much of the story and described Eric's pad as "a kind of combination USO and private home" in a warehouse in the district known as North Beach. The main room, fifty feet long, contained about a dozen beds and mattresses. "The arrangement displeased the Fire, Health, and Police Departments, who said it was a firetrap, a health hazard, a source of juvenile delinquency and further, an unlicensed night club: true, Nord asked a donation of one dollar on admission," said the authors indignantly, but "Eric's Pad was not a disease source, there was little to burn, and a uniformed policeman stood at the door, checking I.D. cards."

"We weren't doing anybody harm," said Eric Nord. "We'd talk and play jazz records and dance, what's wrong with that? But there was a lot of prejudice." The records bear out this modest complaint. So hostile were the newspapers that after a poetry reading in San Francisco, Allen Ginsberg wrote an open letter, phrases of which are significant: ". . . There was no need to insult the audience by calling them 'long-hairs (mostly uncombed) . . . that could be shocked only by the sight of a hair oil bottle' . . . The newspaper cult of sadistic contempt for the egghead is not appropriate on the *Chronicle* front page."

According to Rigney and Smith, the campaign against San Francisco's new Bohemia started in 1957 when about eighty Bohemians were living in the neighborhood of a North Beach bar called The Place, their social gathering-spot. As we know, Bohemians have been a part of the San Francisco scene almost as long as the word has been in use, but before the depression they favored other districts. Only after the Wall Street crash did they discover the Beach with its low rents. Perhaps this change of habitat disturbed the non-Bohemians of the town, reminding them, as it were, of the presence among them of nonconformists: at any rate they began watching the new artist colony suspiciously. Even before the beats gained notoriety, the press was running heavily ironical articles about the Beach. Then came Kerouac's novel *On the Road,* which first attracted San Franciscans because of its local allusions and then shocked them severely. Next, Allen Ginsberg's book *Howl* appeared, published in their own city by Lawrence Ferlinghetti; both Ginsberg and Ferlinghetti were promptly tried on charges of obscenity. The public asked itself indignantly, what was this nest of perverts they were nourishing in their collective bosom? Newspapers were more than ready to tell them. In May, 1958, the *Examiner* ran a series of sensational articles about the Beach community, and the police evidently got orders from on high soon afterwards to do something about it. Not being quite sure what it was they were to do, they let a month go by during which nothing was accomplished but the examination of a number of liquor licenses, the uttering of vague threats, and the charging of Eric Nord with not having enough garbage cans. You can't pull a man in because he wears a beard or doesn't work hard, but it was galling to the police to look at a jaunty beat and know in their hearts that he probably used pot from time to time.

The month passed, and in June they got their chance when a drunk fell off the roof of Eric's Pad and was killed. To be sure, he wasn't a beat — just an ordinary drunk — but it was enough. Then Providence gave them even more ammunition. The very next night the drunk's girl friend picked up a psychopathic Negro sailor, who took her into an alley, raped her and killed her. Who could want more? POLICE CRACK DOWN ON BEAT GEN-ERATION, said the newspapers with rare accuracy. A number of arrests were made — for drunkenness, resisting arrest, obscenity. Few convictions followed, but the arrests continued nevertheless. Many of the police were privately, personally aggravated by a situation that could not be declared illegal — the fact that large numbers of Negroes mixed with whites in Beach bistros — and they made their disapproval known in as many roundabout ways as they could devise. Their biggest triumph was to dispossess Eric Nord of his pad, and to arrest him for having held a public dance without a permit.

Eric and I had dinner at an Italian place. "The town got sore at me all over again, this time on account of my wife," he said. "After we were married her parents came down and made a row, and it turned out she was a good deal younger than she'd claimed to be. I guess we'd committed an offense by marrying without their consent. Her father made a complaint to the police accusing me of seducing a minor and all that. He made her come home with him, but she kept running away and coming back to me. I didn't want it, I didn't want any trouble. There was a lot of adverse publicity." He shook his head at the offer of a glass of wine, and ate a stick of celery instead. Then he brightened. "I'm hoping to get hold of a little island in the West Indies I've heard about, where some of us could start a nudist colony. We practiced nudism here for a while until the police warned us. I'm crazy about nudism."

After dinner we went to see Woody Allen at the hungry i, not so much because of Allen — though he was wonderful — as to give me a chance to look in person at the place that introduced Mort Sahl to the world. Eric said that San Francisco was eagerly waiting for the appearance at Off Broadway, a few nights later, of Lenny Bruce. The late Bruce was very popular, but that wasn't the chief reason for the excitement. The police had been alerted, and it was rumored that hundreds of them were lying in wait, ready to pounce on him at the slightest opportunity. In other states the entertainer had already been warned against the

use of obscene words in his act, and the San Francisco public
looked forward to a showdown in the gladiatorial arena. Next
day I heard more about Bruce from Ralph J. Gleason, columnist
for the San Francisco *Chronicle* and a great jazz fan. Lenny
Bruce was one of his chief enthusiasms, as witness an article he
wrote for the magazine *Contact 5* in June, 1960:

TOTAL SATIRE: The Comedy of Dissent.

> Lenny Bruce is a slim ex-sailor, who in the jazz clubs and
> the jazz-oriented clubs . . . attacks the full spectrum of our
> society, stamping on all the taboos, all the stereotypes and all
> the traditionally sacred cows. His answer to the tranquilizer
> of stage, TV and movie humor . . . is the shock therapy of
> total satire in which nothing — art, politics, human relations,
> religion, sex, age, and color — is sacred and all is viewed from
> the jazz musician's point of view of colossal irreverence — the
> nuclear age equivalent of "show me" . . . "I'm not sick,"
> he says indignantly when labelled as a sick comedian. "It's our
> society that's sick." . . .

> We may not like what Lenny Bruce says — and no comedian
> in memory has had as rough a time at the hands of the critics
> and even the entertainment trade press. He will step on your
> own personal taboo inevitably, but if you can stop screaming
> long enough to think about what he says, we may all end up
> laughing and with the laughter, move things forward a bit.

Fair enough. I'd never thought about all those things before
when watching a Lenny Bruce show — I'd merely laughed,
gasped and laughed again — but now it all seemed clear. I
liked the idea of helping to move things forward, and was more
than ever pleased that I would have a chance to take in a Bruce
show again — for I'd been invited to go with a party from the
university. We found a lively crowd outside the club door, waiting with bright eyes for a police invasion. Some of them were

carrying placards of welcome to Lenny Bruce. Off Broadway was packed; every table had as many sitters as could be squeezed in, and the waiters had to behave like obstacle runners. A roar of welcome greeted Bruce when he walked onstage, trim in high-heeled boots and tight trousers, and began to speak his piece.

Little by little the audience calmed down. I think they were puzzled. I know I was. This wasn't at all the same style I remembered. Bruce was being serious. I remembered Gleason explaining that he is always serious underneath, but this was different — this was not merely an underlying state of mind that showed through now and then: it was on the surface as well, all the time, without sugar-coating. Moreover, Lenny was — not unnaturally — nervous, and that showed too. Doggedly he used the famous four-letter words, the five- and six-letter words, pausing sometimes after bellowing one, and looking toward the entrances for the police. Altogether it was a disjointed, uneasy talk, hardly funny at all. And, in spite of all that courage, no police showed. Gleason next day said in his column that the audience had overtones of the Indianapolis auto races, prize fights and the bull ring; we had gone to see Bruce busted, he said bitterly, and when the plainclothesmen "who were omnipresent" and the uniformed police failed to make their pinch, we were frustrated. Certainly I for one was frustrated, but I'm not sure it was the fault of the police.

As we left the club I said, "Oh well, I guess he's a crusader."

"Yes," said my host, "but it's such an odd crusade to choose, don't you think? Hardly worth the sound and fury."

*   *   *

I'd meant to call on Henry Miller at Big Sur, but I found out in time that he wasn't there; he was staying near Hollywood for a while, partly to get away from people who came to see him at

Big Sur. On the telephone he said I didn't count as a nuisance, however, so I went out to see him in his new house. It was a very nice one, the drawing room hung with his watercolors and paintings by friends, with here and there a piece of sculpture. Everything was so spotlessly in order that I had to make a mental readjustment about Miller, conditioned as I was to his accounts of the poverty and squalor he used to live in in Paris.

"Yes," he said. "At last they've given in, in some parts of the world at least, and my books are selling. I'm legal now in England, and a good deal of my stuff's been cleared even here in America. Funny, isn't it?"

With my mind on Lenny Bruce, I asked Miller if he had ever consciously sponsored a cause. "I know you've fought for your own rights," I added, "but were you ever part of a group — a political one, for example?"

No, said Miller; he'd never had the time or the inclination. "It might have been different if I'd started younger, though I don't think so," he said. "You see, I didn't become a writer until I could give my whole time to it, and I wasn't an adolescent when I gave up my job to go to Paris and write. After that — well, you know all about that." He paused and thought, then shook his head. "No. I'm not a politico. I'm a writer."

"In that case, you might well be the only true Bohemian in the whole bunch," I said. Yes, he said, he might. A few weeks later he sent me a page from the magazine *Genesis West* that he thought pertinent to our conversation, with the comment, "Enclose something (?) from a young poet who thinks he's pretty pure, I imagine." — a letter from Gregory Corso about an unflattering comment on himself that had been made by another poet, Jack Gilbert. Corso was annoyed:

Jack Gilbert is very jealous of me — and I wish he weren't — it spooks me when minor poets complain about my good fortune with the muse — I know myself very well and I know that I am that rare poet everyone imitates . . . I hold that we are all one big great spirit — but I also hold that in comparison I am a better spirit, plus a better man, than Mr. Gilbert — not only because I am Gregory Corso and he is Jack Gilbert, but also because I happen to be Captain Poetry, and I have long since vowed to be the Muse's Champion . . . I hate minor folk, failure folk, complaining jealous creepy folk — and you of the West, it took Ginsberg, me & Burroughs, Easterners all, to wake you up — I've regretted it ever since, because what we woke up were the moribund minors — What good did we by writing some of the greatest and truest poetry this country has ever seen when by doing so we opened the gates of awful poetry — for fact had it that if we, the children of the immigrant, could sing so ethereally, then so could anyone — Never in the history of poetry have poets such as Ginsberg and myself had to bear the muck and slime of jealousy, ignorance, failure, and bitterness . . .

Poets can be the creepiest people alive, as well as the most beautiful —

I say I am beautiful, I say Mr. Gilbert is a creep.

Well, yes, that is the authentic voice that has been heard through the centuries. The vocabulary changes but the spirit is the same, I said to myself, and then I began to wonder. Is it indeed the same? No, it can't be. There are so many more of us — more Philistines, more poets — that of necessity it has changed. Perhaps that is why Corso and Ginsberg and Burroughs and the others join causes. That is why we have group against group, rather than man against man or even school (in the Lake Poet sense of the word) against school. The reasons they give for these schisms may or may not be valid — aren't we all, for instance, children of immigrants? — but the impulse they feel to join a herd is a natural one. An individual has less chance than ever to make his mark, but a group still has power.

But the beat group of Venice West, like that of North Beach, has no core any more. It was dissipated, scattered to the winds in its turn, by the same kind of agency as San Francisco's, the city authorities. The Beat Movement of Venice is so much a matter of history that UCLA is in the process of embalming it by means of taped interviews with those closely involved, the tapes to be transferred in due course to the archives, where seekers after dissertation material can use them. Much of the story, too, has been written by Lawrence Lipton, a kind of self elected leader, non-beat among the beats, in his book *The Holy Barbarians*.

Eric Nord was one of the first beats in Venice, having come down in the vanguard of those who left San Francisco. His primary reason for visiting Los Angeles was to find a lawyer to defend him in case the seduction charge in San Francisco should come to court. During the stay he went to Venice West and saw its possibilities. An abandoned sea resort that had never been successful, full of ramshackle empty houses that were cheap, it was even more of a slum than North Beach. Nord picked one of the largest, the Gas House, and opened up a new pad for lodgers who wanted to paint, recite poetry, or merely listen to jazz records and think. Soon not only the Gas House, but the whole district was filled with artists, poets, sculptors, and teenage rebels who had not yet settled on art or poetry. Lipton set up another community that was more ambitious: under his tutelage the beats started schools for each other and their children in dancing, finger-painting and so on.

For some time Venice swung happily enough, but the San Francisco pattern began repeating itself — tourists came out to gawk at the freaks, and in their wake came merchant adventurers who saw the chance of making money out of the tourists, with giftshops and quaint bars and coffee shops. Layabouts crowded in for food and shelter. The public complained. What about real-estate values? What of their own children, exposed to this moral infection? Once again health authorities went into action, condemning the pads and harrying the inhabitants wherever they saw an opening. Poor Eric Nord was nobbled again, which is why he had taken to thinking of the West Indies when I met him, but Nord was not the only victim. The colony fell apart. Some beats remain, but the spirit has gone out of the place.

Today the most tangible evidence of the original movement in California is the City Lights Bookshop in San Francisco, of which the proprietor, Lawrence Ferlinghetti, is making a very good thing according to his ideas, for it is hardly ever empty of customers buying not only the ordinary publications that any bookstore sells, but the pamphlets and poetry he and his close associates write. Like all good bookshops, City Lights serves as a club as well, with a bulletin board full of posters and notices, some scribbled, some mimeographed:

> Attention! I Need place to stay
> Despertly, getting to cold to sleep
> in Park. Will help out with Rent
> as Much as possible. Male, 21.
> Appreciates Art & culture. Lv. mess.
> Below.
> ATT Females very affectionate & home
> loving
>
> Wanted Girl (or two) to travel through
> Mexico with guy (student, 21) and
> Volkswagen. Plan to tour and camp out
> in remote areas. Points of interest to

include Grand Canyon, Mexico City, and
Yucatan Penin. Share expenses
(150-200 dollars)

23 year old bachelor.
6 ft.
160 lbs.
dark wavey hair
penetrating brown eyes
swift sense of humor
a complete extrovert
acute awareness of circumstances and
situation
wide span of interests
digs sport cars, jazz, the easy life,
flamenco, the study of people and
their motivation, a dedicated
sensualist and seeker of the
unique, with champagne tastes
and beer budget.
Would like to meet a young lady with
tastes that are complimentary or
similar.

E.P. Menon
and Satish Kumar
have walked 2500 miles for Peace

Morning Glory Seeds
"Heavenly Blue"
$1 per 250
Untreated.

*   *   *

Let's move east, first pausing a third of the way across
America. How does New Mexico fare?

Santa Fe has been much affected by the near presence of Los Alamos; so, to a lesser degree, has Taos. The streets of Santa Fe are full of people with that unmistakable stamp of the armed-services-without-uniform, and social parties nowadays usually include a few scientific eggheads who never seem to have anything to say amid the frivolous babble. Both towns are ten times as easy to reach as they used to be: the main roads are paved, and the old highway of La Bajada, with its hairpin turns, has been abandoned in favor of a more efficient, far less picturesque road to Albuquerque. Now and then a plane swoops through the once empty sky and makes windowpanes rattle. But Santa Fe and Taos have always been colonies predominantly of painters rather than writers or other artists, and today, more than in any period of the past, painters are in the happy position of being independent of their surroundings. The moderns need not go out with easel and colors to jot down some picturesque view of mountain or Indian: they sit indoors and interpret their interior vision. What difference does it make to a New Mexico painter if his town is now paved and chock-a-block, ringed with motels, or that little Mexican settlements, sand-choked and parching in the sun as they have parched for centuries, now carry signboards on the general stores that say, "Buy Your Skis and Parkas Here"? None whatever. The air is still clear, and uncontaminated sunlight streams into window and patio. In winter there is still a scent of burning pine-wood. The painter paints.

The artist Raymond Jonson, who once designed scenery for Chicago's little theaters and then went to Santa Fe, long ago moved his residence once more and joined the university faculty at Albuquerque. He has now retired within a museum that bears his name and exhibits his work. Jonson's paintings are so lacking in representation that it is not enough to call them

merely abstractions. As I looked at his latest work I found it
impossible to believe, though I know it as an eyewitness, that
he too in the early days depicted mountains and Indians and
chili-strung adobe houses like everybody else. No, I had to
amend that: it was not like everybody else, because each painter's work is his own. Certainly, however, Jonson used to be
more representational.

A friend who was with me, unhampered by my memories,
simply looked at the pictures and said to him, "I love these
rooms, they're so *withdrawn*."

Jonson nodded. "I wanted it that way, entirely detached
from outside. All one needs is light."

She asked him about a contemporary of his in Santa Fe, who
has continued through the years to paint mountains, still-life,
and Indian dances. "What do you think of Blank?"

He hesitated. "Shall I be honest?"

"Oh yes. Please."

"Well . . . poor old Blank," said Jonson. "He's a very dear
friend of mine, but he never went far enough. That's about it.
He hasn't *freed* himself."

Of New Mexico's writing contingent, never very large, few
of the stars of former days remain; and the only addition I met
was the poet Winfield Scott. Hal Bynner and Spud Johnson
are still there, one in Santa Fe and the other in Taos. Mabel
is dead. So is D. H. Lawrence, if he can be considered a New
Mexico writer: his widow Frieda, who came back after he was
dead and spent the rest of her life on the ranch, has also gone.
The list of New Mexico's dead-and-gone is long, but I think we
must look elsewhere for an answer as to why Bohemianism has
departed from the state. After all, one might justly say, lots of
new painters and writers move in all the time — doubtless

there are more artists in New Mexico now than there used to be in the piping times. Nevertheless, Bohemia no longer nestles in the mountains. I think one reason is that it has become easy to get there: the founders of that particular sort of rebellious community came to their Paradise by wagon-train or on foot. Some of their love of effort, along with a genuinely Old-Western type of life, survived for some years but now survives no more. But there is another reason as well: it must be hard for even the most romantic individualist to take his individualism quite as seriously as his predecessors used to when he knows that up in those mountains, at the end of the road, lies Los Alamos.

CHAPTER 17

Not Quite the Same Thing

"COME UP," called a voice, and I climbed the stairs carefully, for they were steep and irregular. The house was tall and narrow, one of a row in Orleans Alley, alongside St. Louis Cathedral, Jackson Square, New Orleans. Even in that old city there are not many such streets left, with their tiny iron balconies. Occupants of Orleans Alley can see from these balconies, through lush trees and shrubs, the enclosed churchyard across the road. Mrs. John McClure greeted me in a high-ceilinged square room where books filled the shelves and were piled in heaps on the furniture. On one of the heaps an electric fan stood, buzzing and aiming a stream of warm air at us.

"Sit down and slip off your shoes if you like," said Mrs. McClure. "We don't go in for air-conditioning downtown. Well now, you want to know about the *Double Dealer*. If it hadn't been so hot I'd have gone into the room downstairs and dug out some stuff, but I'm almost afraid to open the door, it's so full of John's library. When he died I put it all away there. I know I ought to sort it out some day."

I protested that this would not be at all necessary for my purposes. Just whatever she might remember of some of the crowd —

"Well, there was Faulkner," she said. "He was just about the biggest liar that ever came to New Orleans. You couldn't put faith in a word he said. He didn't ever have a silver plate in his head from the war, the way he claimed. Don't you believe that for a minute." She paused and looked at me severely.

"Did he claim that?"

"Oh yes, and he didn't have any such thing. Anyway he wasn't old enough to have been in the war." For a silent moment she brooded over this breach of faith, then abandoned it. "My husband was a poet first and foremost, you know. The *Double Dealer* took up a lot of time and sometimes he complained about that, but he thought it was fun, too. A lot of people used to come to town just to look up the office. Sherwood Anderson was one — my, that man was conceited, carried a stick and all, but he certainly could write. Ham Basso, you might have known him up in New York. He was just a kid then, playing around with the others. Everybody who's left except me has moved uptown, and I can't blame them, it's changed so much around here. Go down to the river, you can hardly get through the crowd these days, all out-of-towners looking around. But here in the Alley it's just the way it used to be. These are nice houses." She looked out, between the curtains, at the Cathedral and the trees. "John always hoped he could publish one more collection of his poems, but he didn't get around to it. I'd like to get it done for his sake. I sent them to one house up north and they said the poems were dated. That made me sad. Since when does poetry date?"

I had met Mrs. McClure through Harnett Kane, without whose help and that of Mrs. Frances Bryson Moore the New Orleans of Bohemian days would have remained a matter of mere reading. Next day Mrs. Moore took me on a round of visits to other representatives of the *Double Dealer* and its friends. She explained on the way.

"They've all moved out except Mrs. McClure, as you must have gathered. Everybody's gone uptown. The Quarter was all right when we were young, but I guess something happens as you grow older."

"For one thing, people probably need space when they start having children," I said. "There's not much space in the French Quarter."

"There's that of course, but something else happened. The Quarter got too popular. When we all moved in to begin with, we did that as much because it was cheap as because it was pretty. Then it started having a reputation; it got to be the thing for bright young people to take a place downtown. The neighborhood got fashionable, and that was the end. Rents went way up — you'd be surprised what a house in the Quarter costs nowadays. We couldn't afford to stay."

The first house Mrs. Bryson and I visited that afternoon was a very different type from Mrs. McClure's — it stood in its own grounds, with a yard front and back, and was a spacious one-story. Screens enclosed the porch, and through the door we stepped into a blast of cooled air. Our hosts gave us chilled drinks and talked about the old days, about books and plays and cartoons and sculpture that they used to produce, about Lyle Saxon, William Spratling, Flo Field and Aunt Rose's Boarding-house.

"But it's all finished," said my hostess. "Whatever it was back then, call it a renaissance or an eruption or whatever you like — well, it was surprising and we thought it was lovely while it lasted, but it's over. We've scattered. We've — "

"We've grown out of it," said Frances Bryson. "These things happen." We had another round of drinks and I never even thought of asking about beatniks. It was a forgotten word.

Today Chicago's Old Town, which contains Towertown on the Near North Side, is much enlarged. Whole streets of stodgy buildings that used to be outside the boundary, the residences of bourgeois families who couldn't afford lakeside places, have been taken in, turned into apartments, and decorated by their new tenants, who use bright colors and furniture that the departed gentry would have condemned as matchwood. Most of the new tenants are young, hopeful couples earning their livings in advertising or journalism or teaching. The apartments are not cheap: most things aren't cheap in Old Town any more. There is a shopping district that is a departure from suburban centers like Old Orchard outside Evanston; it is something like Greenwich Village's. Shops offer goods from the less privileged foreign lands, offbeat clothes, custom-designed furniture — again, these things are not inexpensive. Old Town restaurants and bars are fancy to look at, though not necessarily ultra-modern: one of the most successful is a nostalgic reproduction of a nineteenth-century tavern. Is this idea derived from "My Fair Lady"? No matter. People come from all over the big city when they are tired of Michigan Boulevard shops and restaurants. They seek something original. Old Town trade is booming.

Here and there one still finds a studio loft — as a matter of fact there are a lot of studios. There are little theaters too, where people can watch Chekhov and such, or plays of the sort that set a new style in the Western world and produced Nichols and May. It was in one of these informal theaters that the British cast of "The Establishment" made such a thundering hit that they were amazed, not having expected Chicago to dig their stuff. As for the genuinely foreign restaurants, there are even more nowadays than there were when the Dill Pickle flourished. Yet, with all this, Old Town could no longer be called one hundred or even fifty percent Bohemian. It is not bourgeois either. It represents a new world where the bourgeois and the artist lie down together, like the lion and the lamb.

Come to think of it, it is becoming impossible to distinguish lion from lamb. The middle classes adopt art, and encourage it, and love it. They buy it. Why, then, should the Chicago artist turn against society? No reason at all, and most of them don't. For beatniks in Chicago one's got to go to the university campus and make do with mere novices. Today's rebels in Chicago are the Negroes, and they are fighting for other things than the right to be Bohemian.

＊　　＊　　＊

On lower Lexington Avenue, in an upstairs apartment that served two men as an office, Harry Baronian, until his death in 1965, edited and published his paper, the *Bowery News*. The *News* could not be called a weekly or a monthly because it didn't come out at regular intervals; when it did appear it was sternly undated. Whenever Harry had enough material to fill a number he put out the paper: it was as simple as that. For distribution he relied on his friends among the hoboes, who bought as many copies as they could carry, as an investment, and moved on to sell them far and wide. Harry was fond of hoboes, and maintained — with the support of Webster's Dictionary — that they are Bohemians, and of the purest sort. Sometimes he went further and called them the only Bohemians left in the world.

Usually when I dropped in at the office I found one of the newsboys resting his feet between trips, but often there were other callers as well. One day I met at the *Bowery News* Prince Robert de Rohan Courtenay, an elderly, bearded gentleman who describes himself as a direct descendant of Their Imperial Majesties of the Byzantine Eastern Roman Empire. The Prince is a Village character — that is to say he spends most of his time there, though he lives farther uptown, on the West Side. A few evenings later I met him on MacDougal Street, walking along as if oblivious to the pelting rain and general gloom of the night: he walked uncertainly, eyes fixed on the pavement ahead of him, and did not seem to be aware of my greeting.

"Well, yes," said Harry uneasily when I reported this. "The Prince is sort of funny sometimes." As if to take my mind off my social failure he brought out an old copy of the *News* to show me a photograph of the Prince, far younger and beardless, wearing a top hat and sitting at the wheel of a luxury roadster full of happy people posing with glasses of champagne. Above the car, evidently a photographer's prop, is a sign, WELCOME HO-BOS! From the legend beneath I gathered that the party was taking place at Palm Beach, Florida. The rest of the paper was as it always is, a mixture of items about the Village — "Al Bank, potter and sculptor in his MacDougal Street Shop. He holds an idol made of clay, which he based on pre-Columbian primitive art." — and articles of life as it seems to a hobo: "On the Skidrow" and "24 hours after you're broke."

The other occupant of the office was Izzy Elfand, who worked as a sweep for New York's Sanitation Department, but also ran a messenger service and restaurant and wrote songs in his spare time. Naturally a man so busy needed a desk, so he had one at the *Bowery News*. As for me, like practically everybody Harry met, I held a card testifying that I was a certified member of the Panhandlers Union — it cost a dollar, as I remember — and this, I felt, gave me the right to drop in from time to time and see how things were going during the *News* office hours, from five to ten in the evening. More than once I found Izzy on his telephone singing a recent composition to some music publisher, but on my last visit things were quiet. Izzy, Harry and a man in motley clothing were all busy eating pink ice cream out of large bowls.

"Bet you never saw a real hobo eating ice cream before," said Harry jovially. "This is Beefsteak Charlie, King of the Hoboes." Every hobo I ever met at Harry's was introduced as the King. Charlie made a bit of small talk for a while as he finished the ice cream, then he shouldered an enormous bundle of papers and took his leave. I asked Harry where he was going.

"Everywhere, anywhere," said Harry. "We might hear from him next in Seattle, but you never know." He went on to talk about the Joe Mitchell articles on Joe Gould, which had recently appeared in *The New Yorker*.

"There was one thing Mitchell evidently didn't know — the last few weeks before he went out of circulation, Gould slept every night on the floor of my office. It wasn't this place then, but over west, and a lot of other people used to spend the night there too. I guess it was a bad time everywhere just then. Gould came in with the others, and they'd lie under the desks and all over the place." He spoke in the impartial tones of a man describing a natural phenomenon over which he had no control. "Well, after a while most of the other guys began objecting to Gould sleeping with them — said he was lousy and shouldn't be allowed. There was one fellow, though, who stood up for him and said he wasn't lousy. It was an out-of-work newspaperman. To tell you the truth I think he had lice himself. Anyway I said Gould had a right to come in like anybody else, and he kept coming. But he wasn't himself, I could see that. He wasn't the old Joe Gould, making jokes and all. He was quiet. Then he stopped turning up, and the next I heard he was in Bellevue. He was in one hospital after another after that and I never saw him again, until he died, like Mitchell says, at Pilgrim State, must have been 1957 or '58. Outlived Bodenheim, as a matter of fact."

*   *   *

"Oh sure, I guess the Village has changed a lot," said the old-timer. "I moved into it in '32 when everything was just happening, and I didn't notice the transition at the time, but anybody would see the difference now—that Coney Island on MacDougal Street and all; isn't that something? I've changed too: I wear a necktie now. Why, do you suppose? What's happened to everybody? My crowd spends most of the time in bars, because a bar down here is more like a Paris cafe than a bar uptown where the waiter keeps twisting your arm. In our bars you can sit around; you don't have to go on ordering. The places I like are what I call loser bars; you know, where a lot of us who never quite made it like to herd together. But we change around, we don't stick to one very long. Take the San Remo, it's an empty hulk now. Remo died and his wife took over, and right away everybody left. You follow your favorite bartender, but that isn't the whole story. It's a funny thing how a bar can drop off overnight, and another one get born as fast. Just a little thing can kill a place—word getting around that somebody's a square will do it. Mind you, the crowd in our bars isn't *all* intellectual; you can meet anybody in the Village, sailors waiting to ship out or unemployed, anybody. Mostly, though, we're a lot of distinguished failures, loners, *you* know. Drink helps us to get together, in a way. The result is, you get tight little circles—same parties, same bars, same faces. We resent it if some flip goes to another bar. 'What the hell are you doing there?' we say. 'That's where the busted skulls go. To be barred from there you'd have to stab the bartender.'

"Yes, there are lots of changes in the Village. Take Negroes, there are plenty of them around nowadays; where the hell do they all come from—Jamaica, Long Island? And the Park's different too. I rarely see a friend in the Park any more. I used to, but now it's all a horde of tourists, Negro winos, ragged rebels with no room for rebellion. People in general are a lot more politically alert than they used to be. Once upon a time you couldn't get a Bohemian to vote, but everybody turned out this last election to vote against Goldwater. I guess they're all anti-war, too. Me, I'm an ex-Commie, kicked out of the Party in '38. I was disillusioned by the invasion of Finland. The Nazi-Soviet pact just about finished Communism around here. None of the old loud-mouthed Reds are still around: nobody even discusses it any more. Everybody's in psychoanalysis nowadays. Group therapy's the latest, very big.

"Then there's the gay boys. The Village has always been a place for gays, but now there must be thousands, male and female. Certain streets you find them standing five deep, where there's no bar or anything, not doing a thing, just standing. Now and then a fellow comes along in a car and picks one up, otherwise nothing. It bothers people, but they don't know what to do about it. I've got nothing against the gays myself. Village sex mores are very loose. I guess they always were, but I seem to notice it more these days. It's got so everybody knows everything about everybody, even before they've been introduced. You develop your own rules in a crowd. For instance, if a couple split up it's considered tactful for them to divide the bars between them, so they won't keep meeting everywhere. Trespassing on the other's territory is no fair. We have our codes.

"Everything's being torn down and rebuilt in the Village, and that helps to make it all different. But it's still a great place for the artists, because nowadays everybody's interested in art. That Outdoor Show they hold every fall and spring, that brings people down here by the thousand. Villagers used to go to Woodstock in the summer; it was a sort of second Village — Bodenheim went, and Hecht, and Puck Durant, and Romany

Marie, and John Rose Gildea. That changed too. Nowadays, I understand, the summer place is Fire Island, but not the Grove end. I can remember Bodenheim and Gildea at poetry meetings in some bar, hurling insults at each other. Gildea was a real flip. Last time I saw him, about fifteen years ago, he was shuffling through the Park delivering other people's manuscripts. He'd become an errand-boy. You know, the other day I ran into a girl I used to know around here, and we were talking about old times and old friends, and all of a sudden we realized that all the people we knew were cooks, bartenders, moving men, pushers, unemployed, waiters — we couldn't remember one artist, one writer, one successful poet. What do you think of that for a record? I used to have a drink now and then with De Kooning, but I didn't know who he was. I took him for a Dutch sailor waiting to ship out. That's what I mean — the Village isn't what it used to be. If you ask me, what's setting in is East Village. People are escaping over there. But I wouldn't move. I still like it here, even if the rents *are* the highest in town."

The old-timer was right about the East Village, as anyone who keeps up with daily and weekly journals could have told him. Eli Waldron in the *Saturday Evening Post* for July 23, 1964, started a flood of information on this subject, describing "a steady exodus of artists from Greenwich Village — bearded lads and lank-haired lassies pushing handcarts and baby carriages loaded with their belongings," concurrent with the invasion of the old Village by "young, snap-brimmed men carrying attaché cases . . . Today only the well-heeled, the very well-heeled, can afford the rates prevailing in Greenwich Village. The ill-heeled and struggling are fleeing to a new Bohemia . . . the former ghetto of the Lower East Side." He names the gathering-places in this new Bohemia — the Metro, the Porpoise, the

Five Spot, the New Bowery Theater and the New American
Cinema, which on the night he visited it was featuring a film
directed by Andy Warhol, "Tarzan and Jane Regained Sort of."
Some months later in the *Herald Tribune* Sunday issue of November 29, John Gruen told of a similar discovery he had
made: "In little less than a year, a New Bohemia has visibly asserted itself in the Lower East Side, with its vital center being
one of Manhattan's largest but least known parks, Tompkins
Square . . . the location of these activities is an area generally
called the East Village, which runs roughly from the East River
to Third Avenue, and from Houston Street up to 14th Street."

A foreigner might marvel at the mentality of New Yorkers,
who make all this fuss over a shift of four blocks from west to
east. But then it is well known that New Yorkers take a lot of
understanding, and in America Bohemia is always news. "This
is the new mecca of artists, poets, dancers, musicians, actors
and film makers," continues Mr. Gruen, raptly. "There are
more beards and black sun-glasses per square foot of the East
Village than fish in a dime-store aquarium. Blue-jeans, sweat-
ers, leather jackets and beat-up raincoats are the accepted mode
of dress for both males and females. Hair grows long for both
sexes." For goodness' sake, imagine that! Finally, however,
the writer comes up with the main point. ". . . The most dis-
tinguishing characteristic of the New Bohemia is its acceptance
of integration as an unquestioned part of the scene. Young Negroes and Puerto Ricans are part of the crowd at the New Bohemian bars, and mixed marriages are common . . . The New
Bohemians are night people, and they move in groups."

Again the reader might pause to wonder. Were the Old Bohemians, all those four blocks to the west, day people? Did they
shun their fellow man? "They form a microcosm of potential
violence, which, more often than not, is expiated by violent

dancing, cool talk, and a 'connection,' be it in the form of dope or sex . . ." It sounds very sinister. It sounds, in fact, like something from the *San Francisco Examiner* back in 1958. And worse is to come. "The East Village abounds in interracial couples, many of them married." After this shocker Gruen goes on to mention the Kerista cult, whose members "congregate in various East Village 'pads,' live and love communally, share expenses and dedicate themselves to 'freedom from repression.' This sexual kibbutz has the fullest support of someone like poet Allen Ginsberg — long an East Villager." In fact, it wasn't merely somebody like Ginsberg, it was Ginsberg himself, who said he supported Kerista, during a visit paid to him by Mr. Gruen at his apartment, in a "five-flight walk-up tenement [that] reeks of garbage and human perspiration. Inside it, the place looked like the next thing to a wall-to-wall bed . . . Books and papers littered a large desk, and strewn about the room were pamphlets and buttons, some of which read 'Let's Legalize Pot,' or 'Smoke Pot, It's Cheaper and Healthier than Liquor!' . . . The East Village and Lower East Side have become a corral of narcotics addicts, predominantly Negroes and Puerto Ricans, but also including numerous New Bohemia 'hippies.' "

On December 13, in the same journal, Isabel Eberstadt had a less sensational article about one of those interracial marriages mentioned by Mr. Gruen: "LeRoi Jones is a poet, is a teacher, is a playwright, is a critic, is a celebrity, is king of the Lower East Side. Is a Flaming Seducer, is a Rabid Racist, who Hates whites, Hates Negroes, Hates homosexuals, Hates intellectuals, Hates liberals, and Watch Out, he's a killer! Not all of these statements are true, obviously (LeRoi Jones is married to a white liberal intellectual for a beginning), but they all exist somewhere in the fantasy and conjecture of the people to whom he has become a cult figure — the denizens of the Lower East Side." And to the *Herald Tribune* as well. In fact, an assiduous reader of the New York Sunday papers would feel justified in deciding that the more things change in Bohemia the more they are the same, were it not for a contradictory note offered by the *Times Magazine* for December 6, same year. In "The College Intellectual, 1965 Model," David Boroff declared that college Bohemia, at least, is really altering, and for good. Values have changed, and yesterday's heroes are forgotten.

"The annals of bohemianism provide interesting insights into the student mind. The beat variety had almost universal authority a few years ago. It offered a ready-made vehicle for rebellion and protest. Disaffiliation was all the rage . . . Today's college intellectuals are far too sophisticated for such simple-minded gestures. Kerouac seems to college students (if they pay any attention to him at all) like a relic from the past. Allen Ginsberg has moved on to other matters, and Gregory Corso is a naughty little boy mouthing dirty words." Here Mr. Boroff comes to a point which I consider very important: "Bohemianism as a cult has virtually disappeared from the campus, yet it is everywhere. It has been assimilated into the mainstream. The young woman with loose-flying hair and black stockings may well be majoring in elementary education, and the young man with a beard is a pre-law student having his last fling. Bohemianism is dead, but its artifacts are all around."

True, yet not true, for the newspapers won't forget the word so easily. Let us say, rather, that *this* Bohemianism is dead. Bohemians are prophets, literally the *avant-garde,* who when their prophecies come to pass drop out of sight, their identity lost in the crowd. The jeering ceases and is forgotten; the new has been adopted, "assimilated in the mainstream," until the next *avant-garde* promulgates a yet newer set of ideas just as outrageous and unacceptable as the old set once seemed. That is the function of the *avant-garde*. This is not to say that every single Bohemian is always right. At the Armory Show back in 1913 the world saw, and maligned, a lot of masterpieces, but also saw — and maligned — more bad pictures than masterpieces. At least that is what we say today: a younger crowd is coming along that may judge the whole exhibition in a different light. Indeed, it is bound to.

*   *   *

A pattern appears. From the 1850s to the early 1890s, American Bohemia had to feel its way with caution. At first it derived wholly from Europe, but American artists and writers soon found their own paths and shook off the influence of the Old World. Late in the nineteenth century, however, there appeared a diversion of direction wholly national in character — a rising interest among Bohemians in the coming struggle between capital and labor. Jack London, who as a youth experienced the pain of being an underdog, openly challenged the art-for-art's-sake concept and in his novels wrote of the social struggle. He had followers: in fact, writers continued to adopt London's youthful ideas long after he deserted Socialism. It was an attitude that many artists found, and still find, inconsistent.

"I am a poet," declares Chaplin in his autobiography. "I am a spiritual anarchist. I am not patriotic. I am amoral." Isadora Duncan said much the same thing. Both artists are defending themselves against the accusation of Communist sympathies: both artists are without doubt sincere. Lenin, for one, knew better than to trust the artist in any shape or form. He said, "Art is a strange and dubious occupation," and when he planned the perfect State of the future he left the artist out.

Nevertheless, the Great Depression convinced a lot of American artists that Socialism was the only hope for mankind. They didn't know Lenin's opinion of them; innocently they thought they could wield great power for good if they bent their talents to spreading the message. Whatever one's judgment may be as to the morality of this belief, there is no doubt that it constricted or suppressed a good deal of art. It is no wonder that Bohemianism languished and grew stale when artists weren't allowed to produce new ideas. The only remarkable factor of the history of Bohemia in America is that the reaction was so long in setting in. Not until the early 1950s, as we have seen, did the beatnik movement manifest itself. Whatever the term "beat" means now — and more and more it seems to be used as a simple synonym for "Bohemian" — in the beginning it stood for something more specific. The beat was not merely out of step with convention: he wanted no part of political causes or, for that matter, any cause whatever, including art for art's sake. In Kenneth Rexroth's term, he was disengaged. In Lipton's he was disaffiliated. In sum, he opted out: retired: went into the silences. He was tired of politics. He rebelled against the rebels.

It's different now: the beats are turning into something else. A one-sheet publication headed "An American Congress of Poets, August-September, 1964" was brought to my attention recently by Mr. Felix Pollak of the University of Wisconsin Library, who collects such things. It reads:

> On the last day of August, a great Rally on behalf of MO-BILIZATION FOR YOUTH convened between Avenues C & D on East 4th St. in Lower Manhattan to protest the mccarthy-ite attacks against MFY by the NY DAILY NEWS and other goldwaterite sources. MFY has, to my own knowledge, rescued youth after youth from despair and drugs with a meaningful jobs program . . . Significant to Poets everywhere will be the

news that many of the Poets of the lower East Side were on hand to support MFY . . . Allen Ginsberg, the revolutionary Poet who uttered the most pertinent social cry of our times ('Fuck America and her Goddamn Atom Bomb!') stood beside me singing, slightly off key, the Star Spangled Banner, as a school band played the anthem slowly, then rocking gently as the Puerto Rican anthem was played. Ginsberg chided some of us quietly for our over-zealous hoots and laughs at certain speakers, urging us to give each man a fair hearing; translated the Spanish of a Puerto Rican member of LENA, listened intently, concernedly, with reverent awareness of what was happening all around.

Does this mean that Allen Ginsberg is going soft? I would say No. I believe that this man whose own zeal helped him out thru the muck of our social order — is now taking another, deeper look into our possibilities. Is it not possible that the same Poet-prophet who warned us with a terrible negation of our emptiness — might now be one, if not *the* one, to find us a challenge of spiritual and social affirmation? . . .

"What does that mean, do you suppose?" asked Mr. Pollak. I don't know any more than he does: the only clear message in that newsletter is that Mr. Ginsberg is changing. But then, everything in Bohemia changes, or ought to. There, if anywhere, history never repeats itself.

Bibliography

Index

Bibliography

Allen, Charles. *See* Hoffman, Frederick John.

Allen, Hervey, *Israfel: The Life and Times of Edgar Allan Poe.* New York: Doran & Co., 1926.

Anderson, Margaret, *My Thirty Years' War.* New York: Covici, Friede, 1930.

Anderson, Sherwood, *No Swank.* Philadelphia: Centaur Press, 1934.

Austin, Mary, *Earth Horizon.* Boston: Houghton Mifflin, 1932.

—— *Land of Little Rain.* Boston: Houghton Mifflin, 1903.

—— "George Sterling at Carmel," *American Mercury.* New York: May, 1927.

Barrus, Clara, *Whitman and Burroughs — Comrades.* Boston: Houghton Mifflin, 1931.

Beer, Thomas, *The Mauve Decade.* New York: Knopf, 1926.

—— *Stephen Crane.* New York: Garden City Publishing Co., 1923.

Bickford, L. H., and Powell, R. S., *Phyllis in Bohemia.* Chicago & New York: Stone & Co., 1827.

Bisland, Elizabeth (Mrs. Wetmore), *The Life and Letters of Lafcadio Hearn.* Boston: Houghton Mifflin, 1906.

Bohemian Club, *The Annals of the Bohemian Club.* San Francisco: Bohemian Club, 1872-1900.

Brett, Dorothy, *Lawrence and Brett.* Philadelphia: Lippincott, 1933.

Brooks, Van Wyck, *The Confident Years, 1885-1915.* New York: Dutton, 1952.

—— *The Times of Melville and Whitman*. New York: Dutton, 1947.

Bunner, H. C., *Jersey Street and Jersey Lane*. New York: Scribners, 1896.

—— *The Midge*. New York: Scribners, 1886.

Bynner, Witter, *Journey with Genius*. New York: John Day, 1951. *See also* Smith, William J.

Chambers, Robert W., *In the Quarter*. New York: Neely, 1894.

—— *Outsiders*. New York: Stokes, 1899.

Churchill, Allen, *The Improper Bohemians*. New York: Dutton, 1959.

Clairmont, Robert, *Quintillions*. New York: MacVeigh, 1928.

Clapp, Henry, *Husband vs. Wife*. New York: Rudd & Carleton, 1858.

—— *The Pioneers*. Lynn, Massachusetts: Tolman, May 7, 1846.

Clare, Ada, *Only a Woman's Heart*. New York: Privately printed(?), 1866.

Coke, Van Deren, *Taos and Santa Fe: The Artist's Environment, 1882-1942*. Albuquerque: University of New Mexico Press, 1963.

Corbett, Elizabeth Frances, *Walt*. New York: Stokes, 1928.

Cowley, Malcolm, *Exile's Return*. New York: Norton, 1935.

De Casseres, Benjamin, "Joel's," *American Mercury*. New York: July, 1932.

De Kay, Charles, *The Bohemian*. New York: Scribners, 1878.

Dell, Floyd, *Homecoming* (Autobiography). New York: Farrar & Rinehart, 1933.

—— *Love in Greenwich Village*. New York: Doran & Co., 1926.

—— "On Being Sherwood Anderson's Literary Father," *Newberry Library Bulletin*. Chicago: Dec., 1961, Vol. 5, No. 9.

Desti, Mary, *The Untold Story* (Isadora Duncan). New York: H. Liveright, 1929.

Dickens, Charles, *American Notes*. New York & Boston: Harper, 1842.

Duffey, Bernard, *The Chicago Renaissance in American Letters*. East Lansing: Michigan State College Press, 1952.

Du Maurier, George L. P. B., *Trilby*. New York: Harper, 1894.

Duncan, Isadora, *My Life*. New York: Boni & Liveright, 1927.

Durrell, Lawrence, *Lawrence Durrell and Henry Miller: A Private Correspondence*. London: Faber & Faber, 1963.

Eastman, Max, *Great Companions*. New York: Farrar, Straus & Cudahy, 1959.

—— *Heroes I Have Known*. New York: Simon & Schuster, 1942.

—— *Venturer*. New York: A. & C. Boni, 1927.

Easton, Malcolm, *Artists and Writers in Paris: The Bohemian Idea, 1803-1867*. London: E. Arnold, 1964.

Falk, Bernard, *The Naked Lady (Adah Menken)*. London: Hutchinson, 1934.

Fay, Eliot, *Lorenzo in Search of the Sun (D. H. Lawrence)*. New York: Bookman Associates, 1959.

Ferlinghetti, Lawrence, *One Thousand Fearful Words for Fidel Castro*. San Francisco: City Lights, 1961.

—— *Unfair Arguments with Existence*. San Francisco: City Lights, 1963.

Ford, James L., *Bohemia Invaded*. New York: Privately printed(?), 1895.

—— *Forty-odd Years in the Literary Shop*. New York: Dutton, 1921.

Furneaux, Rupert, *Courtroom U.S.A., 1*. London: Penguin, 1962.

Garnett, Porter, *The Bohemian Jinks*. San Francisco: Bohemian Club, 1908.

Gaunt, William, *The Aesthetic Adventure*. London: Cape, 1945.

Gilke, Lillian, *Cora Crane*. Bloomington: Indiana University Press, 1960.

Gosse, Sir F. H., *The Life of Algernon Charles Swinburne*. London: Macmillan, 1917.

Gottschalk, Louis Moreau, *Notes of a Pianist*. Philadelphia: Lippincott, 1881.

Grattan, C. Hartley, *Bitter Bierce*. New York: Doubleday, 1929.

Gunn, Thomas, *The Physiology of the New York Boarding-houses*. New York: Privately printed(?), 1857.

Handy, William Christopher, *Father of the Blues*. New York: Macmillan, 1941.

Hanighen, Frank C., "Vance Thompson and 'M'lle New York'." *Bookman*, September, 1932.

Hansen, Harry, *Midwest Portraits*. New York: Harcourt, Brace, 1923.

Hapgood, Hutchins, *Types from City Streets*. New York: Funk & Wagnalls, 1910.

Harland, Henry, *Grey Roses*. Boston: Roberts Bros., 1895.

—— *A Latin-Quarter Courtship*. New York: Cassell, 1889.

Hart, James D., *The Popular Book*. New York: Oxford University Press, 1950.

Harte, Francis Brett, *Bohemian Days in San Francisco*. Boston: Houghton Mifflin, 1903.

—— *Stories, Sketches and Bohemian Papers*. Boston: Houghton Mifflin, 1896.

Hecht, Ben, *Gaily, Gaily*. New York: Doubleday, 1963.

—— *Letters from Bohemia*. New York: Doubleday, 1964.

Hemingway, Ernest, *A Moveable Feast*. New York: Scribners, 1964.

Hicks, Granville, *John Reed*. New York: Macmillan, 1936.

Hoffman, Frederick John, with Charles Allen and Carolyn F. Ulrich, *The Little Magazine*. Princeton: Princeton University Press, 1947.

Horgan, Paul, *The Centuries of Santa Fe*. New York: Dutton, 1956.

Horton, Philip, *Hart Crane*. New York: Norton, 1937.

Howells, William Dean, *The Coast of Bohemia*. New York: Harper, 1893.

—— *A Hazard of New Fortunes*. New York: Harper, 1899.

—— *Literary Friends and Acquaintance*. New York: Harper, 1900.

—— *Years of My Youth*. New York: Harper, 1916.

Huneker, James Gibbons, *Ivory Apes and Peacocks*. New York: Scribners, 1915.

—— *Painted Veils*. New York: Boni & Liveright, 1920.

—— *Steeplejack*. New York: Scribners, 1915.

Janvier, T. A., *Color Studies*. New York: Scribners, 1885.

—— *Santa Fe's Partner*. New York: Harper, 1907.

Jones, LeRoi (Ed.), *The Moderns, New Fiction in America*. New York: Citadel, 1963.

Kemp, Harry, *More Miles*. New York: Boni & Liveright, 1926.

——— *Tramping Through Life.* New York: Boni & Liveright, 1922.

Kerouac, Jack, *On the Road.* New York: Viking, 1957.

Kipling, Rudyard, *American Notes.* New York: Ivers, 1891.

Kreymborg, Alfred, *Troubadour* (Autobiography). New York: Boni & Liveright, 1925.

Krim, Seymour (Ed.), *The Beats: A Gold Medal Anthology.* Greenwich: Fawcett, 1960.

Lang, Cecil F., *The Swinburne Letters.* New Haven: Yale University Press, 1959-1962.

Lawrence, D. H., *The Plumed Serpent.* London: Heinemann, 1955.

Lawrence, Frieda E. J., *Not I, But the Wind.* New York: Viking Press, 1934.

Le Gallienne, Richard, *The Romantic '90s.* New York: Doubleday, Page, 1925.

Leland, Charles Godfrey, *Memoirs.* New York: Appleton, 1893.

Lewis, Oscar, *Bay Window Bohemia.* New York: Doubleday, 1956.

Lipton, Lawrence, *The Holy Barbarians.* New York: Messner, 1959.

London, Charmian K., *The Book of Jack London.* New York: Centaur Press, 1921.

London, Joan, *Jack London and His Times.* New York: Doubleday, 1939.

Luhan, Mabel Dodge, *Lorenzo in Taos,* New York: Knopf, 1932.
——— *Intimate Memories,* New York: Harcourt, Brace:
Background: 1933.
European Experiences: 1935.
Movers and Shakers: 1936.
Edge of Taos Desert: 1937.

Manville, Bill, *Saloon Society.* New York: Duell, Sloan & Pierce, 1960.

McWilliams, Vera, *Lafcadio Hearn.* Boston: Houghton Mifflin, 1946.

Marberry, M. M., *Splendid Poseur* (Joaquin Miller). New York: Crowell, 1953.

Mencken, H. L., *A Book of Prefaces.* New York: Knopf, 1917.

———— *Prejudices.* New York: Knopf, 1927.

———— *The Vintage Mencken* (Ed. Alistair Cooke). New York: Random House, Vintage Books, 1955.

Merrild, Knud, *A Poet and Two Painters.* London: G. Routledge, 1938.

Merwin, Henry Childs, *The Life of Bret Harte.* Boston: Houghton Mifflin, 1911.

Miller, Henry, *See* Durrell, Lawrence.

Miller, Joaquin, *The Baroness of New York.* New York: G. W. Carleton & Co., 1877.

Miller, Perry, *The Raven and the Whale.* New York: Harcourt, Brace, 1956.

Mitchell, Joseph, *Joe Gould's Secret.* New York: Viking Press, 1965.

Monroe, Harriet, *A Poet's Life.* New York: Macmillan, 1935.

Moore, Harry T., *The Intelligent Heart: The Story of D. H. Lawrence.* New York: Farrar, Straus & Young, 1954.

Muddiman, Bernard, *The Men of the Nineties.* London: H. Danielson, 1920.

Murger, Henri, *The Latin Quarter.* New York: Doubleday, Page, 1901.

Noel, Joseph, *Footloose in Arcadia.* New York: Carrick & Evans, 1940.

O'Brien, Fitz-James, *The Diamond Lens.* New York: Scribners, 1885.

O'Reilly, John Boyle, *In Bohemia.* Boston: Pilot Publishing Co., 1886.

Ossman, David (Ed.), *The Sullen Art* (Anthology). New York: Corinth, 1963.

Parkinson, Thomas (Ed.), *A Casebook of the Beat.* New York: Crowell, 1961.

Parry, Albert, *Garrets and Pretenders.* New York: Covici, Friede, 1933. Revised edition, Dover, 1960.

———— "Life in Old Bohemia," *American Mercury,* Nov., 1930.

———— "The Queen of Bohemia," *American Mercury,* Sept., 1930.

———— "Soul Flights of the Village," *American Mercury,* Oct., 1931.

Pennell, Elizabeth Robin, *Charles Godfrey Leland.* Boston: Houghton Mifflin, 1906.

Powell, R. S., *See* Bickford, L. H.

Quinn, Arthur Hobson, *Edgar Allan Poe*. New York: Appleton-Century, 1941.

Rigney, Francis J., and Smith, L. Douglas, *The Real Bohemia*. New York: Basic Books, 1961.

Roche, James Jeffrey, *Life of John Boyle O'Reilly*. New York: Cassell, 1891.

Rogers, Cameron, *The Magnificent Idler (Walt Whitman)*. New York: Garden City, 1926.

Saltus, Edgar, *Imperial Purple*. Washington: Brentano's, 1906.

Saltus, Marie, *Edgar Saltus, the Man*. Chicago: Covici, 1925.

Sanders, Ed, *Poem from Jail*. San Francisco: City Lights, 1963.

Schwab, Arnold T., *James Gibbons Huneker, Critic of the Seven Arts*. Stanford, California: Stanford University Press, 1963.

Smith, Alson J., *Chicago's Left Bank*. Chicago: Henry Regnery, 1953.

Smith, L. Douglas, *See* Rigney, Francis J.

Smith, William Jay, *The Spectra Hoax*. Middletown, Connecticut: Wesleyan University Press, 1961.

Spiller, R. E., *Literary History of the United States*. New York: Macmillan, 1948.

Stein, Gertrude, *Autobiography of Alice B. Toklas*. New York: Harcourt, Brace, 1933.

Sterling, George, "Joaquin Miller," *American Mercury*. Feb., 1926.

Stewart, George R., Jr., *Bret Harte, Argonaut and Exile*. Boston: Houghton Mifflin, 1931.

Stoddard, Charles Warren, "Ada Clare, the Queen of Bohemia," *National Magazine*. Boston, Sept., 1905.

Stoddard, Richard Henry, *Recollections Personal and Literary*. New York: A. S. Barnes, 1903.

Sutcliffe, Denham, "New Light on the 'Chicago Writers,'" *Newberry Library Bulletin*. Chicago: Dec., 1950, Second Series, No. 5.

Swinburne, Algernon Charles, *In the Album of Adah Menken*. London & New York: R. H. Shepherd, 1883.

Taylor, Bayard, *The Echo Club*. Boston: J. R. Osgood, 1876.

Terry, Walter, *Isadora Duncan*. New York: Dodd, 1963.

Toklas, Alice B., *What Is Remembered*. New York: Holt, Rinehart & Winston, 1963.

Ulrich, Carolyn F., *See* Hoffman, Frederick John.

Van Vechten, Carl, *Peter Whiffle*. New York: Knopf, 1927.

Weber, Brom, *Letters of Hart Crane*. New York: Hermitage House, 1952.

Wechsler, James A., *Reflections of an Angry Middle-Aged Editor*. New York: Random House, 1960.

Whittemore, Reed, *Little Magazines* (Pamphlet). Minneapolis: University of Minnesota Press, 1963.

Wilson, Edmund, *Axel's Castle*. New York: Scribners, 1931.

———— *Classics and Commercials*. New York: Farrar, Straus, 1950.

———— *I Thought of Daisy*. New York: Scribners, 1929.

———— *The Shores of Light*. New York: Farrar, Straus & Young, 1952.

Winthrop, Theodore, *Cecil Dreeme*. Boston: Ticknor & Fields, 1861.

Index

Index